Praises for *Arrival of the Gods in Egypt*

"The inherently fascinating story of one woman's exploration of the Egyptian landscape in an attempt to confirm her memories of Atlantis but resulted instead with the unexpected but quite remarkable vision of the Virgin Mary, *Arrival of the Gods in Egypt* offers readers an assurance of the Virgin Mary's powerful ability to bring about peace, as well as touching upon the Copts (who are direct descendants of the ancient Egyptians who were converted to Christianity in the first decades after the death and resurrection of the Christ), as well as the significance of certain artifacts left by ancient Mayans and paintings in the Pharaoh's tombs. *Arrival of the Gods in Egypt* is very strongly recommended for studies of Metaphysics and Christian Mysticism."

    ~ MIDWEST BOOK REVIEW

"This fabulous story of the soul, mind, and body, moving through a world where space and time are irrelevant, brings us face to face with the root races of humankind as they change from light beings to androgynous beings to mixed beings to human beings. Chapman takes us to Eden, Egypt, Maya, and places where apparitions of the Virgin Mary appear. Magnificent!" ~ CAROL HAENNI, PH. D., AUTHOR OF *THE HOLY WOMEN*

    AROUND JESUS

"A fascinating story that makes sense as the basis of our religions, *Arrival of the Gods in Egypt* delves deeply into the mystery of Atlantis and our souls' beginnings on earth. Chapman expertly weaves the tale of a little known Marion apparition with an intriguing quest to discover evidence of Atlantis in the land of the pharaohs. By doing so, she reveals our true relationship with the Universe and offers hope for the future."

    ~ JEAN C. KEATING, PULITZER PRIZE-NOMINATED AUTHOR OF *BEGUILING BUNDLE*, www.astrapublishers.com

CAROL CHAPMAN

ARRIVAL
of the
GODS *in* EGYPT

Hidden Mysteries of Soul and Myth

Finally Revealed

SunTopaz LLC
Light Overcomes Darkness
Foster, Virginia

ARRIVAL OF THE GODS IN EGYPT
Hidden Mysteries of Soul and Myth Finally Revealed

Published by: SunTopaz LLC, P. O. Box 123, Foster, VA 23056, www.SunTopaz.com

The front cover photograph of the Blessed Virgin Mary is of a marble statue sculpted by Jill Burkee displayed at the Mary, Queen of the Universe Shrine in Orlando, Florida, USA

Printed in the United States of America

Disclaimer
The information within these pages is not meant to be used as advice of any kind including medical. It is merely meant to provide information and entertainment. If you suffer with obesity or depression or any other ailment, you should see a qualified medical practitioner.

Publisher's Cataloging-In-Publication Data
(Prepared by The Donohue Group, Inc.)

Chapman, Carol (Carol Anne)
   Arrival of the gods in Egypt : hidden mysteries of soul and myth finally revealed / Carol Chapman.

   p. : ill., maps ; cm.

   ISBN: 978-0-9754691-5-6

1. Mary, Blessed Virgin, Saint--Apparitions and miracles--Egypt--Asyut. 2. Atlantis (Legendary place) 3. Egypt--Description and travel. 4. Egypt--Antiquities. 5. Photographers--United States. 6. Mysticism. 7. Chapman, Carol (Carol Anne) I. Cayce, Edgar, 1877-1945. II. Title.

BT660.A83 C43 2008
232.91/7   2007906438

Cover design © 2007 C. A. Petrachenko
Cover and internal photographs © 2000-2007 Carol Chapman, except:
   Photographs of the Virgin apparition and flashes in Asyut, Egypt © 2000 Wahid Refaat Sedra
   Photograph of the author on the back cover and on page 288 © 2007 John J. Chapman
   Photograph of Carol Chapman coming out of the grotto on page 119 taken by Peggy Day
   Photograph of Peggy Day on page 13 used with permission from Ms. Day
Edited by Clair Balsley and C. A. Petrachenko

Dedicated to my beloved children
Adam, Clair, and Miriam

OTHER BOOKS BY CAROL CHAPMAN

When We Were Gods:
Insights on Atlantis, Past Lives,
Angelic Beings of Light, and Spiritual Awakening
by Carole Chapman
which is the revised, updated edition of:

The Golden Ones:
From Atlantis to a New World
by Carole A. P. Chapman

CONTENTS
Arrival of the Gods in Egypt
Hidden Mysteries of Soul and Myth Finally Revealed

ACKNOWLEDGEMENTS

My experiences in Egypt would not have been possible without the help of my dear friend Hani Ragheb, who very kindly made it possible for me to stay in Cairo with his sister and her family. He was also so helpful in answering my many questions about the customs, clothing, and words of the Coptic Christians and the Egyptians. I also appreciate the many long distance telephone calls he made to Egypt on my behalf.

Hani's sister Mohga, her husband Gad, their daughter Marian, and their son Marcos, were all so helpful and wonderfully welcoming. Because of them, my trip to Egypt became a marvelous adventure. Without them, my Egypt travel would have been the same as any other tourist's, and I would not have had the opportunity to make a pilgrimage to the site where the Blessed Virgin Mary manifested.

A special thanks to Wahid Refaat Sedra for providing the photographs of the Virgin and the flashes preceding the apparition that I have used as illustrations in this book. Wahid and his lovely, friendly wife, Mervat, also made me feel very welcome in Asyut. Their delightful sons Kerolos and Beshoi made me feel at home.

In addition, I appreciate the warm reception and wonderful dinner provided by Hani Ragheb's Asyut sister Nahid, who has sadly passed away since my September 2000 visit. Thanks also to her husband Refaat, plus their son Hani and his lovely wife Sally.

Another person who made this project outstanding was my friend and traveling companion Peggy Day. A person of great spiritual depth, she is also the CPS/Mystic Children's Studio publisher of my first title, *The Golden Ones: From Atlantis to a New World.*

As always, my husband John Chapman supports me in my work. He is also a wonderful traveling companion as I traipse around in various countries taking photographs.

As usual, I appreciate all the help I received from librarians, especially from Linda Caputi at Edgar Cayce's A.R.E's marvelous metaphysical library in Virginia Beach, Virginia.

Again, I am happy to show my appreciation for the fine work of Lynn Redman at Camera City in Hampton, Virginia for his amazing skill in processing my film, especially the low light images taken in the pharaohs' tombs. Because of Lynn's expertise, I have the beautiful photographs that became the cover plus most of the internal illustrations of the book.

Thanks also to Hilario Hilaire for sharing his knowledge of the Maya medicine man explanation of falling into the serpent's mouth.

My gratitude goes to Santiago Domingo of Santa Elena, Yucatan, who graciously shared the stories handed down to him by his Maya grandparents about the witch who hatched a dwarf companion from an egg.

My appreciation also goes out to Pam Bailey for sharing her personal encounter with an apparition of the Blessed Virgin.

Thanks to my proofreaders: Cher Balsley, Jean C. Keating, Cathy Hunsberger, and Lindy van Burik. I am especially grateful to Virginia Hulsey, one of my wonderful proofreaders, who pointed out to me that the pictures in the pharaohs' tombs showed red-skinned individuals in support of Cayce's readings saying that the Atlanteans were the red race. She assumed everyone had noticed this but, as far as I know, no one else has been astute enough to see what was right before our eyes.

Thanks to Adam, Cher, Clair, and Miriam Balsley for their proofing of the cover.

I also feel grateful for her enthusiasm and the changes suggested by Una Marcotte for improving marketing and publicity.

My deepest appreciation goes to Clair Balsley, my editor, for her marvelous editorial skills, creative ideas, formatting abilities, research, writing, and immense patience. She is also the creator of all the wonderful maps including those showing Marion apparition sites.

Finally, my heartfelt appreciation goes to the wonderful power of the female Christ energy, most commonly known as the Mother of God, the Blessed Virgin Mary, and the Holy Mother, for her guidance in this endeavor and also her healing.

PART I

JOURNEY TO THE
LAND OF THE PHARAOHS

Chapter One

UNIVERSE IN CHARGE

I trudged on in the darkness. I did not see another non-Egyptian among the hundreds of people who trekked down the dark, narrow alleyways toward the place where the apparition of the Virgin Mary was to appear.

What was I doing here? I asked myself as I tramped on. My sole purpose in going to Egypt had been to find evidence that people of Atlantis had journeyed to pre-historic Egypt.

Why was I here, walking in the darkness, instead of searching through Egyptian antiquities? I was in a town out-of-bounds to tourists surrounded by hundreds of Egyptians. We all walked to the same place—the place where the apparition was supposed to appear. *The apparition? What was that?*

At first I tried to remember the turns we took so I could find my way back to the car, just in case I became separated from my Egyptian friends. After a while, I lost track of the corners turned, the alleys gone through, and the buildings passed.

We walked on and on. Hundreds of Egyptian men, women, and children flowed around me like leaves floating on a stream. Some wore Muslim finery, some Western attire, and some the long dress-like Egyptian outfits called gallabias. We all traipsed purposefully in the same direction.

It must have been about one in the morning by now, maybe two. Many more strangers streamed in from side streets, most of them striding silently with the crowd. Ancient five-story brick apartment buildings lined the alley making it look like a tunnel.

On that dark night in September 2000, I did not know how long we were going to walk. I did not know where we were going.

I also did not know that Asyut, this town where the apparition chose to appear, had been designated as out-of-bounds for all foreigners—not only tourists. Militant Islamic terrorists had been attacking Christians and tourists there for 25 years.

Neither did I know that six Christian teenagers had recently been murdered because they would not convert to Islam.

Even without this knowledge, I felt afraid. We passed many stairways leading down to below-ground apartments. I realized that someone could grab me, drag me down into a dark basement, and no one would ever know what became of me.

What else could I do but plod blindly on, making sure to keep my Egyptian hosts in plain sight like a small dependent child?

As I tramped along, I thought back to the amazing coincidences that brought me to this experience. My original reason for visiting Egypt had nothing to do with this pilgrimage. Apparently the Universe had different ideas!

Evidence of Atlantis and Our Immortality

My quest began in 1995 when I went to a hypnotherapist for weight control and inadvertently connected with past life memories of Atlantis. While hypnotized, I saw myself travel to geologically stable lands in Egypt when earthquakes began to break up Atlantis. Hence, even though that great island nation had been destroyed, I believed there would be evidence of Atlanteans in Egypt. In books, I had seen pictures of paintings on the walls of the pharaohs' tombs that looked very much like my memories of Atlantis. I wanted to see these images and photograph them.

My hypnosis sessions had also contained dire warnings of upcoming earth upheavals. Because I had correctly predicted an earthquake a year in advance—the month, year, and location—I feared these predictions of earth upheavals might be accurate.

Fortunately, a lot of hope also surfaced in my sessions. The most encouraging information that appeared in my trance sessions had to do with my memories of being a pure soul without a body in Atlantis. This meant I was eternal. I also saw how my soul became enmeshed with the physical.

Since I had seen photographs of paintings in the pharaohs' tombs that looked like my Atlantean memories, I felt excited that by finding these images I would find evidence that we are really souls manifesting in a body and therefore immortal. That is the reason I wanted to find evidence of Atlantis in the pharaohs' tombs and the reason I had to go to Egypt.

Although my original quest had nothing to do with apparitions of the Virgin Mary, as I would soon discover, Mary, Atlantis, and our beginnings as souls on earth are deeply intertwined. The Universe truly was in charge.

The Man of My Dreams

The catalyst for my Egyptian foray occurred when my husband, John, received approval from his employer, the National Aeronautical and Space Administration (NASA), for travel to Barcelona, Spain. He would contribute to a symposium for which he had written a scientific paper, and I would accompany him.

John is literally the man of my dreams. I had a dream that showed me a stranger I would marry before I met him in waking life. I wrote about these experiences in *When We Were Gods,* the updated, revised edition of *The Golden Ones.*

Since I'll occasionally be referring to these titles in the rest of this book, from now on, when I refer to *When We Were Gods*, know that I also mean *The Golden Ones* since the latter is the original edition.

Because Barcelona is close to Egypt, I naturally assumed John would be as excited as I was at the thought of seeing the Great Pyramid and the Sphinx. After his symposium ended, he could take a week of vacation time and the both of us could go to Egypt. It made perfect sense.

"Perfect nonsense!" he said.

Egypt No!

To my amazement, he not only declined to go to Egypt, but he absolutely refused. He cited political unrest, the spread of AIDS, garbage smells, and malaria.

Garbage smells?

"John," I said, "There were garbage smells at the Great Pyramid?"

"No," he looked at me with exasperation. "I was *never* in Egypt," as if it should be obvious.

"Then why won't you come to Egypt with me?"

His exact words were, "I refuse to set foot on African soil ever again."

It turned out he had good reasons for his strong feelings. During his years in the Peace Corps he had taught school in Zaire.

At the same time, the ruthless dictator Mobutu reigned supreme in this central African country, which is now called the Democratic Republic of the Congo. John had been in the midst of some life-threatening situations.

When he told me this, I looked at him dubiously. "Come on, John," I said, "your Peace Corps days were over 30 years ago. Things have changed in Africa."

"You're right," he said, "personal safety is much worse."

"Maybe in Central Africa" I said. "But not in Egypt. Millions of people come from all over the world to see the Great Pyramid."

"What about those tourists that were killed?" he said.

"Which tourists?" I asked.

"It was in the news."

"When?" I asked.

"A number of years ago."

"A number of years ago!" I said. "Who cares? I'm going now, not a number of years ago."

"I made a vow," John said. "I will never set foot on African soil again."

As I have often said in my lectures, when I asked the Universe to give me a man who was the other side of my puzzle—the one who had been with me from the beginning of time, my twin soul—I did not realize I would get someone who shared not only my good qualities but also some of my worst. As John has said many times, he knows of no one more stubborn than he is, except for me.

"OK," I said, "if you won't come with me, I'm going myself."

I waited to hear him offer to accompany me. Instead he said, "Suit yourself, but you're making a mistake. It's too dangerous."

Help From a Friend

I decided I would go to Egypt while John attended the symposium and we could tour Spain for a week afterward. To get a better idea of what to expect in the land of the pharaohs, I telephoned an old girlfriend. She had married a man from Egypt. His name was Hani (pronounced HA-nee). As it turned out, my girlfriend and her Egyptian husband had been divorced for ten years and she had moved away. Fortunately, her now ex-husband remembered me.

"KEH-rol," Hani said on the telephone in his lovely lilting Arabic accent. "How have you been?"

After we spent a few minutes getting caught up on our families' lives, I explained my intention to visit Egypt in the near future. Although I had merely called Hani for advice on how to approach my excursion to Egypt, he, like John, expressed concern that I planned to go alone.

Things were not going well. Hani told me that Egypt was not a country in which women traveled alone. "A camel driver could drag you away," he said.

A camel driver! I thought. *A camel driver? When would I meet a camel driver?* Hani was obviously exaggerating.

But then, I remembered a 1990 movie, *Sheltering Sky*, directed by Bernardo Bertolucci that starred Debra Winger and John Malkovich. In the movie, the Debra Winger character had been marooned in the desert. Members of a camel caravan had rescued her and she had become the sex slave of a Bedouin camel driver.

A camel driver? Of course, the movie was fiction. But, I had to admit that vast deserts flanked the Nile River with the famous and treacherous Sahara Desert on its west. Camel drivers probably still wended their caravans through the sand dunes.

I told Hani that I had no intention of wandering anywhere near the Sahara Desert or a Bedouin camel driver.

At this point, normally, things should *not* have worked out. I should have become discouraged, given up on my desire to go to Egypt, and meekly agreed to travel with my husband to Barcelona. To tell you the truth, I was just about to back down.

However, this trip to Egypt seemed to be taking on a life of its own, because that's when Hani said that if I insisted on stubbornly refusing to see reason, I must stay with his sister and her family.

And that is how I ended up staying with an Egyptian family in Cairo.

Going Solo

The next problem occurred when John's employer suddenly cancelled his travel arrangements. Eek! I would no longer be meeting him in Barcelona. My travel to Egypt had truly become a solo adventure.

Although disconcerting, John's change of plans was nothing new. During my six years of work as a photojournalist under contract to NASA, I had repeatedly had travel arrangements cancelled or established with barely enough time to get packed. With the government there was always the slight chance that the "Powers That Be" might change their minds at the last minute and John would fly to Barcelona after all.

Five days before my flight left for Cairo, there still was no change in plans.

An Unexpected Telephone Call

At the same time, I had been in close communication with Peggy Day, the publisher of the first edition of my first book, *The Golden Ones: from Atlantis to a New World*. Peggy is also the co-author of a wonderful book called, E*dgar Cayce on the Indigo Children: Understanding Psychic Children* which has recently been renamed *Psychic Children: A Sign of Our Expanding Awareness*.

Five days before my scheduled solo departure for Egypt, Peggy called me and said three short words, "I must go."

Confused, I asked her, "Pardon? What did you say?"

"In my meditations the last couple of days . . . ," she began. Peggy made most of her decisions by consulting with Spirit.

"I'm going with you!" she exclaimed in a gleeful voice. Perhaps because I did not reply with equal exuberance—I felt surprised at the news—she added, "if you will have me."

My mind reeled. "Oh!" I said, my heart pounding. I didn't know what to say. I should have been delighted, but instead I blanched.

It would have been OK to be in Egypt with John. However, I had heard that many travelers suffered with the Pharaoh's Revenge, or severe gastrointestinal distress while in Egypt.

"I would love to have a companion," I replied wanly, "but what if we get sick?"

"That's OK," Peggy replied. She told me how during her one previous trip to Egypt, when she went with a tour group, not only did one of the elderly members of their group die suddenly of a heart attack, but everyone who ate a certain tainted chicken dinner spent the next two days sick with diarrhea and vomiting. She said that if it happened again, we could simply take turns using the bathroom. She was sure the experience, if it occurred, would only bring us closer together as friends. Basically, she was game. She'd been through the worst and she knew she could manage it again.

I was not sure if I could. Nonetheless, I did welcome a traveling companion. Furthermore, Peggy already knew my story. What better person to accompany me on a quest to find confirmation of my memories of Atlantis than Peggy—the person who had been so filled with enthusiasm for my story that she wanted to publish it?

"I would love it if you came with me!" I replied to Peggy, once I had finished my deliberations.

A Surprise Development

Now that Peggy was coming with me, I had to call Hani again to tell him I no longer needed to burden his sister with my presence. I would not be alone. Peggy and I could stay in a hotel together.

Again, Hani telephoned his sister in Cairo. When he called me back, he said that his sister Mohga (pronounced MOH-ga) would be happy to have both Peggy and me stay with her in Cairo.

How generous of her, I thought.

"But," Hani continued, "Mohga has a request to make of you." He explained that, by chance, for the last month or so, apparitions of the Blessed Virgin Mary had been appearing in their family's home town of Asyut. Did we want to see the apparition? If so, Mohga would wait until our arrival and take us there with her.

I knew that apparitions of the Virgin Mary were one of the most unusual supernatural events on earth. Were they real? If not, what were they? I am an innately curious person. I thought, *Of course I want to see apparitions of the Virgin Mary. Who wouldn't?*

But would Peggy agree? I telephoned her and explained the latest development. Peggy told me how she had traveled to view apparitions of the Virgin Mary with another author, Jennifer Lingda Tinsman, whose book, *Not My Gift: A Story of Divine Empowerment*, Peggy had published. Unfortunately, she and her friend had not seen the apparition. However, Peggy told me it was the hope of her life to see apparitions of the Virgin Mary.

And that's how my quest to find evidence of Atlantis in Egypt became a pilgrimage.

Chapter Two

CAIRO AT NIGHT

Apprehensions in the Airport

I waited for Peggy in New York City's John F. Kennedy International Airport. Because of Peggy's last minute addition to my excursion, my travel agent had worked hard to get the both of us on the same flight to and from Egypt. Unfortunately, this required that I leave my home in southeastern Virginia at 4:30 in the morning to catch an early flight to New York City. Our flight to Egypt would leave in the evening giving me a whole day to wander around the airport. During that time, I had a lot of time to think about my upcoming adventure.

In addition, a couple of days before I left, John's work had reinstated his travel to Barcelona, which meant that my return flight also had to be reworked. Because of the last minute change in the return flight, I had been up all night repacking my suitcases, this time for two climates—the scorching desert heat of Egypt and the Mediterranean climate of Barcelona. I was exhausted.

Facing the Unknown

I also felt anxious. Talk about leaving many loose ends. Peggy and I would be flying to a Middle Eastern country without the benefit of an organized tour. We would be staying at the home of an unknown woman whose brother I had briefly met more than ten years previously.

Once we arrived in Cairo, we had to depend upon Mohga to be at the airport and for us somehow to recognize each other. Then, we had to depend on Mohga's good nature to pick us up and take us to her home.

Because my travel plans from the U.S. to Egypt changed so much in the week before I left, I did not have the time to make in-country travel arrangements from Cairo to the Valley of the Kings in Luxor, the location of the pharaohs' tombs. During our many telephone calls back and forth, Hani assured me that his family had a cousin in Cairo who was a travel agent. He could make our in-Egypt travel arrangements. I hoped this cousin knew what he was doing. What if Peggy and I did not make it back from the Valley of the Kings in time for our flight out of Cairo?

Furthermore, sometime during our stay in Egypt, we would go to see an apparition—whatever that was.

Fatima and Lourdes

I knew very little about supernormal events. Although articles about apparitions of the Virgin blasted out from the front pages of newspaper tabloids in the checkout line at the grocery store, I really knew very little about the Holy Mother's appearances. The headlines usually contained the words, "Fatima" and "Final Secret," with the sensational pronouncement that the end of the world was at hand. What was I getting into?

I also had a vague recollection of a place called Lourdes in the Pyrenees Mountains in France close to the border of Spain. While traveling in France with John a number of years previously, I had read about Lourdes in a travel guidebook. According to the book, the Virgin had created a spring with miraculous healing powers. This spring still exists and people flock to Lourdes for cures.

My Traveling Companion

I also felt uneasy about Peggy. We had met only once before. All the preparation of my manuscript had been accomplished over the telephone, via email, using the postal service, and through overnight courier. Although it was true that we had become close during this professional relationship, still, she was hardly a person I knew well enough with whom to undertake a week-long travel adventure.

Furthermore, what if I did not find her in the airport? JFK is huge! In the end, it turned out that Peggy and I had circled each other in the terminal for hours without knowing the other was there. I looked for a woman of about five-feet-six-inches (1.7 meters) in height with short ash blonde hair. I had reminded her that I was five-feet-three-inches (1.6 meters tall), chubby, and had dark curly hair.

Peggy Day

When I finally saw Peggy's sweet face, I felt so relieved. We talked as we stood in line to obtain boarding passes. Then, we boarded the Lufthansa plane for a non-stop flight to Cairo.

The Flight to Cairo

As the Lufthansa stewardess tucked soft blankets around us in the dimly lit cabin of the plane, I could not help but wonder. We were supposed to arrive in Cairo in the middle of the night. Would strangers bother to meet people they did not know in the middle of the night?

Hani assured me that all of Cairo stayed awake at night in the hot months. Since Peggy and I would be arriving at the end of September, the days would still be scorching, with temperatures well over 100 degrees Fahrenheit (37.8 degrees Celsius). Hani said his sister and her family would be up anyway. Everyone was. It was the only decent time of day to be awake. I hoped he was right.

The Cairo Airport

As we approached Cairo International Airport, I looked out my window hoping I could see the pyramids from the air. However, I only saw the blackness of night. As the plane descended over Cairo, no pyramids came to view, only city lights.

After we landed I discovered, to my surprise, that the airport was empty . . . totally and completely empty . . . with nothing but white walls, white ceilings, and white floors.

How different. Where were the restaurants, magazine stands, and souvenir shops? Where were the video games, fast food outlets, and gift stores? Where were the neon signs and the hot dog stands? Where were fellow passengers waiting for their flights? I saw nothing familiar.

We were part of a group of about 20 passengers who shuffled along the vacant hallway. Where were the rest of the passengers from the plane? The plane had been full. We huddled together as we walked. Our footsteps echoed along the floor. The tunnel-like corridor curved so we could not see ahead.

As we progressed forward, we encountered a couple of machine-gun-armed guards in the otherwise empty corridor. My mind wanted to make the judgment that Egypt must be a much less safe country than the United States. Then I reminded myself that U.S. airports also contain security guards. Since the terrorist attacks of September 11, 2001, our airports now contain machine-gun-toting National Guardsmen as well.

Back in September 2000, my mind wanted to pronounce Egypt substandard to the U.S. However, I remembered a trip I made to Nicaragua a number of years earlier. I had discovered that, despite the abject poverty, the people possessed a richness of spirit with which I was unfamiliar in the United States in spite of its affluence. I thought about Mohga welcoming me and Peggy— virtual strangers—into her home. Would I do the same given a similar situation?

A swarthy-skinned, black-haired guard wearing a khaki uniform stood beside the wall. He motioned at us with the tip of his machine gun to turn left at a juncture in the corridor. We shuffled past him, keeping well out of the way of the gun.

Before long, the hallway opened up into a large area where a number of men stood on our right. Behind them, I saw painted signs hanging on the wall proclaiming the names of hotels. I guessed that the men must be drivers sent to pick up passengers registered at their hotels. A number of passengers walked over to the drivers. I made a mental note of the sign saying, "Mena House," because I had heard about Mena House before. It was supposed to be a hotel that was situated within walking distance of the Great Pyramid. At the time, I did not know that there are many hotels situated within walking distance of the Pyramid.

My fear that Hani's sister would not turn up at the airport intensified. What if she was not there? How easy it would be to walk over to one of the hotel drivers and get a room at a hotel. I decided that if Mohga did not appear by the time we came to the exit doors, I would walk back through the airport to the Mena House driver and arrange to stay at the hotel.

After we passed the drivers, we saw the lighted booths of money changers on our left. They could change our money from U.S. dollars to Egyptian currency. In all the panic of the last-minute travel arrangements, it had not even occurred to me to get Egyptian money. These money changers were opened in the middle of the night. That suited me just fine.

Alone in Cairo

Once we obtained Egyptian currency, Peggy and I murmured to each other, wondering where and when we would find the place to connect with Mohga. I felt as if we were two little children lost in the woods.

So far we had seen only guards, airport personnel, money-changers, and hotel drivers. Where was the place where friends and family waited to greet loved ones?

In a U.S. airport, people can meet with passengers within the airport at the baggage claim area. But we had long since claimed our baggage and gone through customs. Where was the area in the Cairo airport designated for meeting friends and family?

Hani had said that Mohga would be waiting for us outside the airport. What if she and her family were not there? What if we stepped out of the airport and were not allowed back in? Already we had seen that only passengers and airport personnel were allowed within the walls of the building.

I kept looking for the large floor-to-ceiling glass doors and windows that denote the outside of a U.S. airport. Would Mohga be standing there, her face pressed against the glass, hoping to recognize us?

As Peggy and I searched for the place where passengers greeted family and friends, I suddenly remembered that I had probably met Mohga before. If memory served me right, we had met long ago when Hani and his wife were still married. His now-estranged wife, my friend, was a wonderful cook. Both she and Hani loved to have large outdoor extravaganzas where they roasted a lamb or a piglet on a spit. She would also cook endless delectable cakes and confections. The purpose of one of these super-picnics was to welcome Hani's sisters and brothers-in-law to a vacation in Canada.

If I remembered Mohga correctly, she had an impish sense of humor and dimples. Would I be able to recognize a face I had seen only briefly over 10 years previously? Would I even be able to see her through a glass door as she stood outside in the dark of the night?

As it turned out, I did not need to look through a glass door. The doorway to the parking lot of the Cairo airport did not have doors, glass or otherwise. At the end of the hallway, I saw two openings that represented doorways in the cement walls of the airport. Beyond them, I saw Cairo. Dim lights shone over a parking lot full of cars. The sky looked black.

In front of the open doorways I saw a barricade made of the kind of thigh-high cement barriers you see at construction sites. Leaning over the barricade, various men and women called out in Arabic to friends and loved ones. Most of the women wore long Muslim dresses and head coverings. Many of the men wore turbans.

Anxiously I scanned their faces for a woman with an impish grin and dimples.

She was not there! We were alone in Cairo! Thank God Peggy had come with me. Together we could rent a room at one of the hotels. I hoped the airport officials would allow us to make our way back through the white corridors to the Mena House shuttle driver. Hopefully the hotel had some vacancies.

Just then, from behind the crowd pressed along the cement barriers I heard a lilting woman's voice intone, as if she was calling a child, "Keh-rol . . . Keh-rol."

I swallowed. Could it be? Mohga? Was she hidden in the darkness? Peggy and I crept along the line of people to the end of the cement barrier. Here the people stood three or four individuals deep. We saw three people—a woman and two men. I could hardly see their faces because they stood in darkness. However, I could see well enough to discern they wore smiles and hopeful expressions on their faces.

My heart beat rapidly. Could this be them?

The woman waved to us. Could it be Mohga? When I came closer, she smiled . . . a lovely dimpled smile. Mohga!

She was as I remembered her—a woman of about my height with a dimpled grin. Her eyes, amber-colored as they glistened with light reflected from inside the airport, assured me that she

Gad   **Mohga**

remembered me also and looked forward to our visit.

She wore an ankle-length dress with short sleeves. Her husband, Gad, wore a white shirt and black slacks. Marcos, their son, also wore a business outfit.

Driving in Cairo

In no time at all, they led us to their car in the dark parking lot, loaded our luggage in the trunk, and sped us away through the nighttime streets of Cairo.

When I say "sped" through the streets of Cairo, I mean it. Gad whisked along the dark roads. To my consternation, I noticed that the inhabitants of Cairo have a peculiar way of driving. I do not know if they simply have complete disregard for the lines marking the lanes or if they merely consider the lane markings as inconsequential road art.

Where three lanes are marked on a multilane road, they manage to fit in at least four, sometimes five, rows of cars, all going at breakneck speeds. In addition, most of their cars use standard transmissions. Therefore, Gad, who was at the wheel—Mohga does not drive—had to constantly keep moving his hands and feet as he shifted gears.

When we came into the center of town, his driving style became even more complicated. You have to realize that Cairo is a huge city comprised of a population of over 15 million people.

In the downtown area, as in the downtown of any megalopolis, there are huge avenues made of six to eight lanes of traffic. Three-to-four-lanes are for traffic going in one direction and three-to-four lanes are for traffic going in the opposite direction. At intersections, these large downtown streets are crossed by equally large six-to-eight-lane streets comprised of lanes of cars crossing to the right and left.

However, in Cairo, because of the disregard for lane markings, instead of three-to-four lanes of traffic going in one direction, there were four to six rows of cars going in one direction on a huge downtown street.

In Cairo, intersections are not regulated by traffic lights, as they are in the United States. In fact, they are not regulated at all. No traffic lights. No traffic police. Not even stop signs!

Instead, Cairo drivers weave their vehicles through the intersections. That means that there are no cars stopped at intersections to allow crossing traffic to pass. Instead, the cars going in one direction weave through the cars crossing in front of them in the same way as a line of skaters weaves through another line of skaters at the Ice Capades or a shuttle weaves through woof threads on a loom.

The intersections are always full of cars weaving slowly through cars crossing their direction of travel. The drivers use a unique system of honking horns and, at night, flashing headlights. During the time I spent in Cairo, I did not decipher the honk and flash code. However, I do know that to negotiate an intersection it required that Gad keep his arms and legs in constant motion as he braked, changed gears, honked the horn, and turned the headlights on and off.

I found it quite fascinating to watch him, and even more intriguing to see how four to six rows of cars traveling in one direction managed to weave through four to six rows of vehicles traveling across the road whenever we navigated through an intersection.

The ability to turn left in one of these intersections must have taken consummate skill . . . and thank God, Gad had it. I can only conclude that Cairo natives must possess formidable reflexes and code-breaking abilities as well as a deep trust of their fellows.

As they negotiate a left turn, they inch forward through all the cars in the intersection. I hoped that everyone in the intersection was awake and aware because the grill of one car after another, its headlights flashing on and off, its horn honking intermittently, pointed at the side of the car where I sat.

When we finally made it out onto the open road again I felt exhilarated as we sped along the dark streets of the residential areas. Peggy and I had made it to Cairo safely and had found Mohga and her family! And, they were such nice people.

I had felt an instant rapport with Mohga—as if I'd known her my whole life. Peggy felt it too. We both were relieved that we not only felt at ease in her company but that we also liked her so much.

When Mohga asked us if we wanted to stay up and tour the city or go back to their place, I said, "Let's keep going." I wanted to see Cairo—the sooner the better. I had read that Egypt's capital city was the largest city in Africa. I wanted to see it all—the mosques, the bazaars, the people . . . I had never been in a Middle Eastern city before.

"Are you sure, Keh-rol?" Mohga asked in her lilting voice. "You are not tired?"

"No," I said, "the Lufthansa flight was wonderful. They made our overnight passage extremely comfortable. The food was fantastic. I slept most of the way. . ."

As far as I was concerned, it was one of those time zone mysteries. I had already slept the night on the plane, but when I arrived in Cairo, the night was just beginning. Shouldn't it be the other way around? Shouldn't it be morning? Had I lost a day? Was I just confused? Maybe I was more jet lagged than I thought. Maybe Mohga was just being polite and really wanted to get home to sleep.

"Are you sure?" asked Mohga again.

By the way she said it I suspected that I might be showing signs of drowsiness. At this point I wondered if I might be exhibiting one of my most unsettling characteristics while traveling overseas—an amazing ability to fall asleep anywhere and at any time.

I thought back to the previous week—the hectic last-minute airline changes, John's last minute reinstatement to Barcelona, Peggy's last-minute announcement that she was coming with me, and my early morning flight to New York City. Maybe I was more exhausted than I realized.

"OK, you're probably right," I said to Mohga. "Let's go back to your place."

Mohga and Gad's Villa

I hardly remember Mohga and Gad's home that first night in Cairo probably because I was so tired. I do remember mounting the stairs to the second floor of their house. They lived in a three-story villa. The second floor was the main floor they used. The ground floor was for visitors.

Peggy and I would be staying in the ground-floor apartment, which had previously been inhabited by Hani and Mohga's father before his passing. Peggy and I would sleep in one room, which had two beds. I chose the narrow cot under the window and gave Peggy the double bed.

Wooden slats covered the window diagonally. They were spaced so close together that only a very narrow opening separated them. Although, in the United States we would use a wire-mesh screen to let cool air into the house and keep mosquitoes out, in Cairo, residents often use wooden slats in their windows. This arrangement also provides a barrier against intruders.

Both Peggy and I were taking malaria prevention pills which our doctors had prescribed for us before leaving the U.S. Nonetheless, during the week I spent in Egypt, I never saw or heard a mosquito within the city of Cairo.

I appreciated that Peggy and I had our own bathroom on the bottom floor. Just in case the Pharaoh's Revenge struck, I would be less embarrassed.

Although I felt tired as I lay on the little cot under the window with the wooden slats across it, I could not sleep. Even though the slats provided a safe barrier against intruders, they did not keep out the commotion of the many people living on the other side of the window.

Modern apartment buildings about eight stories high surrounded Mohga and Gad's three-story villa. Our hosts had once lived on a street of villas, but developers had built the apartment buildings around them.

Myriad sounds emanated from the hundreds of people living in the adjacent high rises. A baby howled. A man and woman shouted at each other in Arabic. The hum and roar of the city throbbed all around us. Hani was right. Everyone in Cairo stayed awake in the middle of the night.

The smell of some strange food wafted through the thin spaces between the wooden slats in the window. As I lay in the darkness listening to the people bickering in Arabic high above me, a wave of panic gripped me.

What was I doing in this strange place surrounded by people who were so different from me? Would I get home safely?

Peggy had made only one stipulation of her accompanying me on my quest. She had to get enough sleep. Evidently she is a person who requires more than the usual eight hours of sleep to maintain her health and equanimity. Therefore, she had brought a mask which she wore over her eyes to block out any light.

Light from the wooden slats made stripes across the covers on Peggy's bed. I could not see her face because shadows covered her pillow. I wondered if Peggy lay wide-eyed in the dark like me or if she slept with her mask firmly in place. I felt afraid to say anything lest I wake her. So I said nothing and felt my heart pounding in the darkness.

Chapter Three

FAT KARMA AND DEATH

Baksheesh

The next day, Marcos kindly took Mohga, Peggy, and me for a daytime drive through Cairo. At one point, he turned into a service road and parked in front of a restaurant.

While he went inside to get barbecued lamb, a little boy, dressed in the traditional cotton gallabia, came to the open window of the car to sell us limes. Mohga bargained with the boy and then paid him when he asked for "Baksheesh."

Marcos

Gallabia

Since I'd been warned by an American tour guide to be wary of Egyptians preying on tourists, asking, "Baksheesh," I learned from this interaction that Baksheesh is not only requested from tourists but also from native Egyptians. It is merely the term used to request a payment for a product or service.

We returned to the house and enjoyed a wonderful feast. Mohga and Gad's lovely daughter Rena, short for Marian, had come home from her work as a pharmacist. We talked, ate, and laughed. I felt warmly welcomed.

Rena

Hypnotherapy and Weight Problems

As I described earlier, I originally went to Egypt to confirm my memories of Atlantis in the paintings on the walls of the pharaohs' tombs. To my surprise, I was now about to also experience a validation of another one of my past life memories.

As you know, I went to a hypnotherapist to lose weight. However, I did not mention earlier that I would have never put myself in what I considered to be an extremely vulnerable position while hypnotized if I had not been desperate.

My weight problem had intensified after a miscarriage. Although I had struggled with a tendency to obesity for most of my adult life, the weight gain after the miscarriage exploded uncontrollably. Before the miscarriage, I usually bounced back and forth between about 20 extra pounds of weight. As soon as I hit the upper weight level I would diet until I attained the lower end of my weight range: yo-yo dieting.

After my miscarriage, the weight piled on relentlessly. For a time, I gained a pound a day. In two or three weeks, I had to buy a whole new wardrobe at a larger size. Two or three weeks later, I had to buy another new wardrobe. In no time at all, I had to traipse back to the stores to buy yet another set of clothes, this time even larger than the last group.

Having just married the man of my dreams, I felt panicked. What did he think of me? Could he still love me as I quickly transposed into a blimp?

I had been eating a lot of chocolate for comfort following the miscarriage. When I asked my family doctor if eating the chocolate caused the rapid weight gain she informed me that no one could eat enough food to gain a pound a day. Something had to be out of kilter with my body.

In the end, I went to four doctors—my family doctor and three obstetrician/gynecologists. One ob/gyn gave me a diagnosis of a hormonal imbalance. He said that occasionally women's hormones went awry after a miscarriage with the result that they gained weight at a phenomenal rate. He did not know why this happened and he did not know what to do for me. He did say that usually the rate of weight gain eventually evened off.

"Eventually . . . usually," that was the best he could do for me. However, "eventually" and "usually" were not good enough for me. They sounded like "never" and "hardly ever." I felt terrified. From my point of view, I was doomed to expand until I could no longer fit through a door. Already theater seats had become tight.

That is why I went to a hypnotherapist. A friend suggested that through hypnotherapy I could tell my body I was no longer pregnant and make suggestions to regulate my hormonal imbalance.

At first, the hypnotherapist used conventional hypnotherapy for weight loss, telling my body, and especially my endocrine system, which controls our hormones, to return to a normal rate of function.

When this did not work—I returned the following week seven pounds heavier—the hypnotherapist thought that because I had had a tendency to obesity my whole adult life, the cause of my problem might be due to an incident in my past. She said it might have resulted from something in my childhood—say, if my parents had called me "Chubbo" so that I now subconsciously believed I must maintain a chubby body. Or the problem could stem from an incident further back in my past, that is to say, from something that happened in a previous lifetime.

At the time, I felt ready to try anything. In addition, I believed in reincarnation because as a child I had had a recurring dream in which I lived in France. Therefore, I knew I had lived before.

Mockery and Karma

It turned out that I did have a number of past life memories that had contributed to my present problems with overweight.

For example, throughout my lifetime as a member of the aristocracy during the French Revolution, I had ridiculed fat people. The spiritual rule is: You reap what you sow. By mocking fat people in my past lifetime, I now experienced ridicule as a result of my own fat. Most often, the mockery came from me.

Furthermore, I now lived in a culture that considered obesity worthy of derision. Multi-billion dollar industries flourish as a result of our population's obsession with slenderness.

In my present lifetime, I reaped the result of my mockery. Now I still disliked fat people, as do most people in the affluent West, but now I was one of them. I truly was reaping what I had sown so many lifetimes earlier.

Starvation and Fat Karma

Hypnotherapists who do past life regressions find that one of the reasons people in this lifetime have weight problems is that some people carry a feeling of constant hunger with them, a remnant from a previous lifetime in which they starved. Subconsciously, they feel as if they will never find food again and have to eat all the time.

Though they may be surrounded by plenty of food and know that they need not go hungry, they feel as if they have not eaten for days. Even though they eat more than they need to, the feeling of hunger continues.

During that lifetime in 18th century France, I had been well-fed during most of my life as a member of the privileged aristocratic class in revolutionary France. However, I had also been thrown into the dungeon prior to my beheading at the guillotine.

Throughout the time I spent in the dungeon, my jailers had only fed me the most meager meals of gruel and water. I lived with constant hunger, my shrunken stomach aching for food. As a result, in this present 21st century lifetime, I have occasionally felt hungry even after eating a full-course meal.

Desire and Karma

I also learned there had been lifetimes in which I had actually wished to be fat. Those of us living in the affluent West forget that throughout much of human history, and in many countries in the world today, people are hungry.

During my imprisonment and torture in revolutionary France, I had moaned about the boniness of my hips. Being slender during that time meant that I was poor. As the jeering rabble surrounded the cart that took me to the guillotine, I felt grateful that the thick pleats of my dress hid my emaciated hip bones.

From this incarnation, I had learned that a person has to be careful what they wish for. In my French experience, I had wished to be bigger in the hips. Now I am.

African Lifetime

In yet another lifetime, I found myself a young African woman who lived close to a river surrounded by grasslands. I had a small, nymph-like body, exactly the kind of body I would love to have in this lifetime. My tribe had been attacked by a cannibalistic tribe undergoing a manhood ceremony.

However, the chief's son could not kill me. Instead, he captured me and made me his bride. A number of years later, he became the tribe's chief and invented agriculture so his tribe would not have to kill and eat other humans anymore.

In that lifetime, the people of my husband's tribe were much taller and bigger boned than I was. I often stood in a circle with the other women of the tribe pounding grain, our children playing around us. With each pound of the mortar, I wished to be big like everyone else in the tribe.

Now, in this present lifetime, I was big, but not tall. Instead, I was wide and becoming wider. My wishes from my past lives had come true.

Memories of Death

At the end of my past life in Africa, I experienced my death. The hypnotherapist had asked me to go to the last day of that lifetime.

I found myself on a raised bier breathing my last breaths. After many years as a beloved wife and mother, my coarse hair was now gray. My time had come.

Stars shone in the night sky. The odors of parched grass and dirt filled my lungs with each labored breath. The black silhouettes of scruffy trees and bushes surrounded the clearing where the members of my tribe stood in a group helping me to make the transition. Even children stood quietly with their parents in the darkness. Babies slept in their mother's arms.

This African lifetime, in which I felt so loved and supported by my community, was the sweetest lifetime I remembered in my hypnosis sessions. My husband, who was now the chief of the tribe, sat beside me on the bier. I struggled with one ragged breath after another. Lovingly, he held my hand.

Against the dark night sky I could see that he had put mud in his hair. The mud had dried so his hair looked thick and almost shoulder length silhouetted against the stars.

While hypnotized I kept saying to the hypnotherapist, "He has mud in his hair! He has mud in his hair!" In my memories of this African lifetime, the mud in my husband's hair signified grief and hence, my imminent demise.

I had never heard nor read of this in waking life. That is why I kept saying, while hypnotized, "He has mud in his hair." It seemed so inconceivable yet a part of me "knew" that he had put the mud in his hair to show his grief.

I thought my overactive imagination had produced the mud in his hair. A strong skeptical part of me assumed I had merely made up these memories with an overactive imagination.

However, I was about to receive a validation of that African lifetime in present-day Egypt.

Christina

Mohga employed a young woman from the Sudan as a housekeeper. Christina came in everyday to help with the housework. In honor of Peggy's and my visit, she wore her native dress on our first morning in Cairo. It was a lovely piece of green fabric tied over one shoulder to form a dress.

Sudan is an equatorial country to the south of Egypt, as shown on the map on page six. It is the site of what the United Nations has described as one of the worst human conditions on earth. Because of civil war, many people are homeless, sick, and starving.

Christina, however, in 2000, was tall, healthy, and beautiful. She and her husband had fled from the Sudan for Egypt. Knowing what I now know about the Sudan, I hope she has remained in Egypt.

Christina

When I met her, I felt drawn to her beauty. Tall and graceful, she stood straight and with an easy confidence. She had warm, dark eyes and a friendly mouth. I liked her. Although it made no sense, she looked familiar to me. I thought it was because of her hair.

Where had I seen that kind of hair before? Then I remembered. It looked like the hair of the people in the African tribe of my past life memory. Had I remembered a lifetime in what is now Sudan? Intrigued with her beauty, I took a number of pictures of her.

You know how women are—often within the first 30 minutes of meeting each other we delve into very intimate details about our lives. Often, we blurt out what is bothering us, looking for support and understanding. I have literally had a woman I never met before come up to me, introduce herself, and say, "Hello, I had a miscarriage two months ago and I still can't get over it," followed by a retelling of her misfortune. Any woman knows this is a call for empathy and especially a request to talk about the problem so as to better handle it.

With Christina it was the same. Even though a Sudanese language was her mother tongue, Arabic was her second language, and English her third, within a half hour of meeting her, she told Peggy and me about a terrible misfortune that had befallen her.

In the manner of women all around the world, Peggy and I wanted to support Christina. We sat around Mohga's kitchen table and sipped on hot tea while Christina told us her story.

It turned out that one of the reasons Christina and her husband had fled from the Sudan had to do with their children. They had two lovely children—a boy and a girl.

In one terrible night, both of their children died. Christina's sorrow cut through me as I connected with the devastation she must have felt upon losing her beloved son and daughter. The heartbreak had to be beyond a person's ability to cope.

Without thinking, I blurted out, "Did you put mud in your hair?"

She replied, "Of course."

Peggy and I gasped.

Christina explained that it was an old custom to smear mud and to throw dust on the face and hair to express heartfelt grief. She said that in Sudan and even Upper, or southern, Egypt people had been putting mud in their hair for generations.

Inadvertently, I had just received confirmation of one of my past life memories. Now I knew that my imagination had not made up the memory of my African husband putting mud in his hair to show his grief over my imminent passing.

I had come to Egypt to find corroboration of my Atlantean memories. But before I had been in the country for 24 hours, I had received a substantiation of another one of my past life memories.

Strange as it might appear, it occurred to me that I may have known Christina's ancestors or even been one of them myself. Christina could be one of my descendents. No wonder I felt drawn to her and found her so familiar.

Chapter Four

WAS IT A MIRACULOUS HEALING?

The Church by the Nile

The next evening, Mohga and Gad took us to a lovely church situated along the Nile River. The Christian religion in Egypt is called the Copt Orthodox Church, which is part of the Orthodox Church, the first Christian religion. Only about six percent of the population of Cairo is Christian and most of the Christians are Copts.

The Coptic Church was started in Alexandria, Egypt, by Saint Mark, or, as he is known in Egypt, Saint Marcos. He was one of Jesus' apostles. One of the earliest gospels is attributed to him.

Hani explained that Saint Marcos had been quite young when he and Jesus' disciple, Peter, were in Rome. However, Peter was crucified upside down for trying to ease the pain of Christians as they waited to be fed to the lions. As a result, Marcos fled to Alexandria, Egypt. Sometime between A. D. 48 and 68, Saint Marcos started the Christian church in Egypt.

The Copts are the descendants of the ancient Egyptians. The pharaohs were their kings. After about 700 B. C., the ancient Egyptians were conquered by waves of invaders including the Cushites, Assyrians, and Persians. In 332 B. C., the Greeks, under Alexander the Great, took over Egypt.

The word "Copt" is a derivation of the Greek word for Egypt. However, it was not until A. D. 639 to 642, centuries after the Copt Orthodox Church had been started, that the Arabs and Muslims overran Egypt. The Copts represent those original Egyptians who did not convert to Islam.

There are approximately 10 to 12 million Copts in Egypt and about one or two million more scattered throughout the world, including those who reside in the United States and Canada. In Egypt there are more Copts by percentage of the population the further south you go in the country. In Aswan, in the extreme south close to the Sudan border, about 50 percent of the population is Coptic Christian. Pope H. H. Shenouda III, the Patriarch of Alexandria, is their leader.

Mohga and Gad led Peggy and me through the gate into the church grounds. Immediately, I felt the sense of sanctuary this church provides to the Copts of Cairo. Having always been part of the dominant Christian religion in North America, I had never felt how precious a worship site could feel to its followers until I entered through the wrought-iron gate of the church by the Nile that late September evening.

The sun had set but some light still lingered in the sky as we entered the church grounds. Stars began to pop out in the darkening sky. A feeling of peace and serenity infused the place of worship.

The daytime had been blistering hot, with temperatures well over 100 degrees Fahrenheit (37.8 degrees Celsius). Once the sun set, as is typical in desert areas of low humidity, the evening temperature dropped, and we felt comfortable.

We were not the only people there. Groups of people, many of them young, entered through the gate before and after us. They talked quietly among themselves and milled around the church grounds, which had paved pathways around landscaped beds.

Mohga led us to a long waist-high wrought iron fence. We looked over the other side to see the dark waters of the Nile River. It stretched before us—still, immense, and eternal.

I felt myself sigh inwardly as the hectic traffic and bustling millions of Cairo slipped away from my consciousness. My body relaxed in this tranquil, quiet place. An attractive neon sign in the shape of an arch illuminated the top of a tree in the center of the church grounds providing light as dusk deepened into night. The stars came out in full regalia.

Around us people talked quietly among themselves. I noticed that the area smelled fresh compared to the dusty streets of the city, probably because a buffer of trees and bushes surrounded the church.

As we looked out at the Nile, Mohga explained that the land on which the church had been built was one of the places where Mary and Joseph had stopped with Baby Jesus when they fled from King Herod. The Christian Bible records that Herod had heard that a baby had been born who would become King of the Jews. Therefore, he assumed this baby would grow up to usurp his power. To protect himself, he ordered that all the newborn boys be killed. Fortunately, a dream saved Baby Jesus. His father Joseph was told in a dream to take Baby Jesus out of Bethlehem to Egypt for the baby's safety.

Next, Mohga took us inside the church to see displays of archeological artifacts discovered at the site. We saw an old Bible that had washed up on the shore of the Nile during a very difficult time in the church's history. By chance, its pages had been opened to a page that said, "Blessed my people, the people of Egypt," which brought a renewed hope to the congregation.

After perusing the archeological artifacts, Mohga brought us into the sanctuary. Inside the church chairs had been arranged in rows similar to pews. We sat down to become accustomed to the activities in the sanctuary. A number of other people sat quietly on the chairs.

I discovered that the people sitting on the chairs waited for their turn to pray at the front of the sanctuary. One-by-one, people rose from their chairs, walked to the front of the church where there was a raised platform with a dark navy-colored velvet curtain behind the altar. The people knelt on the platform before the curtain with their backs to us. Mohga said that in the tradition of their church, by praying in front of the velvet curtain, we could receive help from the Holy Mother.

While we waited for our turn, I examined the dimly lit sanctuary. Compared to many Roman Catholic churches I have visited, this Copt Orthodox sanctuary looked plain, old, and worn. The chairs that made up the pews and the carpeting down the aisles had seen many years of use by many parishioners. Unlike a Roman Catholic Church, I saw no statues of saints and no bas reliefs on the walls depicting scenes from the Christian Bible.

I remember feeling disappointed. I expected that a church that represented such a rich heritage should be magnificent and gilded with gold.

Now, as I write these words, I think how much more fitting was the plain and simple sanctuary of this Copt Orthodox Church. It felt devout. The sanctuary resonated with the feeling of hundreds of generations of people congregated in worship within its walls. Here, truly, was a church for the people.

When my turn came to pray, I knelt on the platform in front of the slightly faded deep blue velvet curtain draped there. I found it easy to pray to the Virgin even though the Protestant religion in which I had grown up did not revere Jesus' mother with the same emphasis as the Roman Catholic and Eastern Orthodox churches. I heartily asked for her help, not only with seeing her apparition, but also with my quest to find confirmation of my memories of Atlantis.

When I first knelt to pray in front of the velvet navy curtain, I thought it odd to pray to a blue fabric. However, after a while, I began to feel as if the Holy Mother could be listening to my prayers behind the curtain. A feeling of help, support, and love washed over me. I felt at peace.

The Refreshment Stand at the Church

After praying in the sanctuary, Peggy, Mohga, Gad, and I sat outside in the courtyard enjoying the pleasant relatively cool night air. In this courtyard, adjacent to the church, the light of a small refreshment stand lit the night. Gad offered to buy us drinks. Peggy declined but I walked with Gad to the refreshment stand to choose the flavor of drink I wanted.

Normally I hate sodas. However, here in Egypt, I had been careful not to drink the local water. Therefore, while at Gad and Mohga's house, I either drank tea made with boiled water, the bottled water I had packed in my suitcase, or sodas from bottles.

Operation Smile

I had remembered my experience with Montezuma's Revenge, as dysentery is called in Latin America, when I traveled with an Operation Smile medical mission to Nicaragua. One of my high-school-aged daughters had earned a trip with Operation Smile, a medical mission of plastic surgeons that go to needy countries to help the poor inhabitants by performing free plastic surgeries. The surgeons usually repair cleft lips, cleft palates, and club feet.

In the United States, these operations are so routinely and skillfully performed on newborns that many people here are not even aware that a child is born with one of these abnormalities. In Third World countries, where operations to correct these anomalies are not available, the children often grow up shunned by their neighbors and sometimes are even relegated to a life of shame where their aberrations mark them as "taboo" for life. Both the children and their families suffer lifelong emotional scars.

The Operation Smile doctors, by performing their free surgeries, not only repair the abnormalities, but they also provide the opportunity for miraculous social changes for their patients. No longer do the people have to go outside only under cover of darkness. No longer do they have to skulk around, hiding in the shadows. No longer do they have to fear being jeered at and being shunned. In fact, one of the finest results of the medical missions is that people who would otherwise not have had a chance to have a normal fulfilling life in society are able to marry and get jobs.

During our Operation Smile mission, I traveled as an adult chaperone with my daughter and another high school-aged girl.

The young people presented educational programs on nutrition, dental care, and the prevention of dehydration.

Montezuma's Revenge

As part of our training before we went to Nicaragua, we had to learn that we absolutely must not swallow any of the water in Nicaragua. Even when we brushed our teeth at our motel, it must be done with bottled water brought in from the United States. We were told that while showering we must never let any of the water drip into our mouths and should, in fact, get into the habit of spitting as we showered so we would not inadvertently swallow even a drop of the local water.

When I arrived in Managua, the capital of Nicaragua, I discovered that cleanliness truly was severely lacking. While working in the hospital, both facilitating the educational programs described above and also helping to transport patients from the pre-operation ward to surgery and from surgery to the post-operation ward, I had been shocked and saddened to see the substandard conditions. The nurses' bathroom was so filthy that an American gas station restroom compared favorably.

However, I knew that the hospital administrators could only do their best with the funds at their disposal. Managua had suffered a major earthquake a number of years earlier and all the necessary repairs had not yet been carried out.

Bats lived in the unoccupied third floor of the hospital. You could see bat guano on the stairways leading up to the third floor. At night, the bats flitted about the patients in the occupied first and second floor recovery rooms of the hospital, flying in and out of the windows, many of which were broken. The glass in the windows had not been replaced since the earthquake.

It was my greatest fear that I might become sick and have to stay in the hospital. The last thing I wanted was to succumb to Montezuma's Revenge. Therefore, I meticulously used only the bottled water supplied by Operation Smile to brush my teeth and faithfully spit out while showering.

Unfortunately, one of our mission members inadvertently brushed her teeth with local water from the motel faucet instead of the bottled water. She became extremely ill. All of us could hear her moans followed by explosive vomiting throughout the motel compound.

Fortunately, the Operation Smile doctors and nurses with whom I traveled shared my concerns about the substandard conditions in the local hospital. The medical personnel rigged up a makeshift hospital room in the sick girl's motel room. They had brought with them intravenous bags of nutrients and medicine.

As a result, I knew how bad dysentery could be. I hoped it would not happen to me. However, in Egypt there would be no medical team to put together a makeshift hospital room and no bottles of water shipped in from the United States.

A Delightful Soda Fountain Machine

I looked into the lighted refreshment stand and saw a soda fountain machine. I love these machines. They remind me of 1950s sitcoms and the lunch bar in the old Kresges store in my Canadian hometown. I used to frequent the lunch bar with my aunt when we both worked for my father.

Above the handles that dispensed the soda, I saw labels naming the different flavors available. I felt happy because the one flavor of soda I like at all is orange, and they had it.

When the man in the refreshment stand asked if I wanted ice in my soda, I felt proud of myself because I remembered to decline. Ice is made of city water which would be unsafe for Westerners. I did not want to court the Pharaoh's Revenge and ruin my visit in Egypt.

The man in the refreshment stand held a two-cup size Styrofoam cup under the spout with the Fanta Orange label on it. After he filled the glass with the orange liquid, he placed a plastic lid over the cup and handed me a straw. Gad graciously paid for my drink.

I sipped in the cool sweet liquid. The delightful smell of the Nile River water wafted in on a gentle breeze. It intermingled with the sweet taste of my drink.

Peggy and Mohga already sat on a low brick wall that enclosed the dirt around a tree in the middle of the courtyard. Relaxation showed on their faces illuminated by the soft light from the neon decoration on top of the tree.

By the time I ambled over to Peggy and Mohga, I had swallowed at least a cup of the liquid. When Peggy looked up at me, her face had an unusual expression on it. Instead of her eyes dancing with light, as they usually did, her eyes looked placid and deeply still.

In a low, quiet voice she asked me if bottled sodas were available at the refreshment stand.

"No," I replied, continuing to sip on my straw, "this was from a soda fountain machine, you know, one of those cute machines that mixes syrup with tap water . . ."

Oh my God, I was drinking city water! I thought of all the stories I had heard about the Pharaoh's Revenge. I remembered my friend in Nicaragua who had been so violently ill from brushing her teeth with the local water.

I had just downed more than a cup of it! Would the rest of my stay in Egypt be ruined? Would I spend the next few days wracked with pain? Would I end up in the hospital hooked up to an intravenous drip? Would I lose my chance to search in the pharaohs' tombs for evidence of Atlantis? Would I ruin Peggy's chance of seeing the Virgin Mary?

Peggy continued to look at me with a composed and tranquil attitude. Feeling a bit stunned, I sat down beside her. *How soon will I get sick?* I thought. In the darkness, I unobtrusively poured the rest of my soda drink into the earth around the tree.

In a low, calm voice Peggy began to pray, surrounding me with light and with the protection of the Holy Mother. At the same time, she passed her hand over my torso where the liquid would now be in my body.

"Affirm wholeness," she whispered. "Pray to Mary."

Affirm Wholeness

"Affirm wholeness." That phrase reminded me of a story I had heard many years before from a man who had been driving a number of women to a meeting. He said that a woman who had dedicated many years of her life to meditation and prayer had accidentally placed her hand so that the car door shut upon it. He said that he felt aghast because the dear elderly woman's hand was mangled, slashed, and bruised. He wanted to take her to a hospital but she insisted that he drive on as if nothing had happened. When they arrived at their destination, the driver looked at the woman's hands. Both of them looked the same. He could see no cuts, no bruises, and no sign of injury in the hand that had been damaged. It was as if her hand had not been slammed in the car door at all. In less than an hour, the woman's hand had totally healed.

"How did you do that?" the man asked.

"Years of practice," she said. "I affirmed wholeness."

And so, I thought, *I know it can be done. Instant healing is possible.* Therefore, as Peggy suggested, I chanted the words, "I affirm wholeness," over and over again in my mind, keeping an image of Mary's loving, serene face in my mind. At the same time, I saw myself vibrant, healthy, and fulfilling the purpose of my travel to Egypt.

As I chanted, I recalled my prayers as I knelt before the navy velvet curtain at the front of the church. I thought how I had felt a welcoming acknowledgement as if Mary had heard my prayers. Therefore, I thanked her for healing me.

I also believed that amazing healing could occur because I had read Bernie S. Siegel's *Love, Medicine, and Miracles: Lessons Learned about Self-Healing from a Surgeon's Experience with Exceptional Patients.* I knew that people with incurable diseases could recover. According to Dr. Siegel, these cures resulted when the person maintained a positive determination to heal.

Certainly one way to create a determined, positive mental attitude would be to believe that the Mother of God could heal me.

The peace and serenity of the church grounds infused my spirit. Crickets and frogs shrilled under the starry sky. The night air smelled fresh with the fragrance of the trees and bushes around me. The gentle breeze from the Nile cooled my skin. I thought how much I appreciated Peggy's companionship and her spiritual devotion. I also felt grateful that I liked Mohga and Gad so much.

A feeling of warmth and security permeated my body. I felt as if I reposed in a bubble of light—as if the church grounds represented a haven of safety in the midst of my fear of becoming sick. Security and comfort settled in the core of my being. My muscles relaxed. Fear left me.

And, I did not get sick. I hadn't even seen the apparition yet. Had Mary healed me?

PART II

THE GODS ARRIVE IN EGYPT

Chapter Five

PANIC IN THE PYRAMID

"No! To Tourists"

Our first indication that there might be greater danger than we anticipated at the apparition site occurred during our appointment with Mohga's travel agent cousin.

While Peggy and I made arrangements for our flight to Luxor, Mohga decided to make plans for our trip to see the apparition of the Virgin. Therefore, she asked to rent a van so we could all drive from Cairo to her hometown of Asyut in comfort.

To Mohga's surprise, she was told that Asyut was off-limits to tourists. Her cousin told her that if a van with his company name on it arrived in Asyut, he would lose his license. He explained to Mohga that the Egyptian government selected the places where the throngs of tourists who visited their country could go. Certain areas, such as Asyut, were unsafe because of a high level of violence.

After we left her cousin's travel agency, I asked Mohga about the violence, but she flipped her hand in the air. To me, this said that she felt frustrated that her plans to rent a van had been foiled.

I did not think to press her any further about the violence, perhaps because I felt so focused on my upcoming visit to the pharaohs' tombs.

Whatever the reason, in 2000, if we wanted to go to Asyut, we would either have to take a private car or the train. Since we planned to travel as an entourage of six people, Mohga opted for the train. Her relatives would meet us at the train station in Asyut.

When I look back on it, I find it interesting that I initially did not feel afraid to go into a town forbidden to tourists. At the time, I did not know that all foreigners, not only tourists, were banned from Asyut.

Perhaps it was because I am so familiar with reports of violence in American cities. Perhaps it was because I felt so safe with Mohga. More likely, since everything in this Middle Eastern country seemed so new and different, I believe I simply accepted that in this very different country there were very different rules from the ones with which I was familiar. And that meant that some towns were off limits to foreigners.

First Glimpse of the Pyramids

On our third day in Cairo, we sped along, four cars abreast on a three-lane highway, Gad at the wheel. Mohga drew our attention to the sun setting over the Western horizon. The sky glowed with an orange color. Dust from the road surface danced in the ripples of heat emanating from the hot pavement.

In the distance, beyond the streets and buildings of Cairo, I saw something that did not fit in with the fronds of the palm trees and the square shapes of the buildings silhouetted against the misty orange sky.

Three triangular structures rested on the horizon, almost as if they drifted in the salmon-colored haze of the setting sun. Suddenly, I knew what they had to be. They were the three Great Pyramids.

But they looked so odd—tiny, triangular, and alone. I had always seen photographs of the pyramids looming over the Great Sphinx, or with their massive boulders dwarfing tourists and camels. Seeing them from so far away, drifting on an orange haze, I felt as if I had been transported to another world.

Immediately, I began to take photographs of the amazing sight through the car window. Even if I had not read volumes on the Great Pyramid and even if memories of its construction had not turned up in my hypnosis sessions, I would still have been totally entranced by the sight.

In spite of the pandemonium of vehicles speeding by on all sides of us, Gad noticed my efforts at photography in the back seat. Being the consummate host and gentleman he is, he pulled his vehicle over to the side of the highway so I could more easily take my first photographs of these amazing monuments.

The Great Pyramids drift on the horizon at sunset.

As I snapped the shutter of my camera like a crazed tourist, I felt a tingle within because of how strange these amazing structures looked. They had stood silent and mysterious for millennia. I thought about the millions of people from every nation on earth who had come to see them.

They are the great unknown—inscrutable and enigmatic to the end. Throughout the rise and fall of civilizations all over the earth, during the rise and fall of populations along the banks of the Nile, the three Great Pyramids and the Great Sphinx had remained mute and unmoved through it all.

In my mind I saw desert herdsmen, Bedouin camel drivers, and travelers from distant nations in times past when the sprawling megalopolis of Cairo and its suburbs did not exist. I saw them approach the pyramids, which stood alone surrounded by desert sand. How mysterious these monoliths must have appeared to them. The ancient travelers must have wondered what the pyramids were, why they had been built, by whom, and how.

We still wonder.

I thought about the book and movie *2001: A Space Odyssey* and how the Great Pyramid reminded me of the monolith left by the advanced oversouls to help humanity in its evolution.

The Great Pyramids and the Great Sphinx are the only existing wonders of the ancient world. The ancient wonders include:

(1) The Great Pyramids and Great Sphinx in Giza, Egypt

(2) The Hanging Gardens of Babylon

(3) The Temple of Artemis at Ephesus

(4) The Statue of Zeus at Olympia

(5) The Mausoleum at Halicarnassus

(6) The Colossus of Rhodes

(7) The Pharos of Alexandria

The Seven Ancient Wonders of the World refer to what the ancient Greeks and Romans, around 100 B. C., believed to be the greatest feats in technology, architecture, and art of that time. The Giza greatest wonder is not only the only one that exists today, it is also the oldest.

Indications of Atlanteans in Egypt

Apart from any person's natural inclination to see the only existing wonder of the ancient world, I wanted to visit the Great Pyramids and Great Sphinx to see the characteristics expounded by numerous authors that showed that an advanced civilization may have built them.

Like many others, I believed the Great Pyramids and Great Sphinx had not been built by ancient Egyptians. From everything I read, it appeared that they were built with greater precision than pyramids constructed after their construction date, which meant that whoever built them had to be more technologically advanced than those who followed after them.

In fact, whoever built the three Great Pyramids must have been more technologically advanced than we are today because present-day contractors and scientists cannot explain how multi-ton boulders were fit together with such precision that a knife cannot be forced between them.

Or, anyway, that is what I had read. I wanted to see for myself. Actually, I wanted to see a number of characteristics of these fascinating monuments with my own eyes. These characteristics would show that the Great Pyramids and Great Sphinx had been built before the pharaohs, which would point to the possibility that some advanced, but lost, civilization might have built them.

I also wanted to see indications that they were likely built much earlier than 4,800 years ago, the time determined by archeologists. If the pyramids were built in our pre-history—before the written word—it could also be possible that whoever built these ancient wonders could have been part of a civilization that the ancient Egyptians remembered in their myths. I reasoned that paintings in the pharaohs' tombs could possibly illustrate legendary memories of that time long ago when members of that ancient advanced civilization had been in Egypt.

I had memories of my time in Atlantis that I wanted to have verified in these tomb paintings. First, I needed to see indications that Atlanteans, or some other very advanced civilization in the distant past, could have built the Great Pyramids and Sphinx.

The characteristics I especially wanted to see were:

1. The multi-ton boulders making up the Great Pyramids are placed so close together that you cannot slip a knife blade between them, thereby indicating construction by a civilization with more advanced technology than ours.

2. Some people have unusual, frightening reactions when they explore inside the Great Pyramids, pointing to a possible supernatural connection.

3. The sides of the Great Pyramid are not flat but are indented at the centerline like a crystal. I believe this unusual feature points to the likelihood that the structure was not a tomb but had some other purpose.

4. The stones making up the Great Sphinx show water erosion, not wind erosion, thereby dating its construction much earlier than archeological estimates.

I will discuss these items, among other topics, in the rest of the chapter.

The Location of the Pyramids and Sphinx

The next day Gad drove Mohga, Peggy, and me to the Great Pyramids and the Great Sphinx. These ancient monuments stand on the Giza Plateau, a high desert area in the city of Giza, an industrial suburb of Cairo located on the West side of the Nile.

Although many people believe the pyramids are located way out in the desert, modern life has crept right to the edge of these tourist attractions. With a population of over two million, the city of Giza extends almost to the paws of the Great Sphinx.

The Great Sphinx looks east over the city of Giza.

The Mysterious Great Pyramid

It has always perplexed me that only one of the three Great Pyramids is considered "The" Great Pyramid while the other two do not receive as much attention.

I wonder why. Perhaps it has to do with the intricate passageways within it. Unlike the second and third pyramids, the Great Pyramid contains two large rooms and three main passageways. The other two Great Pyramids have only one main room and a couple of tunnels.

Perhaps it has to do with size. The Great Pyramid or Pyramid of Khufu is the tallest of the three pyramids, standing 455.2 feet (138.8 meters) tall. That is the height of a 40-story building.

But the second pyramid is only slightly shorter. Known as the Pyramid of Khafre, it is 448 feet (136.4 meters) high. However, because the angle of its sides is steeper, it contains less volume than the Great Pyramid. The third Pyramid of Menkaure is much shorter at 215 feet (66.5 meters) in height.

Archeological work continues on the Giza Plateau. The Great Pyramid is in the background.

Why has the Great Pyramid captured the imaginations of people throughout time? It has certainly been and continues to be the object of endless conjecture. Napoleon and his "savants" or learned men cleared sand away from it, measured it, and studied it, noting that, of the three pyramids, its dimensions correlated with the proportions of the earth.

Construction of the Great Pyramid

Ideas vary greatly as to the construction date of the Great Pyramid. Archeologists say that gangs of workers dragged multi-ton boulders up oiled skids from about 2589-2566 B. C. and that it is the crowning glory of the pyramid-builders' art. The skids were placed on the top of a large earthen ramp that the workers built to rise up along the pyramid as it became taller.

Arabian legend, on the other hand, says that supernatural spirits called, djinn, built the Great Pyramid. Some people think that aliens built it.

The great American psychic Edgar Cayce also had much to say about the Great Pyramid. His trance source revealed that it took 100 years to build in 10,500 B. C., which would mean it was built during the time Plato said Atlantis existed.

If the Great Pyramid was built at the same time as the Great Sphinx, geological evidence supports a much earlier construction date of the Sphinx, in support of the 10,500 B.C. date. The construction date of the Great Sphinx will be explored later in this chapter.

Was the Great Pyramid Built in Two Phases?

Authors Robert Bauval and Adrian Gilbert, who co-wrote *The Orion Mystery: Unlocking the Secrets of the Pyramids,* agree with Cayce's date but say that the Great Pyramid was built in two phases: the bottom third first and the top two-thirds later.

In *The Orion Mystery*, Bauval and Gilbert point out that the stones making up the bottom third of the Great Pyramid are a slightly different size and use a slightly different assembly pattern than the stones in the top two-thirds of the pyramid.

In my hypnosis sessions of 1995 and 1996, I had seen the Great Pyramid in use before the top two-thirds of the structure had been built. At that time, the inner chambers had stood free of the stones that presently cover them.

In 2002, a tiny robot was used to explore narrow shafts leading through the Great Pyramid's sides from one of its internal chambers. Researchers discovered that one of the shafts bent around one of the internal chambers, which points to the probability that the internal chamber was built before the shaft was built. This discovery supports the idea that the pyramid was built in two phases.

The Casing Stones Mystery

One of the big mysteries surrounding the Great Pyramid is how the boulders making up this monumental structure fit together so perfectly that you cannot get a knife blade between them. Considering that they weigh at least two tons—some of the internal stones weight more than 70 tons—modern engineers cannot conceive how such a feat could be accomplished even today.

In my Atlantean memories, I had seen the boulders dematerialize as they spun through the air and rematerialize in the exact spot and shape to fit the space where the boulders were meant to be positioned. The Atlanteans did not fit stones closely together. Rather the boulders were molded in place when they rematerialized. The Atlanteans could do this because they worked in agreement with the thought energy of the stones and the earth.

During my September 2000 visit to the Great Pyramid, I found that the Great Pyramid's boulders truly had been put together so tightly that you could not squeeze a knife blade between the stones. There were many examples of stones which fitted together almost perfectly, especially the casing stones, which originally covered the whole structure making the sides flat.

Long ago there used to be about 144,000 casing stones made of limestone, which can be almost white in color. Evidently, the casing stones were highly polished and uniformly flat, and must have reflected light like a mirrored surface. The pyramid truly must have been a magnificent sight glistening in the desert.

Almost all of the casing stones on the Great Pyramid were removed early in the ninth century to be fashioned into building blocks for mosques in Cairo. However, a few remain at the base of the structure. Experts believe the foundation casing stones were protected from the mosque-builders and the elements by being buried in sand.

Each of the casing stones weighs about 15 tons. At that weight, it's amazing that they could fit together so perfectly. In addition, researchers have discovered a scant film of mortar between the tightly fitted boulders—another amazing feat.

Above, the Great Pyramid's multi-ton boulders, the casing stones on the right. Left, tight seams between the boulders.

I wanted to explore inside the Great Pyramid to see if the boulders on the inside passageways, where they were protected from weather, were fitted together as perfectly as some of the casing stones I had seen on the outside of the structure. Whether these stones had been placed together by dematerialization and rematerialization, as I had seen in my Atlantean memories, or whether they had been fitted together by some other method, I needed to see them for myself.

If the inside stones also fit together perfectly, it would point to the possibility that the whole structure had been built using an advanced hitherto unknown technology. In other words, I had my own reasons for exploring inside the Great Pyramid based on the information that came through in my hypnosis sessions.

Next, we were about to discover that some people have intense distressing experiences when inside the pyramids. The person who experienced distressing reactions turned out to be me!

The Third Pyramid

We tried to buy tickets to enter the Great Pyramid but learned that they were sold out for the day. It turns out that the Egyptian antiquities department only allows a certain number of people into the Great Pyramid every day. Moisture from breath and perspiration could produce serious deterioration of the ancient structure.

We would have gone into the second pyramid but it was closed. We concluded that there was nothing left to do but to explore inside the third and smallest pyramid.

Gad generously bought tickets for all of us to tour the inside of the Pyramid of Menkaure. It was also named the Pyramid of Mycerinus by the Greeks.

With tickets in hand, we traipsed over to the third and smallest Great Pyramid. Although it is the smallest of the Great Pyramids, it is still quite large.

I guess it does not matter if the smallest pyramid is damaged by the moisture of breath and perspiration

Crowds pour in and out of the Pyramid of Menkaure.

because the wooden stairs leading up to the entrance of the third pyramid contained a long line of people entering the pyramid and a long line of people filing out. I could see that no limit existed on the numbers allowed inside the Pyramid of Menkaure. We joined the line going in.

Panic Inside the Third Pyramid

Finally, we made it to the head of the line. By now, the sun shone overhead. Even in the shade cast by the pyramid on the north side, where the entrance is located on all the pyramids, it felt uncomfortably hot.

I walked into the Pyramid of Menkaure first, in front of Gad, Mohga, and Peggy. Immediately, as soon as I entered, I discovered that the third pyramid felt even hotter inside than it felt outside. The air also hung with humidity and the smell of human sweat.

I walked into the tunnel that led into the depths of the pyramid following the column of tourists. The line going into the pyramid filed in on the right. Another line of people emerged out of the tunnel on the left. All their faces looked hot and red.

About 20 feet (six meters) into the pyramid, the tunnel dipped down into the earth. It looked dark ahead. The deeper into the pyramid I went, the hotter, more humid, and more unpleasant the smell became. I felt panicked. I did not know how far down we would have to go before we could come out again. However, I did know that once I got deep inside the pyramid there would be no way out except by following the crowd of people jammed up against each other in the line. Although I did not know what to expect ahead, I could imagine a close, dark space crammed with hot, sweaty people, the air so heavy with fetid-smelling moisture that it would be hard to breathe.

Suddenly, I could not stand it another second longer. I had to get out. Like a rubber ball, I bounced out of the tunnel back into the fresh dry sweet-smelling air outside.

I felt guilty that I had wasted Gad's ticket money. I just could not stay inside that oppressive structure a second longer!

Fortunately, I did not have to feel guilty long. Gad, who was right behind me in the line, could not stand it either. He sprung out of the tunnel almost as fast as I did.

So, I had just had my first pyramid experience. Was this only the beginning? Would I find it impossible to enter the Great Pyramid as well when I came back another day?

First in Line

A couple of days later, I returned to the Giza Plateau in the hopes of buying a ticket to the Great Pyramid early enough so tickets would not be sold out.

I arrived before opening time. While I waited for the guard to open the gate, I discovered, to my delight, a dusty yard that contained camels and stables to the left of the gate.

The stables were located below the road and also below the Great Pyramid which loomed in the background. Camel drivers fed their charges and readied their beasts for the onslaught of tourists later in the day. Early morning light made the stable area look crisp and fresh. The Great Pyramid loomed in the distance behind the stables through a faint, glistening mist.

Because it was hidden out of view of the road, I wondered how many tourists had even noticed the camel stables. I loved that the animals could so easily co-exist with humans in such a large and busy city as Giza. The sleepy-eyed creatures munched on large leaves. Camel drivers mingled with their animals, feeding and watering them. The men wore the traditional gallabias with turbans on their heads.

Aha, I thought, *so, these are the camel drivers Hani warned me about.*

On the right, camel drivers rest under a lean-to. In the left foreground, camels eat their morning meal. In the background, the Great Pyramid looms in morning mist.

One by one, a number of camel drivers looked up at me and asked me if I wanted to enter the Giza Plateau before the gate opened. They assured me that they could easily get me in on a camel. Nodding their heads toward the Great Pyramid, which towered over the camp, I realized that they could simply bypass the entrance by mounting the sand dunes surrounding their camp. A number of camel drivers asked me if I wanted to take a ride into the desert to take photographs of the Sphinx and Great Pyramids. They pointed to my camera which, as usual, hung around my neck.

I have seen gorgeous photographs of the Great Pyramids in early morning mist that must have been taken from out in the desert to the south of the Sphinx. To take similar photos, I would likely need to be on a camel.

The desert on the other side of the Great Sphinx where camel drivers often take tourists for dramatic photographs.

However, I remembered Hani's admonition, "A camel driver could drag you away into the desert."

I was pretty sure these men had no intention of dragging me anywhere. They only wanted my Baksheesh. But, I decided to keep to my original plan. What if I was out in the desert taking photographs and other tourists snapped up the last tickets to explore inside the Great Pyramid? Disaster! On my first visit to Egypt, it would be enough to investigate inside the Great Pyramid. Maybe on a future visit, I would tackle early morning photographs and camel drivers.

As soon as the guard opened the gate, I hoofed it up the hill to buy a ticket to enter the Giza Plateau. Tour buses, the stench of their diesel exhaust fumes assailing my nostrils, overtook me. The buses dropped off tour guides who ran to the ticket booth to pay entrance fees for the people on their buses. I had to wait in line. Ahead of me, tour guides bought tickets in bulk. As soon as they bought their entrance tickets, they scurried to the Great Pyramid ticket booth. Would they buy up all the tickets?

Camel drivers make their way up the Giza Plateau.

Tourists enjoy a view of the Great Pyramid from camelback.

Once I bought my entrance ticket, I ran as fast as I could to the Great Pyramid ticket booth. I made it in time! Clutching the ticket in my hand, I headed for the most enigmatic ruin on earth. To reach the entrance doorway, I negotiated a rough path up the bottom third of the gigantic structure. I steadied myself by holding metal railings affixed to the rocks to make the ascent over the huge boulders easier for tourists.

Although it was still early morning, I felt quite warm as a result of the exertion. I joined other tourists waiting at the entrance for the first tour of the day. A guide wearing a turban and a gallabia waited for all of us climbing the boulders to assemble. Then he led us inside the ancient monument.

One of the great hopes of my life had just been fulfilled. I was inside the Great Pyramid. What would I find there? Would I have a terrifying reaction as I had experienced in the third pyramid? I consciously stilled myself and purposefully thought only positive, hopeful thoughts, reminding myself that millions of people had toured inside the Great Pyramid without incident.

Once inside the structure, the air felt cool, refreshing, and even smelled pleasant. Electric lights illuminated the floor. The first tunnel is called the Ascending Passage, and it slants upward at a 26-degree angle. In addition, it is less than four-feet (1.2 meters) in height. Therefore, you have to walk bent over on an upward-slanting stone floor for 129 feet (39.3 meters) before you can stand up straight again. I plodded along the low passageway following in a line with the other tourists, our guide in the lead.

The Grand Gallery

After scrabbling up the Ascending Passage while bent over, I felt as if I had just done an aerobics workout. I wanted to be sure I would not have the same reaction I'd experienced in the third pyramid. Therefore, before I proceeded, I decided to catch my breath.

I still felt a little bit afraid after my experience in Menkaure's Pyramid. On top of everything else, my glasses were fogged up. I stopped and let the group go past so I could rest.

The guide came back through the crowd of people and asked me if I was all right. I said that "Yes," I just needed to wait until I cooled down and my glasses cleared. That must have made sense to him since my spectacles looked like frosted glass.

He left me alone at the foot of the Grand Gallery and took the crowd into the Queen's Chamber which I knew required the negotiation of another squat tunnel. Although the passageway into the Queen's Chamber is built level instead of on an upward slant, it requires 147 feet (44.8 meters) of trudging bent over like a monkey.

To hasten the clearing of my glasses, I took them off and waved them in the fresh morning air inside the pyramid. I felt happy that I had bothered to wake up early because, unlike the Pyramid of Menkaure, which had been so hot in the middle of the day, the Great Pyramid felt cool and refreshing early in the morning.

I smiled to myself and took a deep breath. I remembered that I had read that the Great Pyramid used to reek with the odor of bat droppings. At one time, the nocturnal creatures lived within the pyramid's chambers. I did not notice any unpleasant odor. The bats and their droppings must have been cleaned out years ago.

Pyramid Terrors

While I stood waiting for my glasses to clear, a young man stumbled out of the low tunnel that led from the Queen's Chamber. His breathing sounded labored as if he had just received the scare of his life. He lurched forward, his arms flailing in the air as if pushing some unknown assailant away from him.

His desperate behavior contrasted with the way he looked. Young and attractive with dark hair and a square jaw, his staggering gait belonged to a much older, unsteady person rather than to a person who looked as fit and as healthy as he did.

"I'm getting out of here," he gasped, with terror in his voice. He looked at me with madness in his eyes. "It's boiling hot in there!" He scuttled past me and down the Ascending Passage toward the doorway to the outside of the pyramid.

Well, I thought, *it really does happen. People really do freak out in the Great Pyramid.* I felt happy that I had stopped to cool myself. I also felt compassion for the young man since I had had a similar reaction when I tried to enter Menkaure's Pyramid.

Shortly afterward, the tour guide emerged out of the tunnel from the Queen's Chamber. The rest of the group followed behind him, straightening to upright height as they turned the corner out of the squat passageway.

The guide asked me if the young man had left the pyramid. I told the guide that the young man had headed down the Ascending Passage toward the outside opening.

My answer must have satisfied him because he next explained to the group that people often felt that the rooms in the Great Pyramid were hot. However, the rooms were not actually hot. The people only felt hot because of the exertion they had been through.

Who knows what terrors had been awakened in the young man upon entering the Queen's Chamber? If it had been a mere question of heat, the young man would have cooled down after a few minutes in the Queen's Chamber, just as I had cooled down after waiting for a few minutes at the foot of the Grand Gallery.

I knew from my experience in the Pyramid of Menkaure that something else—some fear, some unconscious reaction, some connection with a lingering past—can distress a person when entering one of these very ancient, mysterious structures.

I have since read in *The Traveler's Key to Ancient Egypt* by John Anthony West that Menkaure's Pyramid has a reputation for creating a feeling of intense power. West says that a twelfth-century doctor from Iraq who visited the Giza Plateau felt that the third and smallest pyramid conveyed a feeling of oppression, ostensibly because it is constructed of very hard red granite.

West points out that each of the pyramids is known to create different effects in people, and that many people find that the third pyramid brings up intense negative feelings. I definitely agree.

In addition, he says that many people do not feel comfortable in the second pyramid. Perhaps we were lucky that it was closed to tourists and under renovation.

Chapter Six

THE ATLANTEANS AND THE GREAT PYRAMID

The Great Pyramid as a Power Plant

In my hypnosis sessions, I said that the Great Pyramid had been built as a power source. It was modeled on a rough imitation of the Atlantean towers used to create the crystal power in Atlantis.

I had said that because we, from Atlantis, were unfamiliar with the vegetation in Egypt—it being of a more cyclical nature than in Atlantis—our construction of the Great Pyramid had been coarser than we would have liked it to be. We had to proceed quickly to build the immense structure because we needed the help of the energy produced in the towers in Atlantis before earth upheavals destroyed our great island nation.

The existing towers on our home continent were used to levitate multi-tonned boulders through the air to their positions in the Great Pyramid. In that memory, I had worked in one of the Atlantean towers and knew that they looked somewhat like our present-day optical telescopes.

Because earthquakes had started to break up Atlantis, the Atlanteans had constructed towers that produced earth-friendly power in the nearby lands of Egypt and Yucatan. The Atlanteans wanted to safeguard their technical knowledge just in case Atlantis was totally destroyed, which it was in the end.

Optical telescopes on Kitt Peak in Arizona. They look similar to the Atlantean towers in my memories.

Although I had not read the book until after I returned from Egypt, I was delighted to discover that engineer Christopher Dunn also believes that the Great Pyramid was constructed to be a power plant. In *The Giza Power Plant,* he says that the ancient builders of the Great Pyramid constructed a machine that used sound vibrations in resonance with the earth to make power.

As I said in the previous chapter, "Panic in the Pyramid," my memories of the Great Pyramid under construction had shown the structure in use while only the first third of it had been completed. The so-called Grand Gallery rose like a ramp above the bottom third of the Great Pyramid. The top two-thirds of the pyramid had

The McMath-Pierce Solar Telescope at Kitt Peak National Observatory in Arizona.

not yet been built over the Grand Gallery. It looked similar to one of our modern-day solar telescopes. If a building were built on top of the solar telescope at left, it would look similar to my memory of the Great Pyramid under construction with the King's Chamber on top of the ramp of the Grand Gallery.

In trance reading 877-26, Edgar Cayce said influences from the sun had been crystallized through the crystal which had been used to create power in Atlantis. In reading 519-1, he called it "the mighty, the terrible crystal." Unfortunately, it had been misused for selfish reasons, leading to a further destabilization of the already geologically active land in Atlantis.

Since Cayce said the crystal had used influences from the sun, could the Grand Gallery have been used to harness solar energy?

According to Peter Tompkins in *Secrets of the Great Pyramid*, some researchers think that because the Grand Gallery rises at a 26-degree angle and its sides telescope in, if its top were opened, it could be used as an astronomical observatory.

What about a solar observatory? It looks more like our modern-day solar observatories than our astronomical observatories.

Future Use of the Great Pyramid

While under hypnosis, I had also said that the Great Pyramid would not become operational until the capstone, which contained a crystal similar to the crystal used in the Atlantean power towers, was put in place. Unlike Christopher Dunn who believes the Great Pyramid had been used as a power plant in the distant past, I had said it was meant to operate in the future.

Furthermore, while hypnotized, I had said that a more spiritually developed version of our present human beings, the fifth root race, would know where to find the capstone, which presently is buried somewhere on the Giza Plateau. The fifth root race (more on them in Chapter Thirteen, "Psychics, Mystics, and the Root Races") would know how to levitate the capstone to the top of the pyramid.

I suspect that the capstone is likely near or part of the Atlantean Hall of Records that Edgar Cayce says can be reached through a passage-way accessed at the right forepaw of the Great Sphinx. So far, no one has found the Atlantean Hall of Records. According to Cayce, it contains material left by the Atlanteans that describes information explaining how to activate the Atlantean crystal power. Since he also calls it the Pyramid of Records, I wonder if the capstone is actually the Hall of Records. The capstone would be in the shape of a small pyramid. Amazingly, the Hall of Records is also supposed to contain a description of the person who will discover it and open it.

Here is an excerpt from the Cayce readings about the more spiritually-developed individuals called the fifth root race and their relationship to the records left by the Atlanteans. In reading 5748-6, Cayce's trance source says that the Atlantean Hall of Records "may not be entered without an understanding, for those that were left as guards may NOT be passed until after a period of their regeneration in the Mount, or the fifth root race begins."

There will be more on the root races in Chapter Fourteen, "Serpents, Root Races, and Myths."

The Walls of the Inside Chambers

One of my purposes in negotiating the inside passageways of the Great Pyramid had been to see for myself that the boulders inside the structure had been placed so close together that you could not get a thin knife blade between them. Some of the boulders inside the Great Pyramid weigh 70 tons.

In fact, it was so. All the walls inside the Great Pyramid looked so uniform it was hard to believe they were made of multi-ton boulders. They looked so flat and uniform that they could have been the internal cement walls of a modern-day multi-story building.

Because the boulders fit together like placed concrete, I felt that it supported my past life memories of how the multi-ton stones had dematerialized and rematerialized into their correct positions. Now I felt satisfied that it could be so.

The Unusual Shape of the Great Pyramid

When I finished my tour inside the Great Pyramid, I wanted to confirm something I had read in Peter Tompkin's *Secret of the Great Pyramid*. I felt his observations supported the concept that the Great Pyramid had been built to be something other than a pharaoh's tomb.

The sides of the Great Pyramid, unlike any other pyramid, buckle in like a crystal. The following rough diagram of the footprint of the Great Pyramid, drawn by yours truly, shows the indent in the Great Pyramid's sides. The indent in the diagram is exaggerated.

Because of the size of the structure and the relative small indent at the centerline, this buckling in of the sides is not visually obvious. You have to take a measurement from one corner of the Great Pyramid to the other with a surveyor's theodolite and then compare this number with a measurement of the exact footprint of the side on the ground to see that it buckles in.

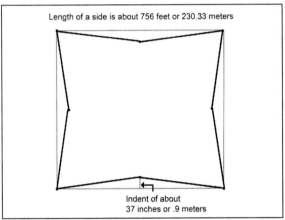

Length of a side is about 756 feet or 230.33 meters

Indent of about
37 inches or .9 meters

A not-to-scale footprint of the Great Pyramid.

Since I was not going to go to Egypt with a theodolite—even if I knew how to use one—I had to devise some other way to determine if the sides of the Great Pyramid truly buckled in.

I had seen an excellent aerial photograph of this characteristic on page 109 of the *Secrets of the Great Pyramid* and decided that if I ever had the opportunity to take photographs of this indent, I would do so.

But first, I would have to develop a way of showing the indent without a theodolite and without hiring a plane to take an aerial photo. This is what I conceived. I figured that at a certain time of the day, the sun would shine in such a way that it would light one half of the north side of the pyramid and not the other half.

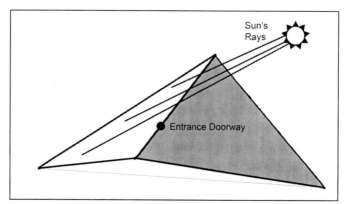

The left or eastern half of the north face should be lighter if that side is turned toward the westerly sun.

At the right time in the afternoon, I set up my camera to photograph the north side of the Great Pyramid. Sure enough, the sun lit one half of the north face more than the other half.

In the photograph I took, displayed below, you can see that the left side of the Great Pyramid is lighter than the right side. The sun, shining from the right, as in the diagram above, shows that the left side is turned slightly toward the direction of the sun. This could only occur if the pyramid side is buckled in at the centerline.

The north side of the Great Pyramid showing that it is slightly indented at the centerline.

Theories on the Unusual Shape of the Great Pyramid

Why is the Great Pyramid built with its sides indented? There are many theories, including that it was built as a measuring device for future generations. I do not agree with this theory but let me explain why some researchers believe this idea.

The circumference of the Great Pyramid compared to its height creates a mathematical relationship that is the same as the relationship of the circumference of the earth at its widest part—the equator—with the vertical distance from the equator to the north pole. In other words, it is as if, proportionally, the Great Pyramid is a miniature of the Northern Hemisphere of the earth.

Note that the Great Pyramid would not be as accurately proportional to the earth's size if the pyramid's sides did not buckle in. Nineteenth century researchers believed that the builders of the Great Pyramid made the sides indented at the centerline so that the structure would be a more accurate measuring device and future generations could use the Great Pyramid's measurements to calculate the size of the earth.

This theory does not make sense to me. If the ancient architects of the Great Pyramid wanted it to be an accurate model of the earth, why not make the sides of the pyramid buckle outward? That way it would look more like the earth than with it buckled inward.

Furthermore, can you imagine someone today going through the trouble of constructing a 13-acre (5.26 hectares), 455.2-foot (138.8 meter) tall structure made from two and a half million blocks that weigh an average of two and a half tons each as a measuring device for people 5,000 years from now? What a waste of time, energy, and money!

Some Ideas Why the Great Pyramid's Sides Buckle In

To me, the information that the sides of the Great Pyramid buckled in at the centerline was very important. It provided another indication that the structure had to have some purpose other than that of a tomb for a pharaoh. I cannot imagine the ancients, or anyone today for that matter, going through the trouble to make a three-foot indent in the sides of a structure 40-stories tall for no good reason whatsoever if the structure was truly meant to be a tomb. It would have been so much easier for the ancients to have built the Great Pyramid with straight walls. Did it matter to the pharaoh's mummy whether or not the sides were flat or indented? Not at all. There had to be some other reason.

This buckling reminded me of a carved crystal. I wondered if the indented sides focused some kind of waves penetrating into the center of the pyramid. Or, did the indented sides focus outgoing waves?

It made me think of my memories of the triangular windows on top of the Atlantean tower, which were necessary to focus the beamed radio-type waves that produced the energy in Atlantis. That the sides indented meant that the peak of the pyramid was not made out of four triangles but eight—a number more like the triangular openings at the top of the tower in Atlantis as I saw in my trance memories.

Could it be that the Great Pyramid is built with indented sides like a crystal because it is meant to transmit or receive some type of invisible waves?

Chapter Seven

THE SPHINX AND THE WOMAN
WITH THE GOLDEN HAIR

The Great Sphinx

The next day, I decided to tackle the final item on my list. I had read that geological evidence points to an earlier construction date of the Great Sphinx. Therefore, my next stop was the most mysterious statue on earth.

Although the Sphinx had not come up in my trance sessions, my memory of the Great Pyramid under construction did include a different climate in Egypt than at present. I saw the structure that would become the Great Pyramid surrounded by grasses. It was not in the middle of a sandy desert as it is today. Therefore, during the time the Sphinx had been built—if it was built at the same time as the Great Pyramid—according to my hypnosis-induced memories, it had to be at a time when the Cairo area had more than its present yearly precipitation of less than one inch (one centimeter).

Geologists . . . not archeologists . . . agree with my memories. They believe the Great Sphinx was built during a time when Egypt had a much greater annual rainfall.

Dating the Sphinx by Water Damage

According to John Anthony West, author of *Serpent in the Sky*, the Sphinx is at least 12,000 years old, a time when Egypt had a lot of rainfall. If it was built as long ago as 12,000 years ago, it would have been built during the time Plato said Atlantis existed. John Anthony West explains the research of R. A. Schwaller de Lubicz indicating that the type of erosion on the stones of the Sphinx is caused by water, not wind, damage.

I wanted to photograph the water damage. To do so, I needed to get inside the fence around the Great Sphinx. Where would I find someone to let me in the gate? I remembered that I had emailed Ahmed Fayed, a well-respected Egyptian tour guide who has led tours for Edgar Cayce's Association for Research and Enlightenment for years. Sadly, he has since passed away.

He emailed me back saying that I could find him at his home, which is close to the Giza plateau. However, when I went there, his wife and mother said he had just left to lead a tour.

Without Ahmed's help I did not know what to do. Therefore, I decided to shop for souvenirs. While browsing in the shops, I experienced one of those strokes of good luck that characterized this whole trip.

The proprietor of the shop tried to aggressively interest me in one trinket after another. Practicing my bargaining techniques, I remained uninterested. In an attempt to impress me, he lifted up a pile of letters from the top of his display counter. He shoved them in my face and challenged me to open and read them. He assured me all the letters contained appreciation for his fine wares.

To my surprise, I saw the name, "Fayed," on the envelopes. It was the same last name as Ahmed Fayed's.

"Are you a Fayed?" I asked him.

"Yes," he replied.

"Do you know Ahmed Fayed?" I asked him.

"Of course," he replied, "He is my cousin. Why do you ask?"

"Because I want to find him. Do you know where he is?"

We were standing so that my back faced the open doorway to the man's shop. He stood facing me and the open doorway

"There he is, right now!" he exclaimed.

"Where?" I spun around but saw no one on the sidewalk outside the shop.

"He just drove past." The shop owner ran past me and out the door into the street. He disappeared from my view.

A couple of minutes later, the owner of the shop returned followed by Ahmed. The shop owner explained that Ahmed was leaving for a three-week tour. He only had a couple of minutes to give me.

Fortunately, Ahmed remembered me from the emails we had exchanged. I asked him how to get into the chain link fence surrounding the Great Sphinx.

"Ask Hawass," he said.

Dr. Zahi Hawass is the Secretary General of the Supreme Council of Antiquities and the Director of the Giza Pyramids Excavations. He is also one of my heroes. A celebrity, he appears on television in National Geographic Specials. He is also a sought-after lecturer. I heard him speak at the College of William and Mary in Williamsburg, Virginia, where the audience roared with laughter at his amusing anecdotes and soaked up his up-to-date information on the archeological excavations in Egypt.

The next day, I made an appointment with Dr. Hawass. After receiving an audience with the delightful man, Dr. Hawass arranged for me and a couple of other photographers to have a uniformed guard take us within the fenced enclosure.

Our guide took us to the side of the Sphinx. There, he unlocked a gate. We went past a temple under reconstruction to the stairs leading down to the foot of the Sphinx.

The Temple on the side of the Sphinx in the foreground.

Standing at ground level looking up, I discovered that the Sphinx is much larger than I expected. It towered above me. The paws were almost twice as tall as I am.

It measures 65 feet (20 meters) high, is 200 feet (60 meters) long, and 20 feet (six meters) wide. The huge face is 13 feet (four meters) wide. Amazingly, the eyes are six feet (1.8 meters) in height—a gargantuan statue!

I am 5 feet 3 inches, (1.6 meters) tall.

The giant paw of the Great Sphinx.

To my delight, I discovered that both the back of the Sphinx and the stones surrounding it did look as if they had been eroded by water, not wind. Since the Sphinx is made of the rock quarried out of the pit in which it is located, it makes sense that both sets of rocks show similar erosion characteristics.

When wind causes erosion, stones are uniformly worn away. However, these stones exhibited greater erosion at the top than at the bottom, as would be accomplished by the dripping of water.

You may be wondering why the stones do not show the effect of wind erosion over the succeeding centuries when the climate changed and Egypt became a desert. It is because during much of that time, most of the Sphinx was covered by sand. Desert sandstorms filled in the pit containing the statue. When Napoleon and his men first saw it in 1798, they could see only the head sticking out of the sand.

The stones behind the Sphinx show water erosion. Bricks have been used to reconstruct the back paw and tail.

Another interesting tidbit: On the previous page, note the photo on the left. Behind me and between the paws of the Sphinx there is a stele or stone plaque. The stele records the dream of Thothmose IV (1425-1417 B.C.) who, before he became king, had a dream when he fell asleep at the foot of the Sphinx which, at the time, was only a head sticking out of the sand. The statue told him that if he dug it out of the sand, Thothmose would become king. This means that the pit in which the Sphinx is situated has repeatedly filled with sand, there-by protecting the stones from wind damage. By the way, Thothmose IV fulfilled the Sphinx's request and the Sphinx kept its promise to him.

Why doesn't the head show more wind damage if it has been exposed to the elements for so long? The head was carved from much denser stone than the body so it did not erode as easily.

Why weren't the stones making up the body covered during the millennia when Egypt had a much wetter climate? Sand was not blowing around because vegetation held the soil in place leaving the stones exposed to rainfall and water erosion.

I felt happy to see that the Sphinx showed geological evidence of a construction date coincident with Plato and Cayce's dates for the existence of Atlantis. This meant that images in the pharaohs' tombs might represent the ancient Egyptians' memories of that long ago time.

An Unusual Dinner Companion

That evening, Peggy and I dined with Peggy's friend, a lovely young woman with striking long reddish-blonde hair. She had come from the United States to study Arabic at the University of Cairo. We ate outside on the patio at Mena House, where Peggy had arranged to meet the young woman.

The Mena House patio.

After the meal, we relaxed on easy chairs enjoying the view of tropical flowers and palm trees framing the Great Pyramid in the distance. In reply to the waiter's request, I asked for some tea.

When the waiter asked the young woman if she would like anything, she said that she wanted a smoke. She specifically asked for a certain type of tobacco and a certain type of pipe, which I believe was called a "sheesha."

To my surprise, the waiter brought her a knee-high tall water pipe, which he placed on the ground beside her chair. It was one of those ornate pipes that consist of a glass jar containing water at the bottom, a long metal column with beautiful scrollwork, and a long flexible tube with a metal tip, which is used to suck in the fragrant hot air over the water in the glass jar. It reminded me of the hookah smoked by the caterpillar in the Lewis Carroll classic, *Alice in Wonderland*.

It steamed with a pleasant odor. I have since read that tobacco-producing companies have started to add sweet fruit flavorings to water pipe tobacco so that it appeals more to women.

While the waiter looked on, the young woman sucked on the metal tip of the long tube. The water in the bulbous bottom of the pipe bubbled.

"Yes," she told him, she was satisfied. The waiter made a small bow with hands clasped, just like a wine steward, and left us.

The young woman told us that usually only men smoke these pipes. At one time, men would smoke these pipes while gathered together in men's clubs. Only recently have women begun to smoke the water pipes. It was sort of an "in" thing with young women. She said that it took her a long time to get used to the pipe. She used to choke when she first smoked it.

When she asked me if I wanted to try a puff, I declined.

Cairo Drinking Water and Foreigners

My after-dinner conversation with her, as she puffed on the "sheesha," brought me closer to a realization that I likely did receive a healing from the Holy Mother when I drank the soda fountain drink at Mohga and Gad's church in Cairo.

As we sat on the Mena House patio sipping tea and smoking, our conversation drifted to problems she was having in Egypt. She said that she still suffered with stomach distress whenever she ate raw vegetables. Then she explained how she would soak the vegetables she bought in a mild bleach solution to counteract the effects of the water used to wash the vegetables. Even when she towel-dried the vegetables, after their soak in the disinfectant solution, she still experienced gastro-intestinal discomfort.

I thought back to the two-cup container of soda water, most of which I had downed at the church in Cairo. Since that amazing night, I had wondered if perhaps I had been spared a bout of the Pharaoh's Revenge because the city water in Cairo was actually safe for Americans. However, after hearing the young woman's experience with the local water, I realized that I had been very fortunate and very much protected. I felt as if I likely did receive a healing from the Holy Mother.

The Workings of a Soda Fountain Machine

However, my skeptical nature resurfaced when I returned home. I wondered if perhaps I do not understand how a soda fountain machine works.

In a conversation with my husband, he said that a soda fountain machine is hooked up to a large metal bottle, which he assumed must contain carbonated water that is mixed with the syrup at the fountain spout. If so, I had not drunk the local water, but instead had drunk bottled carbonated water.

I wanted to make sure. Therefore, I called a local Coca-Cola bottling company to find out how a soda fountain machine works. The employee at the company told me that although she had no way of knowing just what system the Egyptians used, with Coca-Cola, carbonation from a tank of gaseous carbon dioxide is mixed with tap water and syrup to produce the drink at a soda fountain.

I asked her if a soda fountain might use a tank of carbonated water to mix with the syrup. She explained that a tank of carbonated water would likely lose its carbonation or go flat over time. That was why sodas were bottled—to keep the carbonation in the drink. That was why a tank of gas, rather than a tank of carbonated water, was mixed with tap water to make a soda drink at a soda fountain—so the carbonation would not go flat.

From this, I realized that likely I did drink at least a full cup of the local water in Cairo . . . and without suffering any gastrointestinal distress whatsoever.

Just in case you are thinking that I must have an iron-clad stomach, I have experienced some intestinal distress from eating a salad in Mexico. The amount of water clinging to the lettuce leaves was much less than the cup or more of water I drank in Cairo.

Based on the young American woman's experience with the Cairo drinking water, I can only conclude I must have experienced a genuine healing when I drank over a cup of it.

Again I wondered, *Did Mary heal me*? I have to admit that something of a miraculous nature likely did occur.

Chapter Eight

RUSSIAN AIRCRAFT AND
EGYPTIAN TANK TRUCKS

Air Flight to Luxor

I felt happy to find indications that the Great Pyramid and Great Sphinx may have been built during the time Atlantis was supposed to have existed. I had also seen for myself that a very advanced civilization may have built these ancient ruins. Hence, I believed it possible that the images painted on the walls of the pharaohs' tombs in the Valley of the Kings might illustrate the ancient Egyptians' legendary recollections of that time. I also hoped that these tomb images might illustrate my memories of Atlantis. Therefore, our next stop was the pharaohs' tombs in the Valley of the Kings.

Many tourists who visit Egypt travel to the Valley of the Kings on a cruise ship that sails down the Nile to Luxor. We would not have the time to take a leisurely sightseeing cruise along the river.

We flew to Luxor instead. When I think back on it, I am again amazed that everything worked out so well for us. As Hani had promised, his cousin in Cairo owned a travel agency, and he had arranged our travel. As this was an in-country travel agency, we naturally flew Egypt Air.

I found our flight to be a new experience. Most of our fellow passengers were Egyptians. And, they were almost all men. Except for a couple of young women tourists who traveled with husbands or boyfriends, our fellow passengers had swarthy skin, jet black hair, and looked like they might be relatives of that dashingly handsome and famous movie actor of Dr. Zhivago fame, Omar Sharif. It was quite a difference from the blondes, brunettes, and blacks of the United States.

In addition, Peggy and I found it just a little bit disconcerting that all the signs in the plane such as "Exit" and "No Smoking," were written in large graceful Arabic characters, and, in equally large and prominent letters, in Russian. Under the Arabic and Russian we found very tiny English lettering.

This could only mean one thing. The Egyptian aircraft on which we flew was not an American plane. It was Russian! Nonetheless, the flight was lovely—comfortable, enjoyable, and delightful—everything a person would want in commercial airline service.

Because we flew at night, the lights in the cabin were dimmed. Although Peggy and I should have felt apprehensive or even sleepy, because it was such a new situation for us, we felt like children who have been allowed to stay up later than our usual bedtime. We talked with energy and animation over the roar of the engine for the whole flight.

Luxor at Night

We arrived in Luxor in the middle of the night. The men with whom we had shared our flight deferred to us with consideration and politeness because we were women.

Our driver waited for us on the tarmac in the spotlight created by a light on a tall pole. This was not a big bustling airport. We walked off the plane, down a moveable ladder, and picked our luggage out from a pile on the tarmac.

All the other passengers scattered, leaving Peggy and me alone with the driver who loaded our luggage into his vehicle, which he had driven onto the tarmac. I felt grateful to have Peggy's companionship, thankful she had offered to come with me.

It must have been quite late at night because we did not pass a single other vehicle on what seemed like a long drive from the airport to our hotel in Luxor.

The name, "Luxor," is often used to signify the entire area of Egyptian ruins at the location that used to be the ancient city of Thebes, instead of just the town of Luxor. In cases where Luxor is used to describe the entire region, it is common to use the location descriptions of "West Bank" or "East Bank," such as "The Temple of Luxor is located on the East Bank."

Both the Temples of Luxor and Karnak are located on the East Bank of the Nile. However, most of the burial tombs of the pharaohs are located on the West Bank, many of them in the Valley of the Kings and the Valley of the Queens. The ancient Egyptians chose to bury their dead on the west side of the Nile because the sun set, or died, in the west.

Cruise Ships in the Nile

As we drove from the airport on the West Bank to our motel in the city of Luxor on the East Bank, we crossed a bridge over the Nile River. Everything—the bulrushes along the water, the moonlit road and the black water itself—felt quiet and still as if we drove through a museum display.

Anchored in the dark water below, I saw the lights of dozens of cruise ships. Probably hundreds, maybe even thousands, of tourists slept in these floating motels.

It all looked so crisp in the moonlight. The air smelled fresh but dry even when we crossed the bridge over the river. In the headlights of the car, everything looked brown, including the low scruffy bushes along the road.

As we drove along in this unfamiliar land, I realized that, for the first time, we were totally disconnected from the safety of our umbilical connection with Mohga. We had felt nurtured and safe with her. Now, we were on our own. What would we do if there was a problem with the hotel? Who would we call? Who would help us? Who would care?

Compared to Cairo, Luxor is a small town. Once inside the town, we drove along an empty street that paralleled the Nile. In the darkness, we could only see sleeping buildings on our left and a row of palm trees on our right, which I assumed lined the river. Everything in this desert area looked brown, even in the city.

As we approached the hotel, golden lights that beamed through the glass doors beckoned to us. When we checked into the hotel, the attendant gave us the choice of paying a slightly higher fee for a room with a view of the Nile. We opted to pay the higher fee.

It turned out that I wasted my money because I never inhabited the room in the daytime when I could have seen the Nile from my motel room. Instead, I spent all of my time exploring the nearby ruins.

From Luxor to the Valley of the Kings

As prearranged, the next morning our driver arrived before first light. Streetlights at the hotel entrance lit up his car parked by the curb. The sky had lightened to a dark gray by the time we drove out of town.

The driver seemed especially anxious to get to the entrance of the Valley of the Kings as quickly as possible. Not having been there before, I did not understand why he appeared to be in such a hurry. I could only think that he wanted to get us to the antiquities site while the air temperature was still comfortable.

The Valley of the Kings is an area rich in ancient Egyptian artifacts, located between the towns of Luxor and Karnak. Many pharaohs who lived from around 1540 to 1075 B. C. were buried in this area. Of these pharaohs, the best known to modern people is probably Tutankhamen or King Tut.

Nobles and their families were also buried in this area, as well as pets. The majority of the tombs have been ransacked by grave robbers, Tutankhamen's to a much lesser extent than others. Because he was a minor king during his lifetime, experts believe that the treasures found in his tomb are merely a glimpse of the amazing artifacts originally contained in other pharaohs' tombs.

Although several tombs are closed to the public, the extensive abundance of Egyptian monuments leaves a plethora of tourist-friendly places.

Nearby is another area of ancient Egyptian artifacts named the Valley of the Queens, since it was the area designated as the burial ground for important queens, such as Queen Hatshepsut.

Extra Security

The drive from the hotel to the entrance of the Valley of the Kings site appeared to be much shorter than the drive from the airport to the hotel. Once at the entranceway we quickly purchased our tickets. Only a few other people, all men, queued up with us at the ticket window. Perhaps they were all tour guides.

As I turned from the ticket window, I saw something I had not noticed in the darkness of the early morning shadows. Crouched under the overhanging rooftop of the building that housed the ticket sellers loomed an army truck with a gun turret on its roof. The gun pointed at the parking lot. A couple of military policemen, armed with machine guns, hovered at the ready nearby.

The tank-truck at the Valley of the Kings entrance.

Until this moment, I had dismissed the number of military police in Egypt as equivalent to the number of policemen we have in the United States, believing that I had become so accustomed to police in our own society that they have become transparent to me.

However, the tank-at-the-ready produced a shock that made me realize that the situation in Egypt is much more dangerous than on U.S. streets. Of course the pyramids and the many other precious archeological sites in Egypt attract throngs of people from all over the world, so there is need for heightened security.

At the time, I did not know that 58 foreigners had been massacred by terrorists at the Valley of the Kings in 1997. No wonder John had been wary of visiting the land of the pharaohs. No wonder the Egyptian government needs to keep a tank-truck and machine-gun toting soldiers at the ready at the Valley of the Kings. I appreciated that they did.

The sun broke through the palm fronds at the horizon and at the same time, I heard the grumbling of a bus engine. I turned to observe the stinking behemoth swing into the dusty road alongside the parking area. The tourist bus took its place behind three cars parked in front of the closed entrance gate. Our driver scurried up to Peggy and me. He motioned anxiously to us, begging us to hasten into his car.

At first I could not understand why he was so anxious. As our driver frantically motioned toward his car, I saw the reason for his alarm. Rumbling on the road from the Nile River, a convoy of tourist buses bore down upon us, the fumes from their diesel engines causing dust to plume in clouds along the road.

I realized that they carried the hundreds of tourists who had spent the night on the dozens of cruise ships anchored in the Nile. I felt thankful that our driver knew to get us into the queue ahead of the buses. If we had had to wait for all the people on the buses to get off, our delay before we could enter the archeological site might have become interminable. By the time we got into the site the desert sun would have been frying us alive.

We ran to his car and made it to the entranceway before the buses. We were some of the first people to enter the premises.

Ahead of us, we saw walls of barren desert cliffs, which surrounded a valley. Along the floor of the valley, dry gravelly pathways wound from the entrance of one tomb to another.

As I walked through the gate, I saw a sign saying that the use of flash photography was prohibited inside the pharaohs' tombs. I felt happy that I had consulted a guidebook before I left the United States and so knew to bring film and lenses suitable for low light photography.

The tall desert cliffs in the Valley of the Kings.

The Tomb of Thothmose III

Through research, I had learned that many of the images I sought could be found in the tomb of Thothmose III. Therefore, aware that the desert sun rose steadily in the sky, Peggy and I passed the crowds moseying along from tomb to tomb. Instead, we used the map of the Valley of the Kings in our guidebook and headed straight to the entrance of King Thothmose III's tomb.

As king of Egypt, Thothmose III brought great wealth to the country. He conquered Syria and most of the Euphrates Valley. He was the son of Thothmose II and a minor wife, Isis.

Although Thothmose III became king when his father died, he had to share the position with Thothmose II's royal wife, Hatshepsut. During Hatshepsut's approximately 22-year reign, Thothmose III had very little power. However, after her death, Thothmose III ruled Egypt for the duration of his life.

Peggy and I knew that once the crowds arrived, the atmosphere in the tomb would become increasing warmer, both from warm bodies and from the gain in heat from the relentless desert sun. In addition, I did not want to have to deal with people standing in front of the images I wanted to photograph.

I am happy that we rushed ahead because of a detail I had not anticipated. Thothmose III's tomb has a false floor built about a foot high above the original stone floor. My guess is that this wooden platform is built to keep the many shuffling feet from stirring up dust in the enclosed space. Therefore, instead of walking on the actual floor of the tomb, visitors walk on this false floor made of wood. It looked somewhat like an indoor boardwalk.

Although the wooden floor created a pleasant walking surface, I had not anticipated the bounce created by the wooden planks. Once crowds started to pour into the tomb, I found it increasingly difficult to take photographs since the wooden platform bounced as the visitors tramped through the manmade cave.

Since the walls of the tomb were lit with only one row of fluorescent lights placed at the level of the false wooden floor, the paintings were not lit as well as I had hoped. Even with my fast film, I needed a very long exposure time.

With all the people bouncing on the wooden floor, I could not keep the camera steady enough for a long exposure no matter how tightly I jammed my elbows against my sides or how long I held my breath. Even when I held the camera like a rock, the floor beneath me caused the image to bounce. When I looked through the viewfinder to focus the image it appeared as if I stood on a trampoline.

That first hour or so in Thothmose III's tomb, during the time when Peggy and I almost had the tomb to ourselves, was the best. I saw many images that corroborated my memories of Atlantis.

Chapter Nine

WHO WAS EVE?

Recollections of Atlantis

My journey to Luxor not only confirmed my memories of Atlantis, they also helped me understand why Mary is often called the New Eve. In *God Sent*, Roy Abraham Varghese says that the first outstanding principle about Mary formulated by the founders of the Christian Church is that Mary is the New Eve. In addition, she sometimes calls herself the New Eve during her manifestations.

Since I believe Adam and Eve were originally spiritual beings in Atlantis—more on this in Chapter Twenty-one, "Amilius and Atlantis"—the information on Atlanteans which came to light in the pharaohs' tombs helped to better clarify how Mary could have been Eve in Atlantis and reincarnated to be Mary in the Holy Land.

Atlantis Memories Are Very Different from Past Lives

As you know, I originally went to a hypnotherapist to lose weight. My purpose in visiting the hypnotherapist had nothing to do with Atlantis. But sometimes the Universe has different ideas.

Once the hypnotherapist had put me in a deep trance, I began to recall past life experiences contributing to my phenomenal weight gain.

To my amazement, my recollections of Atlantis turned out to be quite different from my past life memories leading to my problems with weight described earlier. I had expected to confront incarnations similar to the ones described in Chapter Three, "Fat Karma and Death."

While under trance in the hypnotherapist's office, my conscious mind, which was awake enough to hear and answer questions, could hardly believe what I was seeing and feeling.

To my surprise, I was not human. I relived my own personal "Fall" from pure spirit to a soul enmeshed with the physical on earth. I learned that my present overweight provided a constant reminder of the weight of the physical. It motivated me to discover a better understanding of my relationship to the Creative Forces.

In Atlantis I found myself to be a curious frog-like being. This bizarre creature had frog legs and sticky, long-fingered hands. Its skin appeared to be green with mottled brown patches like a frog. Its face was an even brown tone. However, the little creature had a human-like face instead of a frog's face. It did have large black eyes which were slanted like a frog's but not bulbous. Instead, its eyes glistened like a "gray" alien's eyes or a Disney cartoon character. Straight black hair covered its head. A swath of hair fell over its forehead.

While hypnotized, I thought it looked cute, with its pixie-like face and the large cartoon-character black eyes. It also had a tiny nose, a pointed chin, and a sweet little mouth. Because of its cute human-like face, I called it a pixie-faced frog being.

Animal Mixtures

Hawks with human heads.

Based on my memory of having been a mixture of a human type with a frog type (the pixie-faced frog being) I assumed that some Atlanteans were mixtures of human and animal types. Or anyway, I hoped to find images of human/animal mixtures in the pharaohs' tombs.

I found this to be so. I saw

many images of human/animal mixtures. There were hawks with human heads, humans with hawks' heads, men with rams' heads, a woman with cow horns, and many more. I just kept snapping the shutter of my camera and changing rolls of film.

Human/animal mixtures in Thothmose III's tomb including creatures with a human body mixed with the head of, from L to R, a falcon, a cow, a ram, and a dog.

Of course, the most outstanding example of an ancient Egyptian illustration of a human/animal mixture is the Great Sphinx. In *Heaven's Mirror*, co-authors Graham Hancock and Santha Faiia say that the word Sphinx is derived from the ancient Egyptian words "sheshep ankh," which means "living image."

I wondered, a "living image" of what? Interestingly, John van Auken, author of, "Weird Times: Ancient Human/Animal Mix," an article in the September 2005 issue of *Ancient Mysteries*, an Edgar Cayce's A.R.E. membership newsletter, says that "We cannot leave this brief study of human and animal intermixing without noting that the Cayce readings make an important reference to the Sphinx as a symbol of this intermixing. The reading is 5748-6." It makes sense that the Great Sphinx represents the ancient human/animal mixtures since the Great Sphinx is a mixture of a human head with a lion's body. Therefore, the Great Sphinx is a living image of a human/animal mixture.

In trance reading 5748-6, Cayce goes on to say that there are many more sphinxes, not only the Great Sphinx and not only in Egypt. They can also be found in the Middle East and Greece.

During our visit to Luxor, we found many smaller sphinxes, for example, a row of sphinxes leading to a Luxor temple. We also saw sphinxes depicting the supreme deity worshipped by the ancient Egyptians in the Luxor area. He is known as Amon and is depicted as a ram-headed human/animal mixture.

A row of human-headed, lion-bodied sphinxes lead to a Luxor temple.

The god Amon—a ram-headed, lion-bodied Sphinx.

A human-headed Sphinx.

Androgynous Atlanteans

Not only was I a frog/human mixture in Atlantis, I was also androgynous. When the hypnotherapist asked me whether I was male or female I at first replied that I did not know. Then, when I thought about it for a while, I replied that I was both.

Six male stamens surround one female pistil in the center of a lily.

The dictionary defines androgynous as having the nature of both male and female. My trusty Webster's Dictionary uses flowers for an example, because many flowers have male stamens and female pistils.

This is not to say that the Atlanteans were flowers. But I mention flowers to show that even today there are androgynous species in the natural world.

I am not the only one with Atlantean memories of having been androgynous. Since my Atlantean hypnosis sessions, I have read Shirley

MacLaine's *The Camino*. To my delight, I discovered that she also has recollections of having been an androgynous being in Atlantis. In fact, MacLaine wrote about the process she went through to separate into two bodies: one male and one female.

Does this story of two separate sexes coming from one individual remind you of anything? It should because it parallels the story of the creation of Eve in the Garden of Eden.

Was Adam Androgynous?

Genesis 2:21 describes how God takes out of Adam a rib which is used to make a woman. I believe this is the story of the separation of the original androgynous individual into male and female.

Without getting into a discussion about: "Was it really a rib?" I would like to look at this ancient Christian story in a new way. Instead of assuming that Adam must be a male since he is referred to as "he," I would like to consider that "he" might mean a universal "he" in the same way that "man" can refer to mankind or all human beings. By so doing, it can free us to consider that Adam may not have been specifically male.

Because I remembered being androgynous and Shirley MacLaine remembered her experience of separating into male and female, I would like to consider that Adam was originally androgynous, that is to say, having both male and female in the same body.

Therefore, I believe the Genesis 2:21 story is actually the handed down account of the time when our souls inhabited androgynous bodies.

Interestingly, Pope John Paul II agrees with the concept that Adam had to be something other than our present-day human male. In *The Pontiff in Winter* by John Cornwell, John Paul II is reported as asking in his writings that we consider the loneliness of the sexually undifferentiated Adam in the Garden of Eden. The Pontiff goes on to say that he sees Adam, before Eve, as being neither male nor female.

In further support of this concept, if you consult the Old Testament, in Genesis 5:28 you will see that an individual named

Lamech who is a descendent of Adam and Eve, had his first child at the age of 182 years. His father, Methuselah, lived 969 years. These people were obviously not the kind of people we are today. Furthermore, they came *after* Adam and Eve.

Adam and Eve were likely at least as unusual as Lamech and Methuselah . . . or more so . . . and also very different than we are now.

It follows then that it is possible that Adam could have been an androgynous being and that the story of the creation of Eve in the Garden of Eden is actually the story of the separation of Adam's androgynous body into male and female.

Therefore, Eve could actually be a female expression of the original androgynous Adam.

Remember this because in Chapter Twenty-one, "Amilius and Atlantis," I will continue on this theme. It is important in this book about Mary since Mary is sometimes called the New Eve.

The Serpent

In *When We Were Gods*, I looked at Jesus in a new way: that he had been a spiritual being named Amilius who entered the material world as Adam to lead us out of the physical.

In this chapter, I looked at the origin of Eve in a new way: that she was the female half of the sexually undifferentiated Adam.

In the following chapters, I intend to look at the serpent in a new way. First, I will discuss the feathered serpent of the ancient Maya, then the winged serpents in the pharaohs' tombs, and finally, mythological serpents, especially the one that might have become the cunning serpent in the Garden of Eden famous for beguiling the very innocent and newly separated individuals Adam and Eve.

Mary and the Serpent

I emphasize the serpent in this book about Mary because the Holy Mother's purpose is intimately tied with the serpent. If she truly is the New Eve . . . and I show that she is in Chapter Twenty, "Twin Souls and Serpent Gods" . . . it means that Mary, as Eve, had been seduced by the serpent in the Garden of Eden. If you remember, the serpent enticed Eve by offering her the fruit of the tree of the knowledge of good and evil.

I believe the Garden of Eden represents that time in Atlantis before we knew death, explained in Chapter Twenty, "Twin Souls and Serpent Gods."

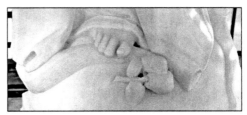

Mary's foot crushes the head of the serpent holding the fruit in its mouth, a statue displayed at the Our Lady of Fatima Shrine in Lewistown, New York.

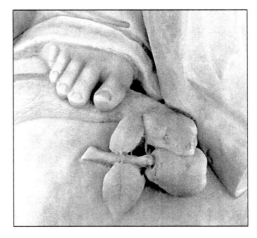

In addition, in Genesis 3:15, it is prophesized that Eve's "seed" or descendent will crush the head of the serpent. Since Mary is the New Eve, it follows that Mary's Son, Jesus, is the "seed" who crushes the head of the serpent. Some believe that this verse was incorrectly translated and originally meant that Eve would crush the head of the serpent.

Because of Mary's associations with the serpent, in the next two chapters I will discuss images of serpents in the ruins of both the ancient Egyptians and the ancient Maya in Yucatan, Mexico. Both civilizations flanked Atlantis when it existed in the Atlantic Ocean. And both civilizations, according to Edgar Cayce's trance source, experienced an influx of Atlanteans when Atlantis began to break up due to earth upheavals.

Aside from historical interest, I also had my own personal reasons for investigating images and myths of serpents. My scariest memory of Atlantis involved a serpent.

Chapter Ten

SCARIEST MEMORY OF ATLANTIS

Encounter with an Atlantean Serpent

The encounter with the serpent occurred during a series of earth upheavals that ultimately destroyed Atlantis. As the earth began to break apart with the force of gargantuan earthquakes, I traveled to Egypt where the land was stable.

To get to Egypt, I had traveled in a most unusual manner. This recollection turned out to be my scariest Atlantean memory.

I had seen myself fall into the huge open mouth of a giant serpent. While hypnotized, as I relived the experience, I did not feel frightened as I fell headlong into the serpent's waiting jaws. In fact, in my memory, I felt keenly aware as if I was doing something I had practiced many times before.

Furthermore, I felt sincere and knew I had to be careful to adopt the correct attitude. I told the hypnotherapist that to do this, one had to be an especially "letting go" kind of person.

However, when I first had the memory, I felt afraid to tell her anything. I feared she might think I was crazy. In fact, I felt sure that she would think I was imagining such a silly scenario as falling into a serpent's mouth.

Even though I willingly believed the memory of having been an African maiden or something as odd as a pixie-faced frog being, when I saw myself fall into the serpent's mouth, I could not accept it. Eventually I was able to tell the hypnotherapist, and she helped me to come to terms with my memory.

While in trance, I saw the wide-open mouth of a huge snake below me. Two large fangs extended down from the upper jaw. It looked as if the serpent's head had been fashioned as the entrance to an underground tunnel because only the neck and head protruded above the earth.

Immediately after I fell in the serpent's mouth, I found myself flying through space.

Was It an Underground Shamanic Journey?
People who attend my seminars have asked me if I traveled through the earth after I fell into the serpent's mouth. Many of them have read about shamanic journeys through tunnels in the earth. However, I do not remember going through the earth.

Furthermore, a number of my readers have shared their own memories of encounters with magical serpents. These people have had memories or recurring childhood dreams of falling into a serpent's mouth and then being inside the serpent's body. Some people recall traveling through the serpent's body in the earth.

However, my memories from the hypnosis sessions were different. Immediately after falling into the snake's mouth, I found myself flying through space, not in an underground tunnel.

Today we would use a solid rocket booster or a jet engine to provide the momentum necessary to overcome gravitational force. However, in Atlantis, I had seen that Atlanteans somehow used serpent energy to propel themselves into flight. I believe it was the serpent's strike ability that the Atlanteans employed to provide momentum.

This memory—of flying through space after falling into the serpent's mouth—motivated me to visit ancient Mayan ruins.

Feathered Serpents in Yucatan
A number of years prior to my visit to Egypt, I had traveled to Yucatan, Mexico, which I described in my first two books. My

purpose had been to see stone carvings of men in feathered serpents' mouths.

No one knows why the ancient Maya created so many images of men in the mouths of feathered serpents. No one knows why the ancient Maya appeared to be obsessed with feathered serpents.

I thought I might. These images likely showed the method by which the Atlanteans traveled to and from the Yucatan.

According to the world's best-documented psychic Edgar Cayce, the Atlanteans traveled to safer lands in Yucatan and Egypt when Atlantis began to disintegrate. Cayce says that Atlantis used to be situated in the middle of the Atlantic Ocean, between Central America and Northern Africa. Therefore, it made sense that the Atlanteans would have fled to lands that were closest to their homeland—Northern Africa on the east and Yucatan on the west.

To the indigenous people of Central America and Northern Africa, the Atlanteans must have seemed like magicians, the memory of their arrivals and departures continuing on as legends in the indigenous people's mythical traditions. Very likely, the native people saw the technologically advanced Atlanteans as gods. Probably, they commemorated the seemingly magical exploits of the Atlanteans in their art.

One of the most powerful images the indigenous people must have seen would have been the method by which the Atlanteans arrived and left the Yucatan and Egypt.

If my memories of Atlantis are correct, the Atlantean method of transportation to and from the Yucatan and Egypt would have been by falling into the serpent's mouth and then flying through space.

Mayan God Arrives on a Raft of Serpents

The indigenous people would have remembered transportation via serpents in stories that were passed down in their oral history. And indeed, the ancient Maya have a legend that their god Kukulkan arrived from the East—the location of Atlantis—on a raft made of serpents.

Recently an isolated tribe of primitive people who worshipped a statue of a wooden airplane were discovered. They had made the statue out of local materials in imitation of the aircraft they saw flying overhead—it looked like a plane, but it could not fly. To them, the aircrafts they saw flying overhead appeared to have god-like qualities. Therefore, they made a representative image out of natural materials and worshiped it.

In the same way, the indigenous people in the Yucatan must have made images of the amazing Atlantean transportation system. They probably passed down their memories by telling stories from one generation to the next. The image became a part of their religious practice, and, therefore, as their civilization flourished, they incorporated the image in their buildings and art.

Stone Carvings of Feathered Serpents

I believe the ancient Maya showed the flight ability of the magical Atlantean serpents by giving the serpents feathers. This image was the mystical feathered serpent.

Before I went to the Yucatan, I researched various books on the ancient Maya, such as Peter Tompkins' *Mysteries of the Mexican Pyramids*. In doing research, I discovered a curious fact.

I noticed that most of the sculptures of men in feathered serpents' mouths were described as being exhibited in museums and private collections. Indeed, zealous explorers and collectors had even lifted bas reliefs from their original locations on the sides of buildings to reinstate them in museum displays.

Likely, the explorers and collectors did not consider the background on which they found the bas reliefs as relevant. In fact many of the explorers merely saw the stone carvings as artifacts of superstitious primitive people, rather than as historical evidence of a lost continent. They did not think that the background on which they found the carvings might explain the image.

Because I believed that the background contained clues as to the meaning of the stone carvings, I hoped to find one of the ancient Maya's sculptures or bas reliefs in its original location.

Whenever I arrived at a Mayan ruin during my first visit to the Yucatan, as described in *When We Were Gods*, I inquired of the present-day Maya guides, "Is there a sculpture of a feathered serpent with a man in its mouth here?" When I asked in Tulum, Coba, and Chichen Itza the guides said, "No."

Finally, in Uxmal, the guide said, "Yes." He led me to the Nunnery Quadrangle, a group of four, long, narrow buildings arranged around an open square. I followed him across the grassy square to the building on the west side of the quadrangle. He pointed to the top half of the building where I saw an image of a feathered serpent carved along the length of the building.

The serpent had its mouth open. In its wide-open mouth a man's face looked out as if he watched the scenery from a commercial airline window.

Most significantly, in front of the figure of the feathered serpent the ancient Maya had carved images of stars. The guide said the star images were pictures of Venus. In effect, the whole scene showed a feathered serpent flying through space with a man in its mouth!

This, exactly, had been my experience in Atlantis. By falling into the serpent's mouth, I had flown through space. Here, on the side of a building in a Mayan ruin, I found a stone representation of my Atlantean memory.

More Feathered Serpents with Men in Their Mouths

I have since returned to the Yucatan. Although I did not find any more pictures of serpents against a background which included stars or planets, I did find a number of sculptures showing clearer images of the man in the feathered serpent's mouth.

For example, I visited the Merida Museum of Anthropology and History where I saw a magnificent stone carving of a man's head in the wide-open jaws of an amazing feathered serpent.

On the next two pages, please find photographs of the feathered serpent with the man in its mouth flying through the stars in Uxmal and the serpent with a man in its mouth displayed at the Museum of Anthropology in Merida, Yucatan.

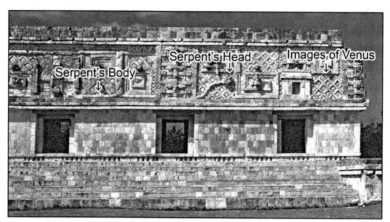

The west building of the Uxmal Nunnery Quadrangle.

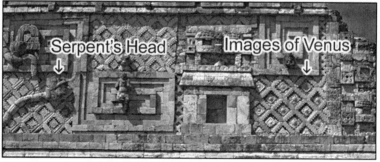

A closer view of the feathered serpent and Venus images.

Left, a close up of the man in the serpent's mouth. Below, an enlarged Venus image.

A man's head juts out of the wide-open jaws of a stylized feathered serpent on display in the Museum of Anthropology and History in Merida, Yucatan.

A visit to the archeological site at Labna, which is not very far from Uxmal, provided an image of another reptile with a man in its mouth. Archeologists believe it is the mouth of a lizard rather than a serpent. However, since lizards look like dragons and I believe dragons are also mythological memories of the flying serpents from Atlantis, I include the photograph at right. There will be more on dragons in Chapter Fourteen, "Serpents, Root Races, and Myths."

A lizard with a man in its mouth in Labna, Yucatan.

During my second visit to Yucatan, I discovered that there are actually images of men in feathered serpent's mouths at Chichen Itza. Since my first visit, Chichen Itza has been named one of the New Seven Wonders of the World in a ceremony in Lisbon, Portugal on July 7, 2007.

The New Seven Wonders of the World (in alphabetical order):
1. Chichen Itza, Mexico
2. Christ Redeemer, Brazil
3. Colosseum, Italy
4. Great Wall of China
5. Machu Picchu, Peru
6. Petra, Jordan
7. Taj Mahal, India

The images of the feathered serpents with men in their mouths are on the walls at the top level of the Temple of the Warriors in Chichen Itza. They are pictured on the opposite page.

These are magnificent images. Behind the serpents' heads, carved in bas relief, are elaborate wings and hawk-like claws, showing that these serpents can fly because of their bird-like characteristics.

The Temple of the Warriors in Chichen Itza. The bas reliefs of the men in the feathered serpents' mouths are on the sides of the top level of the structure.

Close ups of the man in the feathered serpent's mouth. Note the elaborate feathers and the hawk claws carved on the wall.

During my second visit to Yucatan, I also found an amazing free-standing statue in the Museum of Anthropology in Merida. It looks like the same god that is carved in bas relief on the wall of the Temple of the Warriors in Chichen Itza illustrated above.

Amazingly, this individual and two of his companions are called, "Atlantes," which sounds exactly like Atlantis. The plaque accompanying the display says that the Atlantes are mythological creatures who separate heaven from earth. These statues were used to support tables and altars.

One of the Atlantes statues illustrated on the following page appears to be a statue of a human/serpent/bird Atlantean mixture similar to my memory of being part frog and part primate in Atlantis. The statue is shown in three close-up views.

Here is an interesting tidbit that I learned from a guide during my second trip to Yucatan. I have always wondered why the very long-tailed exotic bird, the Quetzal, is associated with the feathered serpent god Kukulkan, mentioned earlier. In fact, the Aztecs' name for this god is Quetzalcoatl after the Quetzal bird.

The figure on the far right of the three Atlantes figures is shown in close up views below.

This Atlantes figure has feathered wings and a serpent mouth opened wide with a man's face inside the mouth.

The guide explained that because the Quetzal has such a long tail, when it flies, it proceeds in a wavy fashion similar to the way a snake slithers. In effect, the ancient people of Mexico showed that since the feathered serpent few through the air it flew like a Quetzal bird—as you would expect a serpent to fly—with an undulating motion.

The Descending God
During my second visit to Yucatan, I came across bas relief carvings of another god I had encountered during my first Yucatan visit. This was the descending god. I had first seen the descending

god in Tulum. Amazingly, the ancient Maya carved this god upside-down. He hung head down, his legs splayed wide apart.

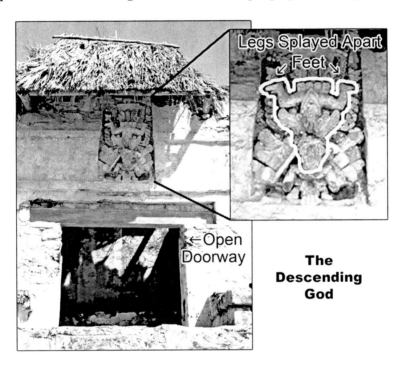

The image reminded me of my memory of falling into the serpent's mouth. I had plunged head first also. This descending god certainly looked like a "letting go" kind of a person. He appeared to be very relaxed with his legs wide open.

I liked the image for another reason. The ancient Maya had carved the descending god over an open doorway. Had they meant the doorway to represent the open mouth of the serpent? During my second Yucatan visit, I found two more descending gods falling into open doorways in the ruin at Sayil. These carvings left no doubt that the descending god fell into a wide open mouth.

The Palace in Sayil with descending god images over the fourth and eleventh doorways counting from the left.

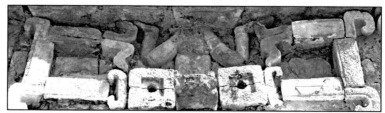

The descending god between large serpent eyes and nostrils.

The descending god falls headfirst into the open mouth of the large-eyed serpent. Its mouth is represented by the open doorway below. The large serpent eyes flank the splayed-apart legs of the god. The nostrils have holes in them and are smaller than the eyes.

A Yucatan Guide

In *When We Were Gods* I wrote about finding confirmation of my Atlantean memories in the Yucatan. However, I did not write about a very interesting person I met there. He was a guide named Hilario Hilaire.

Hilario was a non-Maya, but he had lived in a modern-day Mayan village for ten years while married to a Maya woman—an arrangement the Maya usually do not allow. As a result, he knew much more about the Maya's customs than do most American guides.

He happened to live in Akumal within walking distance of the motel where John and I stayed. We had met Hilario at a dinner in which we were served modern-day Mayan foods. Hilario followed the meal with a slide presentation which showed the activities in a typical modern-day Maya community. When we talked with Hilario afterward, he invited us to visit him in his apartment.

During our visit, I wondered whether I should say anything to Hilario about my Atlantean memories of falling into the serpent's mouth. Almost as if in answer to my mental deliberations, Hilario spontaneously began to talk about men in serpent's mouths. He told me that the modern-day Maya medicine men say that if a person ever has a vision of falling into a serpent's mouth, the next thing they see will be truth.

"Oh my God!", I said.

Hilario stared at me with a quizzical look on his face.

Now I knew I had to explain my hypnosis sessions to him. When I finished, he asked me to tell him what I had seen after I fell into the serpent's mouth. I explained that I had seen myself speeding through space and then had landed in Egypt during the time the Great Pyramid was under construction.

Hilario said that according to the Maya medicine tradition, whatever I had seen after falling into the serpent's mouth had been truth. If the Maya medicine men are right, I had just received another validation of the memories that surfaced in my hypnosis sessions. Atlanteans had used serpents for flight.

2012 and the End of the World

During my hypnosis sessions in 1995 and 1996, I had mentioned that there would be earth upheavals. In trance, I even correctly predicted an earthquake that I said would be the gentle beginning of widespread earth changes. The earthquake occurred in the month of August in 1997 at exactly the place on the west coast of Australia that I said it would. Furthermore, I said the earth changes would be over by the end of 2011.

This date correlated with the Mayan Long Count Calendar. It says that a new cycle will begin on the winter solstice of 2012 or December 21, 2012. Each of the Long Count Calendar cycles lasts 5,125 years. The previous one began on August 11, 3114 B.C.

Some people think the world will end on December 21, 2012. Obviously, it did not end on August 11, 3114. Furthermore, the date is a translation of ancient Mayan texts, most of which were destroyed by a Spanish priest who rewrote the Mayan texts from memory. The date has also been found on a couple of stone stele in Mayan ruins. However, the date could be wrong because the carvings on the stone are difficult to decipher and because the Mayan date has to be correlated with the Gregorian calendar.

Nonetheless, I wondered if the modern-day Maya had any sense of this date having any importance. Therefore I asked Hilario, "Are the modern Maya aware of the 2012 date? Are they preparing for a new world or the end of an old one?"

He told me that he had not been invited into their religious practices. However, he did say that the modern Maya murmured among themselves about "2000 and then a little bit" as if they looked forward to some kind of event.

Chapter Eleven

WINGED SERPENTS IN
THE PHARAOHS' TOMBS

Images of Serpent Transportation in Egypt

In Yucatan, I believe that the ancient Maya put feathers on their sculptures of serpents to denote flight. As a result of my second travel to Yucatan, I also saw ancient bas relief images that showed serpents with wings and talons. This could mean that the ancient Maya had used wings and talons as well as feathers to show that serpents could produce flight like a bird.

When Peggy and I went to explore the pharaohs' tombs in the Valley of the Kings, we went to find evidence of the Atlanteans' serpent transportation system. I wondered, *What symbols would the ancient Egyptians use? Would they, like the ancient Maya, also stylize their serpents with feathers? Would their serpents have wings?*

In John Anthony West's *Traveler's Key to Ancient Egypt*, I had seen images of serpents with wings. Therefore, I expected that I would find paintings of serpents with wings in the pharaohs' tombs.

As in the Yucatan, I wanted to find these images in their original settings to see what backgrounds the ancient Egyptians had given the winged serpents. Would they show stars or planets as had the ancient Maya in Yucatan?

Who Made the Images in the Pharaohs' Tombs?

Before I go any further, I want to make it clear that these images, whether in the ruins of the ancient Maya or in the tombs of the Egyptian pharaohs, were not created by Atlanteans. They were images created by the ancient Maya and ancient Egyptians.

For example, pharaoh Thothmose III lived from 1479 to 1425 B. C. That is about 3500 years ago. Atlantis, according to Plato, existed until about 9,000 B.C. That is 11,000 years ago.

Therefore, the ancient Egyptians lived during the time that human beings, not Atlanteans, lived on earth. However, it does not mean that the ancient Egyptians did not remember the time that came before them.

In the same way, 2000 years after Jesus the Christ lived on earth, Christians adorn their walls with His images. Similarly, we no longer live during the time of Siddhartha Gautama, the Buddha. Nonetheless, many people today have statues of the Enlightened One even though he lived over 2500 years ago. In the same way, although Krishna has not been on earth for the last 5000 years, people of the Hindu faith still produce images in remembrance of their spiritual leader.

Just because images of Buddha, Jesus, and Krishna are still manufactured and used by devotees today does not mean that these spiritual leaders are still walking in the flesh among us. They did long ago, and we remember them for the great things they did and the wonderful lessons they taught us.

In the same way that we carry on the memory of great and important events from our spiritual past, so too did the ancient Egyptians and ancient Maya. Therefore, the images I hoped to find in the pharaohs' tombs would be images of an event or events that occurred long before the time of the people who painted the images.

Would Peggy and I find any images of serpents denoting the Atlantean method of flight in the tomb of Thothmose III? We were about to find out.

The Tomb Overseer

An attractive young Egyptian man with a black moustache and full sensuous lips approached us. He wore a turban and a gallabia and looked as if he could have belonged to a camel caravan.

One of my favorite books is called, *Drinkers of the Wind* by Carl R. Raswan. It describes the origin of elegant Arabian racing horses which were initially cultivated by Bedouin nomads. This young man, with his exotic good looks, aquiline nose, black moustache, and turban, looked like he might own a splendid Arabian racing mare.

He probably lived in an apartment in Luxor, but he looked very much like the smoldering Bedouin camel driver who had taken Debra Winger as a sex slave in *Sheltering Sky*.

Because of the movie, I glanced at him warily. However, he smiled at us with a welcoming air and acted the epitome of courtesy, as did so many of the Egyptian men we met on our travels. In lovely lilting English, similar to Hani's and Mohga's, he told us he was at our service and asked if he could help.

It turns out that each tomb has an overseer to guarantee that no one defaces the priceless artifacts and to provide helpful information to visitors. I asked him to please show us an image of a serpent.

"Oh," he said, fixing me with his deep, dark eyes and speaking softly, "there are many serpents painted on the walls here." He extended his arm in a gesture that included all the walls in the tomb.

Winged Serpents

He was right. Everywhere Peggy and I looked, we saw stylized serpents painted on the walls.

The first images that caught my eye were two huge undulating serpents whose bodies extended about 12 feet (3.7 meters) in length along both sides of one section of the long tunnel that made up the tomb.

My heart leapt with joy when I saw that these large serpents had wings.

One of two huge winged serpents on each side of the tomb.

I heard a squeal of delight from Peggy who stood behind me. She pointed to a serpent with wings . . . and feet. Then she saw another serpent with a man riding on its back as if riding on a cart.

Peggy squealed again. I followed her pointing finger to a boat made in the form a two-headed serpent with the heads of the serpents at the prow and stern—back and front—of the boat. They were serpents used to carry people over the water.

We saw images of serpents used for transportation all around us—serpents with feet, with wings, used as carts, and used as boats—all images that said that serpents had been used for transportation. We both could hardly contain our delight at finding so many images that supported my memories of Atlantis. Peggy actually leapt up and down with joy, very uncharacteristic for this self-contained, strong-willed woman.

The young Egyptian stared at us. I could see his mind working. Why were these women jumping up and down? Tourists usually did not act in this ebullient manner when visiting the tomb of Thothmose III. And why were they so excited by images of serpents?

A three-headed serpent with wings and feet.

Two-headed serpents used as carts.

Serpents used for transportation over the water.

Men Inside Serpents

Now that I had found images of serpents used for transportation, I wanted to solve another question. I had seen myself fall into the mouth of the serpent. In the previous chapter, I described how I had found two images in Yucatan that showed the ancient Maya's depiction of men falling into the mouth of the serpent: one, a man in the feathered serpent's mouth and the other, a strange upside-down god called the descending god.

Would the ancient Egyptians also create some way of showing that Atlanteans fell into the serpent's mouth? Although Peggy and

I did not find paintings of men in serpents' mouths in Thothmose III's tomb, we did find images of men inside serpents. We also found paintings of a man's head traveling down the length of the serpent's body.

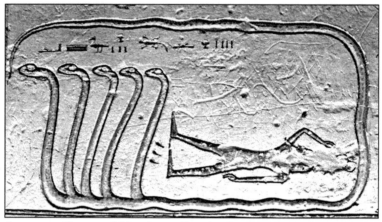

A person floats within the coils of a five-headed serpent.

The head of a man appears to travel through the serpent's body as if the man's body is within the serpent.

A serpent carries a man on top of its head—probably the one image that comes closest to the Maya feathered serpent with a man in its mouth.

Because these images showed men inside serpents, I wondered if perhaps, after falling into the serpent's mouth, I did travel through the serpent's body before flying through space. As a result, I look forward to delving further into this memory during a future hypnosis session.

Our young guide continued to watch us with fascination. After I had exposed a roll of film and while I reloaded my camera, he sidled up to me and said in a low secretive voice, "Why you take picture of snake? You like Satan?"

Because I thought an explanation of my Atlantean memories would be too complicated and also take up too much time—time I would rather use to take photographs of these amazing sights—I at first did not answer the young man. Already I could see hordes of people darkening the bright sunlit entrance to the tomb. However, he had been so good to us. He deserved some kind of explanation. Therefore, I just said, "Those serpents aren't Satan. They mean something else."

The young man looked long and hard at me with his deep, dark eyes from under his black eyebrows. I could see he still wanted to engage me in conversation, but I did not have the time. The other tourists were already pressing forward into the tomb. I felt so excited, and I did not want to miss a single image. The platform bounced as the tourists walked into the tomb.

Hastily, I looked around for another set of images I had seen in John Anthony West's *The Traveler's Key to Ancient Egypt*. They were from the Book of the Gates.

The Book of the Gates

As you know, a gate is a device that makes it possible for a person to go from one place to another. You open the gate and you can enter or exit. I assume, therefore, that the Book of the Gates has something to do with traveling from one place to another—exactly my experience of serpent travel in Atlantis.

Significantly, many of the images illustrating the Book of the Gates show a long yellow gate. Each one of these gates contains the body of a snake extending down the middle of the gate from top to bottom. The head of the snake hovers above the top of the gate and the tail extends to the bottom of it. The gate looks like the kind of swinging gate you would see leading into a saloon in an Old West movie.

Peggy and I saw numerous images of these gates. Since a gate takes you from one place to another and the Egyptians put a snake

down the middle of the gate, it looked to me as if the ancient Egyptians chose to show that a serpent took you from one place to another.

In other words, the ancient Egyptians used three ways to show that serpents were used as transportation:

1. Serpents with appendages such as wings and feet.
2. Serpents drawn as transportation devices such as a serpent in the shape of a cart or a boat.
3. The image of a serpent painted in the center of a gate.

Time to Move to another Tomb

During this initial visit to the tomb of Thothmose III many tourists eventually pressed forward into the tomb. They made photo-taking impossible, partly because they caused the wooden planks of the false floor to bounce and partly because they stood in front of all the images I wanted to photograph. It was a full house.

An image from the Book of the Gates.

Peggy and I decided to make our way to a less accessible tomb where we hoped to find less people. Therefore, we said good-bye to the young overseer and headed out into the brilliant sunshine.

We planned to visit the tomb of Amenhotep II next. This pharaoh was the son of Thothmose III and a minor wife, Merytra.

A warrior and a diplomat, he was the first known pharaoh to sign a peace treaty.

I had read that to reach his tomb you had to climb up a ladder and then stairs because the entrance to Amenhotep II's tomb is up the side of a cliff. Due to its inaccessibility, I hoped that this tomb would be a less popular destination for the throngs of tourists that presently poured into the Valley of the Kings. I could probably take photographs without the press of people around me.

However, I also had some fear that it would be too hard for me to climb up the cliff face into Amenhotep II's tomb because of the desert heat. The time was about 11 a.m. and the golden cliffs surrounding us glowed like an oven. We trudged along the walkways between the tombs to a distant section of the valley where our map said we should find the tomb of Amenhotep II.

To my delight, when we rounded the bend of a cliff, we saw that shade covered the cliff face ahead of us. According to our guidebook, the ladder and stairs rising straight up the cliff led to the tomb we sought. What a relief. We could climb in the shade.

The Grotto

I experienced an unusual incident before we entered Amenhotep II's tomb, something that I call "part of that weirdness," meaning all the strange things that have happened to me, starting with dreaming about my husband before I met him in waking life.

Prior to leaving for Egypt, I had scheduled a hypnosis session to see if there was anything specific I needed to do in Egypt. Once under trance, I felt surprised when spiritual guides appeared and told me that I had a task to accomplish in the land of the pharaohs.

This would be at the Valley of the Kings. While hypnotized, I was shown the opening to a small grotto in the stone face of a cliff. I was told this grotto would be found to the right of one of the tombs Peggy and I would explore.

There were only two tombs we meant to visit: Thothmose III and Amenhotep II. Since Amenhotep II's tomb was located up the side of a sheer cliff face, it made sense that if the information in this hypnosis session was correct, I should see the opening of the grotto to the right of Amenhotep II's tomb.

When Peggy and I arrived at Amenhotep II's tomb, I scanned the face of the cliff to see if there really was a grotto to the right of the tomb. To tell you the truth, I really did not expect to see anything. The cliff walls all around us were sheer and flat.

However, my heart skipped a beat when I saw an opening in the cliff wall to the right of the tomb, just as I had seen it in my hypnosis session. I did not say anything to Peggy, hoping she would not notice it. She had asked me about my most recent hypnosis session while we flew on the plane from Cairo to Luxor. Therefore, she knew about this grotto. I hoped she had forgotten what I had told her.

I had also told Peggy that the guides in my hypnosis session had told me that once I got inside the grotto, which did not look to be more than ten feet (three meters) deep in the hypnosis session, I should place my hands on the stone wall in front of me. Under trance, I felt a response from the stone. I felt as if an ancient energy in the grotto had waited millennia for me to return. Because of my return, it would know it was the time for the fulfillment of its purpose.

According to the information in my hypnosis session, I was supposed to acknowledge this energy. Once the communication occurred between us, the walls of the grotto would begin to move.

Then, the ancient energy would travel with me to Giza, home of the Great Pyramids and the Great Sphinx. It would wait on the Giza Plateau in a cave until it was time for the opening of the hidden room left by the Atlanteans. As I mentioned earlier, this room, called the Hall of Records by the sleeping prophet Edgar Cayce, was supposed to contain artifacts left by the Atlanteans.

Of course, after the hypnosis session, I thought all of this to be absurd. An energy left from Atlantean times awaiting fulfillment of its purpose? That the walls of the grotto would move? It sounded like total and complete lunacy—obviously a figment of my imagination.

Unfortunately, Peggy also noticed the indent in the cliff face. She nodded toward the cave. "Carol," she said, "There's your grotto."

"Yeah," I said, trying to act as if I did not care, but feeling at the same time excited and afraid.

"What are you going to do?" Peggy said.

How much I wished I could just avoid it. The task seemed so silly. I did not want to walk over to an opening which was not a tomb and which was not designated as a site to visit. I would look like an idiot.

It was too bizarre. As an excuse I nodded toward the guard who stood beside the ladder leading up to Amenhotep II's tomb. "There is a guard," I said, inferring that I could not go into the grotto because the guard would stop me.

Peggy made that same calm, still look she had bestowed upon me when I drank the city water at the church in Cairo. She did not have to say anything. I knew what she was thinking. *Why not just do it?*

"I might regret it if I don't," I said, surprised at my desire to go ahead with the foolish task.

"It's up to you," she said in her still, calm voice. I liked that she did not push.

I took a deep breath. "But the guard . . . ?"

"Well, look at that," Peggy said, inclining her head toward the guard, "he's leaving."

Rats! I thought. *Now, I don't have any excuse. What if the rest of the information in this hypnosis session is true also? What if the walls start to move? What if I start to move? What if I end up spinning? What if I feel an energy? What if it goes with me to Giza?*

Peggy's voice broke into my musings. "You'd better go now," she said.

The coast was clear. I heaved a huge sigh, handed Peggy my camera, and trudged over to the grotto.

Why not? I thought. *It doesn't hurt anybody to do this. Probably no one will even notice.*

And, I continued in my ruminations, *it is a good idea to show my unconscious that I want to work with it. Someday, it might give me a hunch or an intuition that will be really valuable.*

I walked to the grotto on dry crumbled rock that crunched under my feet. The shallow cave was about four or five feet (1.5 meters) up the cliff face so I had to walk up a steep little hill to access the opening. When I heaved myself inside, I felt disappointed to see pieces of crumpled tissue paper and a couple of soda bottles. I could also detect the faint odor of urine.

Someone had used the grotto as a bathroom and trash can. Nonetheless, I walked into it, faced the rough stone wall that looked like tiny sharp stones sticking out of cement, and placed my hands on the hot cliff face. I stood with my face on the hot, sharp pebbles with my arms raised. My palms lay flat against the stones and I prayed, just as I had been told to do in my hypnosis session. I stayed in this position for a couple of minutes and waited for the sensation of movement as I had experienced under hypnosis. At the same time, I hoped no one could see me.

But nothing happened. To my surprise, I experienced some disappointment that I had not felt any movement. In the hypnosis session, it had felt as if the walls of the grotto had spun. I had wondered if an opening would appear in the cliff side, just like it did in the Arabian myths, with the words "Open sesame."

But, nothing happened. The sun beat down on my head. The stones felt as hot as beach sand on my palms. Because I stood so close to the cliff face, I could see that the stones glistened with salmon, ochre, and cream colors. The earth in the cliff wall smelled warm and comforting but the miasma of urine fumes rising from the floor of the grotto detracted from any pleasure I felt.

There! I thought, *I have done it and nothing happened.* Relieved, I edged down the steep slope of the hill leading out of the grotto and back to Peggy. The guard returned at that time. My window of opportunity to step into the grotto had passed perfectly.

As it turned out, the spinning sensation did not occur until a couple of weeks after I returned home from Egypt. At the time, my mother was sick with cancer. I thought the dizziness I felt must be the result of my feelings of help-lessness and grief. However, a friend recently pointed out to me that, whatever the cause, after I went into the grotto I did experi-ence a spinning sensation. Would I have experienced the dizziness anyway because of my grief? I do not know.

Climbing out of the grotto.

I have no idea what purpose the spinning sensation could have produced—a change in consciousness? The opening of a spiritual center? Inner ear problems? Just another one of the mysteries of life, I guess.

A couple of days later, when Peggy and I returned to the Giza Plateau so I could take photographs of the Great Sphinx, I spied a cave-like opening under a huge boulder.

Immediately, I remembered my experience in the grotto beside Amenhotep II's tomb. Had an energy that had waited for me since Atlantean times come with me from the Valley of the Kings to the Giza Plateau?

As I said earlier, it all seemed silly to me. Nonetheless, upon seeing the opening in the rock, something within assured me that this would be a good place for that energy to hide until the time came for it to partake in the purpose it had waited so long to fulfill.

And who knows? Maybe this thought came to me because the Atlantean energy had mentally communicated with me, and it had gone into the cave-like fissure in the rock.

The arrow points to a typical cave-like opening on the Giza Plateau.

Even though I felt the grotto and the Atlantean energy were "part of the weirdness," some aspect of me could relate to the concept of an Atlantean energy when I thought of the strange creatures I had seen in my memories and also on the walls of the pharaoh's tomb. It could very well have been one of the Light Beings that will be described in the next chapter, "Light Beings in the Pharaoh's Tomb."

Flying Serpent

When I emerged from the grotto in the Valley of the Kings, Peggy and I walked over to the ladder fastened to the cliff face and began to climb up to the tomb of Amenhotep II. After my encounter with "part of that weirdness," I felt relieved to mingle among the other tourists.

As I ascended, I hoped that in Amenhotep II's tomb I would find the image that is on the cover of *The Serpent in the Sky* by John Anthony West. It showed a man flying through the stars on a serpent's back. In fact, it was this image that had originally motivated me to come to Egypt. The stars in the background left no doubt that the serpent flew through the air. Because the man sat on the serpent, the image conveyed the idea that the serpent provided flying transportation for the man. It beautifully illustrated my Atlantean memory of serpent flight.

I had to see the real image with my own eyes. In West's *The Traveler's Key to Ancient Egypt*, I had found the picture in a series of images accompanying a summary of the Book of What is in the Duat, an ancient Egyptian text that is part of the Book of the Dead. I discovered that this image could be found in a number of the pharaohs' tombs in the Valley of the Kings.

This image was very important to me because I felt it would be an Egyptian counterpart to the feathered serpent flying through space, an image of which I had already photographed in Uxmal, Mexico, illustrated on page 98.

The Tomb of Amenhotep II

Once we climbed to the top of the vertical ladder and then mounted the stairs, we discovered that Amenhotep II's tomb was not as impressive as King Thothmose III's tomb. Our first glimpse inside the tomb showed bare walls . . . and also, another ladder. We discovered that after climbing the sheer cliff wall, the inside of the tomb also required more climbing from one level to another.

I noticed that this tomb had a pleasant dry earthen smell. I saw with relief that this dark, cool tomb did not have a false wooden floor and was almost devoid of tourists.

Once we entered the inner chambers of the tomb, we found images painted on the walls. Many of these images appeared to be the same or similar to what we had previously seen in the tomb of Thothmose III.

Because the images are from the book of what has been popularly named the Book of the Dead, and because these books are painted on many of the walls of the pharaohs' tombs, archeologists believe that they are funerary texts, helping the deceased pharaoh on his voyage to the afterlife.

The images in Amenhotep II's tomb were drawn with less substance and embellishment than the same images in Thothmose III's tomb. In fact, the Amenhotep II figures almost looked like stick figures in comparison.

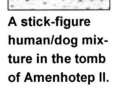

A stick-figure human/dog mixture in the tomb of Amenhotep II.

When we came to the inner sarcophagus room, we found it to be extremely dark. However, to my delight, I found a likeness of the image I had seen on the cover of John Anthony West's *Serpent in the Sky*.

Unfortunately, I could not steady my camera enough to take a crisp picture. There simply was not enough light.

The guide in Amenhotep II's tomb came over and trained his flashlight on the image. A tourist who also had a flashlight helped too. Between the two of them, they produced enough light to take a photograph.

Now you know why the next image appears to be lit so poorly. It was illuminated by two wonderful people—one a tourist, the other an Egyptian—who kindly held the light of their flashlights on the image while I held my breath and clicked the shutter.

I feel so grateful for the help I received to get this photo. When I look at it, it reminds me of the darkness of the tomb, the stone floor, the labyrinth of rooms, the cool temperature, the smell of the earth, and the delightful people who helped make it possible.

The magic carpet serpent.

I love the picture. It illustrates my Atlantean memories so well. The serpent in this image is carrying a man through the stars. The image also reminds me of the magic carpet of the Arabian Nights legends. I wonder if the flying carpet legend actually refers to the Atlantean method of using serpents for flight.

Powerful Serpents Revered by Many Cultures

The ancient Egyptians and ancient Maya are not the only cultures in our historical past that revered powerful mythical serpents.

In *Heaven's Mirror: Quest for the Lost Civilization*, Graham Hancock writes about the Nagas of India. The greatest and most powerful of these Nagas is Sesha who is similar to the many-headed serpents in the pharaohs' tombs, except that Sesha is sometime depicted with as many as 1000 heads. Sesha is responsible for the creation of the world and spits out fire at the end of each age to help destroy the previous world so the new one can be created.

Among the Indian pantheon of serpent gods, Ananda Lahara, an eleven-headed Naga, sounds like the Indian version of the Egyptian magic carpet serpent because it is supposed to be a wave of bliss that carries the gods into eternity. Agni is another Indian serpent god who is supposed to be a manifestation of divine fire. A discussion of the Indian Nagas would not be complete without mentioning the many-headed Muchalinda, guardian of the Tree of Enlightenment, who protected Buddha by wrapping itself around him.

Many more cultures throughout the world revere powerful mythological serpents. Many of these serpents are gods and goddesses. There are also many mythological Chinese serpents such as Shen Lung, a spiritual serpent controlling wind and rain. Tien Lung is a Chinese sky serpent who protects the gods and Nu Kua is a serpent god-dess who made the first people.

In addition, Cecrops, the Greek creator of civilization, sounds like an Atlantean mixture because he is half human and half serpent. Ouroboros is the name of a great serpent who, according to the ancient Vikings, encircles the earth. The Australian aborigines believe that a Rainbow Serpent is the mother of the world—both heaven and earth.

Dzyu is the Tibetan serpent power of creation. Iara is a great serpent goddess from Brazil who is mother of the water. A serpent goddess from Central Africa is called, Moma.

Seraphim are divine creatures from Hebrew mythology sometimes described as fiery serpents or serpentine in form and associated with fire because they are so immensely bright with light. They also sound like third root race beings because they are described as mixtures of animals with tall serpent bodies, four-heads, and with six wings, one set of which is used for flying.

In Chapter Twenty, "Twin Souls and Serpent Gods," I will discuss good and bad serpents. But first, I will examine a very unusual god painted on the walls of the pharaoh's tomb. This god provides the verification of our beginnings as souls on earth.

Chapter Twelve

LIGHT BEINGS IN THE PHARAOH'S TOMB

Back to Thothmoses III's Tomb

When we left Amenhotep II's tomb, Peggy and I still had some time left before our prearranged rendezvous with our driver. I noticed that, as the lunch hour approached, the crowds of tourists in the Valley of the Kings had begun to thin out. I assumed they had returned to their buses to have lunch on their cruise ships, which were still anchored in the Nile.

On our way back to the entrance gate, where our driver would soon be waiting for us, we walked past Thothmose III's tomb. Peggy must have had the same idea as I did because she said, "Want to look in here again? The crowds seem to be leaving."

When we walked into the tomb, I saw to my delight that she was right. The tomb was almost empty. Only about six tourists remained. The good-looking young Egyptian guide recognized us and greeted us as if we were long lost friends. Since I had taken an immediate liking to him as well, I felt happy with our reception.

"Come," he said and led us through the tunnel of the tomb. His gallabia flounced behind him as he strode ahead, directing us into the back recesses of the tomb. This was the sarcophagus room that had held the body of King Thothmose III. Although the mummy no longer rested there, the walls were more elaborately decorated than the walls in the rest of Thothmose III's tomb.

In the sarcophagus room, I saw many more images of serpents. Therefore, I assumed our young guide had brought me into this room to show me these serpent images. However, it turned out he had brought us here to tell me something in private.

In this room where the pharaoh's mummy had lain, the earth had been hewn out to make a larger room than the tunnel-like rooms of the front part of the tomb. Because the sarcophagus room was wider than the forward parts of the tomb, parts of this large room were not visible from the narrower sections of the manmade tunnel.

As soon as Peggy and I entered the sarcophagus room, the young guide led me around the corner of the room beside a wall that could not be viewed by any of the lingering tourists in the front part of the tomb. Then he turned to me and, speaking in a low voice, whispered, "The serpent is the Ka."

The Serpent as Ka

Aha, I thought. *While we were gone, he has been thinking.* All the time while Peggy and I had searched in Amenhotep II's tomb, he must have mulled over our visit in his mind trying to decipher why two American ladies would be so excited about finding images of serpents when most Americans were repulsed by images of the reptiles. He must have wondered why I had not agreed with his first exploratory statement about the serpent being Satan.

Now, in the sarcophagus room, he spoke so low that even Peggy could not hear what he said to me. By his secrecy, I knew he must be taking some kind of risk, but I did not know what. I did know that according to ancient Egyptian tradition, the Ka represents the spiritual essence or soul part of us.

How interesting, I thought. *He has made some kind of connection with ancient Egyptian tradition and my fascination with the serpent images.*

It intrigued me. Why did he associate the Ka or spiritual essence with the images of the serpents? Why did he act with such secrecy?

At the time, I had not read an online report by Moira Timms, author of *Beyond Prophecies and Predictions,* saying that the serpent decoration on the pharaoh's headdress refers to a solar serpent that symbolized the Ka or soul essence of the sun. She goes on to say that because the serpent represented the Ka or soul essence of the sun, the pharaoh wore a headdress that included a serpent.

I wish I could have discovered why the tomb overseer acted with such secrecy, and I wish that a couple of tourists had not walked into the sarcophagus room at that very moment. Immediately, he returned to being a protective guardian of the premises. He no longer acted like a co-explorer with me. Our discussion was over.

The arrow points to the serpent Ka's face on the pharaoh's headdress.

Was this an important opportunity I missed? Could I have learned something from him that would have shed light on my Atlantean memories? Should I have returned to the Valley of the Kings after lunch instead of going on my pre-arranged tour of the Temple of Karnak? I will never know.

On the other hand, our tomb overseer may have known from experience that tourists who were interested in the paintings of serpents were also interested in the Ka. I must admit that I gave him a generous amount of Baksheesh for the extra attention he gave us.

Although I may have missed an opportunity, I felt so happy that I had found the many images that corresponded with my memories of Atlantis and the Atlanteans. Furthermore, I had photographed many different examples of serpents used for transportation including cart serpents, boat serpents, and magic carpet serpents.

Thoroughly content with my discoveries, I did not expect to come upon the next two images that would mean even more to me.

They were paintings that said to me without a doubt that my unconscious, for some inexplicable reason, reverberated with the truth of some long ago past—a past that possibly contained the key to unlocking one of our greatest mysteries: the mystery of who we really are. These two images showed that we are immortal souls.

The "God is Greater" Sunrise Image

After the handsome tomb overseer busied himself with the tourists who had wandered into the sarcophagus room, Peggy and I scanned the walls of the room to see if we could find any more images that illustrated my memories of Atlantis. We found many pictures of serpents in the sarcophagus room, but none showing them used for transportation with wings and feet.

The "God is Greater" sunrise greeting on the cover of *When We Were Gods*.

Therefore, we drifted back into the front area of the tomb, scanning the walls to see if we had missed anything.

The first image I saw amazed me because it mirrored the photograph I had created for the cover of my first two books, *The Golden Ones* and its revised and updated edition, *When We Were Gods*.

I had set up this image with my son on the beach at sunrise to show how the light of the soul fills up the physical body. I also took the photograph because the guides in my hypnosis sessions had emphasized the importance of greeting the rising sun. Under trance, my spiritual guides said they had a message for all people. We would all benefit from greeting the sunrise. It would help to overcome the soul sickness of disobedience that separates us from oneness with God.

The spiritual guides told me to raise my arms and say, "God is greater" three times as the sun rose. I intended to duplicate the "God is greater" pose in my photo shoot.

It was not until long after I took the photograph that I learned that a similar composition, with the sun on the top of the head, denotes a god in ancient Egyptian tradition. The Egyptologists call the sun in the ancient paintings a solar disc.

Because the sun shone on top of my son's head in the photograph used for the cover of the book, I had inadvertently created an image that showed an Egyptian god.

You can imagine my delight when I saw the same image on the walls of Thothmose III's tomb. The ancient Egyptians had painted a man with his arms upraised in the "God is greater" pose with a solar disc poised on the top of his head.

Amazingly, the image in Thothmose III's tomb showed more than the solar disc. At the feet of the god, stood a serpent with wings and feet. In front of this transportation serpent, the ancient Egyptian artists had painted stars which meant that this serpent had been used for transportation through space.

The "God is greater" greeting in Thothmose III's tomb with a winged and footed serpent that flies through the stars.

Here was another flying serpent that flew a man through the stars. This meant that I had found another image that paralleled the Mayan stone image of the man in the feathered serpent's mouth flying through space, illustrated on page 98.

Gods and Goddesses

My first two books deal with the concept that in our Atlantean experience we had been godlike. In fact, when the hypnotherapist asked me who I was in Atlantis, I had replied, as if it should be obvious, "a goddess." By goddess, I meant that I still knew who I was—in essence, a Light Being made in the image of the Creator, hence the title of the second edition, *When We Were Gods*.

Our Light Being Soul Essence

In the previous chapter, "Winged Serpents in the Pharaohs' Tombs," I described how I had fallen into the serpent's mouth and then flown through space. In Chapter Ten, "Scariest Memory of Atlantis," I had also said that in Atlantis I had been a pixie-faced frog being.

What I had not said—and it is explained in greater detail in *When We Were Gods*—is that when I fell into the serpent's mouth, I had *not* been a pixie-faced frog being or even a human being. I had been a glowing ball of light.

When I flew through space, I looked like a glowing spinning fireball similar to a miniature sun flying through the air. My companions who traveled with me to the geologically safe lands in Egypt also looked like glowing spheres of light.

How could this be? As I said in the previous section, in Atlantis we called ourselves gods and goddesses because we knew who we really were. We were not the bodies we temporarily inhabited, but Light Beings made in the image of the Creator.

In this day and age, to separate out of the physical, a person needs to have an out-of-body experience when the soul lifts out of his or her body for a short time. Or, a person can have a near-death-experience, which occurs when a person clinically dies and is revived. Today, for our soul to separate from our body, it is a monumental event. People write about their experiences. They speak about these events because they are so unusual.

In Atlantis, it was commonplace. We did not spend as much time in physical bodies as we do today. Now, most of us do not leave our bodies until we are asleep and dreaming. Today, our souls do not leave our bodies permanently until we die.

In Atlantis, we could leave a physical body at will. We did not have to die first to do so. In fact, much of the time, we, as pure souls, remained separate from the physical. We looked like Light Beings, or miniature suns made in the image of our Creator.

Therefore, when I left Atlantis for safety lands in Egypt, I did not go as a pixie-faced frog being. My soul pulled out of the creature I called a pixie-faced frog being.

A Semi-solid Encapsulated Light Being

When I fell into the serpent's mouth, I traveled in my pure soul form—a spinning, glowing ball of light. I called myself a semi-solid encapsulated Light Being. Now, as Peggy and I ambled along the manmade tunnel of Thothmose III's burial chamber, I was about to see illustrations of this Light Being painted in the tomb.

We walked past one of the large winged serpents I had seen when we first visited the tomb of Thothmose III early that same morning. This time, I noticed something I had missed the first time we had walked through the tomb. The ancient Egyptians had painted the image of a semi-solid encapsulated Light Being floating in between the wings of the serpent.

Peggy and I looked around the tomb. Surrounding us, we saw more images of semi-solid encapsulated Light Beings. They hovered over the heads of the mixtures of humans with animals. I realized these images must have been the ancient Egyptian artists' way of showing that the light essence could leave the god or goddess at will.

A Light Being floats between the wings of the serpent.

One image showed a woman with cow horns on her head. She looked like a human and cow mixture. I learned from my guidebook that she was Hathor, the goddess of the arts, love, and fertility. She was also the wife of Horus, the falcon god, and the daughter of the sun god, Ra (pronounced RAY, like a sun ray—perhaps the Egyptian sun god is the origin of the word, "ray"). In between the points of her cow horns, the ancients had painted a round disc that looked like a semi-solid encapsulated Light Being.

Hathor   Khenmu   Ra

Did the disc denote that she could still pull her Light Being-soul essence out of the physical as I had seen myself do in Atlantis? Is that why the ancient Egyptians called her a goddess as I had called myself?

In another part of the tomb, we again saw the boat made of a two-headed serpent. Again, I saw the image of a ram-headed human. This time, however, I noticed, hovering over the head of this human/animal mixture, another solar disc, reminiscent of a semi-solid encapsulated Light Being.

After I returned home I learned that the ram-headed character was also considered a god. He was called Khenmu, the "Great Potter," because he was the creator of people. He made them by sculpting them out of Nile River clay and held them up so that Ra, the sun god, could shine life into them. Then, Khenmu put them into their mother's wombs to be born.

This sounded very much like the original idea behind my "God is greater" photograph in which the light of the sun illuminated the body to create a human. Of course, this light is actually the light of the soul that illuminates the physical body.

The tomb also included a painting of Ra. He was portrayed with a falcon head and a huge glowing ball over his head, with a serpent encircling the glowing ball.

I realized that this image—of the glowing ball encircled by the serpent—represented an excellent portrayal of a semi-solid encapsulated Light Being inside a serpent. In other words, instead of showing a man's face inside a feathered serpent's mouth . . . the way the ancient Maya had portrayed it . . . the ancient Egyptians actually put the semi-solid encapsulated Light Being, or soul essence, inside an encircled serpent.

In my Atlantean memories, I had seen myself, as a glowing ball of light, fall into the mouth of the serpent. Here, in Thothmose III's tomb, I saw an image of the memory I had experienced painted over the head of Ra. You can see the image of the Light Being inside the serpent on the opposite page and also on the prow of the boat in the image on the next page.

Interestingly, Ra, Hathor, and Khenmu were supposed to be very old gods who were worshipped from the earliest days in Egypt, which also points to their being Atlanteans.

You may also be interested to know that included among the ancient Egyptian pantheon of gods and goddesses, I found a human/frog mixture goddess named Heqet. She was supposed to have been associated with Khenmu, because she was the goddess of childbirth and infinity. Although Heqet was female, Egyptian mythology also includes four male frog gods who also existed in the earliest time.

A serpent-encircled Light Being leads a boat carrying gods with "solar disc" soul essences over their heads.

Unfortunately, I did not see any paintings of Heqet or any other frog-type gods or goddesses in either the tomb of Thothmose III or Amenhotep II. However, I have read in the *Secret Doctrine*, by the mystic Helena Petrovna Blavatsky, that the ancient Egyptians decorated their coffins with an image of Heqet. Perhaps we did not see any images of the frog goddess because we did not visit any museums with mummy cases on display.

An Amazing Light Being

Satisfied with our latest discovery, Peggy and I decided to leave King Thothmose III's tomb. We felt hungry for lunch. Soon, our driver would arrive at the entrance to the Valley of the Kings. We turned toward the glowing sunlight at the opening of the cave-like tomb.

For some inexplicable reason, one of us looked up at the ceiling of the tomb. Perhaps our handsome young guide pointed it out to us.

Whatever the reason, there on the ceiling of the tomb, painted to look as if it was flying over us, I saw the most amazing image. I had seen it before in books and magazines. This image stretched all the way across the ceiling of the burial chamber.

Like the Yucatan bas relief of the feathered serpent with a man in its mouth, this was the first time I had seen this famous Egyptian image in its original location. Like the feathered serpent in Mexico, the background of this image helped to explain its meaning.

If you remember, I had seen myself as a shining, glowing ball that spun through space. After dropping into the serpent's open jaws, I had flown through space calling myself a semi-solid encapsulated Light Being.

The image we saw on the ceiling of Thothmose III's tomb showed a shining, glowing ball—the semi-solid encapsulated Light Being. The ancient artists had painted long outstretched wings on either side of it, which could have meant that the round ball was flying. The artists had painted two serpents, which stretched their heads out from the glowing ball as if the serpents were leading it.

To me, the symbols said that the semi-solid encapsulated Light Being (the glowing sphere) flew (the wings) by using serpent power (the serpents). This image beautifully illustrated my Atlantean memory of flying through space as a glowing, spinning ball of light after falling into the serpent's mouth.

The image even has a name: The Disc of Ra. As I said earlier, Ra was the Egyptian supreme god, the god of the sun. Ra is portrayed as an image of a glowing ball or a Light Being.

This image is a common image. I have seen it illustrated in books about ancient Egypt and the pharaohs' tombs. Modern-day people like this image. It fires our imaginations and, I believe, awakens unconscious soul memories of our experiences as pure souls. I have seen the image illustrated in modern-day magazines and even as a decoration on fabric.

However, this image is often portrayed separate from its background. In the tomb of King Thothmose III, I saw the Disc of Ra in its original location and this time I saw it in context with its background.

The ancient Egyptian artists had painted stars in the background. This Light Being is flying through the stars.

The semi-solid encapsulated Light Being, powered by two serpents, flies overhead through the stars.

By taking these photographs, I felt that I had accomplished what I thought was my purpose in coming to Egypt—to find evidence of Atlantis and Atlanteans in the pharaohs' tombs and to validate my trance memories.

I felt especially happy because these images showed our beginnings as souls on earth.

Those Amazing Atlanteans

There is, of course, much more to this story. For example, the Atlanteans were not all combinations of humans with animals. Some had human-like bodies, others the bodies of animals.

In my own memories, I had not only been a pixie-faced frog being. My soul, while an Atlantean, could be in three different bodies at once. As well as a pixie-faced frog being, I had also been a human-like scientist and also a human-like mother with a little boy. I described both of these more fully in *When We Were Gods*.

However, the most important concept to grasp in this description of the Atlanteans is that they did not consider themselves to be humans, animals, or combinations of both. They knew themselves to be souls—the semi-solid encapsulated Light Beings—made in the image of the Creator. They saw themselves as Light Beings that interacted with the physical on earth, albeit in human, animal, or human/animal mixtures.

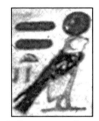

Atlanteans in animal and human-like bodies.

In addition, not all Atlanteans could pull their Light Bodies out of the physical bodies with which they interacted. Some had become permanently encased in matter. These, I believe, are depicted on the walls of the pharaohs' tombs as human-like or animal beings or human/animal mixtures without the glowing balls or solar discs over their heads. They were no longer gods and goddesses, but had become permanently bound to matter.

All of these concepts are described more fully in *When We Were Gods* including the marvelous story of how we became human beings. As you may well imagine, this is a story that requires its own book because it includes the saga of the amazing cooperation between our souls and the nature kingdom.

The "Halo" in the Sphinx and Pharaoh's Headdress

There is actually more evidence of the soul's connection with the body among the antiquities in Egypt. For example, in their statues, the ancient Egyptians depicted the glow of the Light Being soul by carving rays, similar to a halo, emanating from the head of the Sphinx and on the headdresses worn by the pharaohs.

**Light beams out
from the head
of the Sphinx.**

**The pharaoh's
headdress shows
soul light rays.**

**Mary and Jesus
emanate the light
of the soul.**

The conventional opinion is that the rays emanating from the head of the Sphinx and pharaoh represent either the sun or a divine origin. However, it is my belief that all three images above show the same concept as the Light Being flying on the ceiling of Thothmose III's tomb: definitely a divine origin and also a divine Light Being soul that is actually integrated with the physical body and is shining through. Some people can see this aura.

Therefore, finding evidence of Atlanteans in the land of the pharaohs meant the most to me because it showed the stages our souls took from Light Beings to the human beings we are now.

Most importantly, the images show that there are records in ancient ruins that we are immortal. It is not a matter of faith. It is not a matter of believing the words of a psychic. The images of our beginnings as Light Beings . . . from our earliest experiences on earth as Light Beings through mixing our energies with earthly creatures to our present experience as human beings . . . are all recorded on the walls of the pharaohs' tombs and in Egyptian antiquities.

Chapter Thirteen

PSYCHICS, MYSTICS, AND THE ROOT RACES

The Root Races

In my hypnosis sessions, I called my soul's different stages of involvement with the physical the root races. Human beings are the fourth root race. The three previous root races can be listed as:

- First: Light Being
- Second: Wisp-of-Smoke, Amber Translucent Being
- Third: Animal Mixtures, Gods and Goddesses

In the first three root races we did not know death. Instead, we knew ourselves to be immortal and made in the image of the Creator. Just as Adam and Eve knew they were immortal until they ate the fruit of the knowledge of good and evil, so did we.

In the previous chapters, we saw that the ancient Egyptians recorded their memories of the times when we were still immortal in their paintings and statues. In addition, they recorded the different types of beings . . . what I call the root races . . . in their cultural memories of the time before we became human.

What is a Root Race?

By the words "root race" I do not mean anything to do with our present concept of race, which relates to zoological divisions of humankind based on superficial physical features such as skin color or eye shape.

The important word in "root race" is the word, "root," meaning a derivative or original type of being. You could say it was the representative model of a certain type. For example, the human "race" is a derivative type of organism unlike any other type.

These root races displayed characteristics very different from each other, much more different than a few mere physical features. For example, a first root race being is pure light, glows, floats, travels through Star Gates, and melts into vibrations. It is very different from our present or fourth root race human being, which is deeply mixed with the physical, does not appear to glow (unless you can see auras), cannot float or melt into vibrations, can only leave the atmosphere of the earth in a space vehicle, and needs to experience the world through the senses of the body.

The Bliss of the First Root Race

In my memories of Atlantis, I was at first a Light Being. I also lived in bliss—an amazing all-pervading ecstasy. My whole world consisted only of vibration. *I* was only vibration.

My purpose was to explore the universe and bring a record of His Creations back to the Creator. I did not explore as we do today—in a body that tramps around the earth or in a body protected by a space suit tethered to a space shuttle.

Being without a body and being pure light, I knew my world only as vibration. I had no sensors—eyes, ears, nose, skin or mouth—with which to explore my world.

When I explored the world, I merged my Light Body with constantly moving vibrational energy vortices, feeling them swirling around and within me. Every energy pattern I merged with felt wonderful. My understanding of the vibrations involved no judgment—no discernment of good or evil. All felt delightful. All was one. I lived in constant bliss.

The Second Root Race "Wisp-of-Smoke"

I have described at length the third root race beings. They are the Atlantean mixtures —both those that are stuck in matter and those that can go in and out of physical bodies, the gods and goddesses.

Until now, I have not described the second root race in this book but I did describe them in my first two books. Briefly, when I first became caught in the physical, I was a being that really had no more impact on the physical than an idea or a thought.

In explanation, although a recipe is not the finished meal, it is the idea of that meal. The recipe makes it possible to make the meal. Therefore, as a second root race being, I did not exist in matter except as an idea, similar to a blueprint.

After I "fell" into the physical from my usual environment of pure spirit, I first became a thought or idea. I looked like a wisp-of-smoke and floated like a genie rising out of Aladdin's lamp. Like a genie, I looked amorphous and constantly changed shape.

As a pure Light Being I had explored my world by merging with vibrations. Not surprisingly, as a wisp-of-smoke, I also explored my physical environment by merging with it. By so doing, I became the third root race. In my hypnosis session, I said I merged with matter in an agreement with nature.

In summary, the first three root races did not know death. Only we, the fourth root race, experience death. In addition, our souls only leave our bodies during sleep. We permanently disconnect from our bodies at death. However, because our souls are immortal, death for human beings is actually part of the life/death/life reincarnation cycle.

In my previous two books, I mentioned that I had at first been very distressed at the unusual memories that surfaced in my hypnosis sessions. I received solace when I researched the work of psychics such as Edgar Cayce. I found that Cayce too discussed the history of the soul on earth through different physical stages. However, Cayce only specifically names the upcoming fifth root race as a "root race." Therefore, I have correlated his descriptions of the stages the soul took in its interaction with the physical with my understanding of the previous root races.

Edgar Cayce, the World's Best-Documented Psychic

Edgar Cayce was born near Hopkinsville, Kentucky on March 18, 1877. He died in 1945. When he was a young man, just starting out in the work force, he lost his voice. He tried to get help from doctors and a hypnotist with no success. Then he discovered that he could diagnose and cure his own ailment while under self-induced hypnosis.

When people heard about his abilities, they began to ask him to go in a trance to see if he could correctly diagnose and prescribe cures for their illnesses. Because of the success of his trance information, his fame spread far and wide. During the 43 years he gave psychic readings, he gave over 14,000 trance readings and helped thousands of people.

Although Cayce gave his first psychic reading in 1901, it was not until 1923 that he made a reference to reincarnation. After a period of soul-searching, because Cayce was a devout Christian, he began to give not only physical readings, but also life readings, which described the person's previous lives and their effect on the inquirer's present life.

With the life readings, Cayce touched on some of the basic issues underlying the human condition: Who are we? What are we doing here? Where are we going? These questions are the foundation of the hidden or esoteric aspects of our religions. They deal with the question of our beginnings as souls on earth.

Cayce on the First Root Race

What does Cayce say about the history of the soul? In reading 1231-1, he says that the soul, which lives forever, is the real self. Furthermore, it was this real self, the soul, which was made in the image of the Creator.

In reading 262-89, Cayce says that man's natural state is soul, implying that our present state is not natural for us. In addition, this reading makes it clear that our real body is a spiritual body.

"Man in his former state, or natural state, or permanent consciousness, IS soul. Hence, in the beginning all were souls of that creation, with the body as of the Creator – of spirit forces . . ." (262-89)

These readings describe what I call the first root race as a being made in the image of the Creator. This is the Light Being of my trance memories and the "solar disc" in the pharaohs' tombs.

Cayce on the Second Root Race

Cayce refers to the second root race as a thought form. In the 364 series of readings dedicated to Atlantis, Cayce says in the third Atlantis reading 364-3 (hence the "3" added on to 364) that the physical form the souls took were thought forms, implying that a thought, although it is not a material object, has enough substance to be considered physical. He also says in this reading that these thought forms took shape by pushing themselves in the direction that thought took them. In other words, they were not a stable form but amorphous and constantly changing.

In the hypnosis session that dealt with my experience in the second root race, I had seen myself as a wisp-of-smoke. You know that smoke keeps changing. It billows and shifts and moves. Although the wisp-of-smoke looked like a woman's upper body, the shape of my torso, arms, and body kept changing the way oil alters its shape while floating on water.

In reading 364-3, Cayce also refers to an amoeba pushing through water as an example of the way a thought form pushed into matter. An amoeba also constantly changes shape.

In reading 262-89 Cayce said that the thought forms could change their color dependent upon their surroundings, similar to a chameleon today. For example, in my trance memory, the color of my body had been amber, which is why I had called myself an "Amber Translucent Being." I had been inside a cave, the walls of which were the color of a reddish-brown-colored earth.

Cayce on the Third Root Race

The Cayce readings refer to the third root race as projections into matter. Cayce's trance source usually associates third root race beings with Atlantis.

In describing these projections into matter, Cayce says in reading 1472-10 that souls experimented by mixing together with animals, including birds, and even plants. He says that memories of these mixtures have been handed down to us in legends of mythological beasts such as mermaids (primate and fish), satyrs (primate and goat), and centaurs (primate and horse).

In 275-33, Cayce describes Atlanteans who had extra appendages such as feathers, claws, bills, and hooves as a result of these mixtures. In reading 1472-10 he adds that even segments of the vegetable realm might be seen in the bodies of the Atlanteans. He also mentions, in reading 5748-6, that most individuals at that time had tails. The third root race beings are the mixtures of animals and humans drawn on the walls of the pharaohs' tombs.

Interestingly, he also says that the Atlanteans were the red race.

The Red Race

The Biblical story of creation says that God made Adam out of the dust of the ground (Genesis 4:7). According to the Baby Zone web site, Adam means: son of the red earth. It is generally agreed that Adam was made of red dust or red earth.

Cayce describes Atlanteans in reading 364-3. He begins by talking about the second root race projections into matter which, as we have already seen, he calls "thought forms."

> "As to their [the Atlanteans'] forms in the physical sense, these were much RATHER of the nature of THOUGHT FORMS, or able to push out OF THEMSELVES in that direction in which its development took shape in thought . . ." (364-3)

In the next part of the same paragraph, he goes on to describe how the second root race or the thought forms became the third root race:

> "of their own desire . . . they became hardened or set . . ."
> (364-3)

Then he describes these Atlanteans as being:

"... much in the form of the existent human body of the day ..."
(364-3)

But do not assume that because he uses the word "human" that he is referring to the present-day human body. He specifically uses the words, "human body of the day." Remember, he said in reading 1472-10 that souls experimented by mixing together with animals, including birds, and even plants and, in reading 5748-6, that most Atlanteans had tails.

In the same paragraph of reading 364-3 quoted above, he continues by describing the color of these thought forms that had projected into matter. He says that when they became hardened or set they had:

"that of color as partook of its surroundings much in the manner as the chameleon in the present." (364-3)

If you have ever seen a chameleon, you know that if it sits in one place for any length of time, its skin begins to change color so it becomes camouflaged against the background where it is sitting. I have also seen spiders change their color according to the hue of the background on which they stood.

Cayce completes this paragraph by stating that the Atlanteans came:

"... into that form as the red, or the mixture peoples ... known then later by the associations as the RED race." (364-3)

In a subsequent reading in the Atlantis series, the conductor of the trance sessions asks Cayce to verify the skin colors of the thought forms that eventually became human beings. Since they took on the color of the earth where they were located, the conductor wants to know if:

12. (Q) Are the following the correct places? Atlantean, the red.
(A) Atlantean and American, the red race. (364-13)

I am discussing this topic at length because many of the
paintings of gods and goddesses in the pharaohs' tombs show
individuals with red skin. Because the photographs illustrating
this book are in black and white, you cannot see the skin colors of
the various individuals. That is why I have also included the
photograph below in color on the back cover. However, even in
black and white, you can see that some of the individuals in the
photograph below have skin colors of various intensities.

**Taken from the right, the first and third indivi-
duals are red-skinned, the second and fifth
are black-skinned and the fourth, who hap-
pens to be a woman, is lighter skinned—
from Thothmose III's tomb.**

The individual on the right is Ra, the falcon-headed Atlantean-
mixture whose image is also on page 132. I find it interesting that
even the semi-solid encapsulated Light Being floating over Ra's
head is a red color as you can see in the extreme left thumbnail
photo on the back cover. The black and white versions of the three
thumbnail photos of red-skinned Atlanteans are on pages 86, 129,
and 137.

Since we are on the topic of the different skin colors of the
individuals painted on the pharaoh's tomb, I would next like to

quote Cayce's reading 364-13 in which he says that the black race originated in the Western portion of upper Egypt—that would be in the southwest of Egypt close to what is now the border of Sudan on the south and Libya on the west of Egypt. As I understand the following reading, the white and yellow races were also in Egypt as well as in India, Persia, and Arabia.

> 13. (Q) Upper Africa for the black?
> (A) Or what would be known now as the more WESTERN portion of upper Egypt for the black . . . the white and yellow races came more into that portion of Egypt, India, Persia and Arabia. (364-13)

Since, according to Cayce, all of the races except for the brown-skinned were in Egypt, it explains why there are red, black, and light-skinned individuals painted on the walls of the pharaohs' tombs.

Gods and Goddesses

Cayce also refers to the gods and goddesses. He says that because the Atlanteans wielded so much control over the physical, they called themselves gods and goddesses. In reading 364-11 he says that the Atlanteans decided they must be gods and goddesses since they had dominion over animals, birds and fishes. He also says the Atlanteans varied in size from giants to midgets. At that time, when the first earth upheavals had begun, the separation of male and female had begun according to Cayce.

Cayce's Root Races Timeline

In the September 2005 issue of the *Ancient Mysteries* monthly newsletter, John van Auken, author of many Cayce books including *Ancient Egyptian Mysticism and Its Relevance Today*, provides a metaphysical timeline. The time chart shows that first root race beings, which Cayce calls "Morning Stars" entered into the earth as long ago as 4.5 billion years ago.

The first thought forms, or second root race beings, belong to the Mu or Lemurian era. They emerged about 12 million years ago. Lemuria was a continent that disappeared under the sea in the Pacific Ocean before Atlantis sank. The Atlantean era of the third root race beings, including the projections into matter, began about 200,000 years ago.

The Location of Atlantis
Reading 364-3 describes the location of Atlantis. According to Cayce's trance source, it occupied the area between the Gulf of Mexico and the Mediterranean Sea, which contains the Atlantic Ocean and also the Bahamas and Caribbean Islands.

Cayce also says that evidence of Atlantis can be found in the Pyrenees Mountains, which are on the border between France and Spain in Europe, and also Morocco in northern Africa. In addition, evidence of the continent of Atlantis can be found in North and Central America, Yucatan, British Honduras, which is now called Belize, the Bahamas—especially the Bimini Islands—and the Gulf Stream area.

Cayce and the Safety Lands
In psychic reading number 1007-3 Cayce said that because the Atlantean leaders realized that the Atlantean lands would break up and Atlantis could possibly no longer exist, many inhabitants evacuated to safety lands. Reading 801-1, says that Atlanteans were sent to both Yucatan and Egypt for safety.

As you have seen, in the previous chapters we found drawings of the Atlantean mixtures painted on the walls and ceiling of the pharaohs' tombs and stone carvings of Atlanteans flying via serpent power in the ruins of the ancient Maya.

Rudolph Steiner, Mystic Philosopher
Rudolph Steiner was born in Kraljevec, Austria, now Croatia, in 1861 and died in Dornach, Switzerland in 1925. He is best known for the Waldorf Schools, of which there are about 150 at the

present time in the United States and Canada, with about 800 worldwide in 32 countries.

Steiner is also known for a unique agricultural system. Biodynamic farming and gardening supports a belief that vitality in a person stems from vitality in the food he or she consumes.

From his earliest years, Steiner knew of a separate reality. He possessed clairvoyant talents such as the ability to see elemental beings and to communicate with those who had passed on.

A brilliant, multi-dimensional person, Steiner gave thousands of lectures and wrote hundreds of books on topics as diverse as archangels, architecture, nature spirits, and medicine. He called his new branch of spiritual exploration Anthroposophy, or wisdom of man, meaning the whole man, including humanity's spirituality. He is considered a Christian mystic.

Besides all of his many diverse interests and clairvoyant abilities, he, like Cayce, could access the Akashic Record, a spiritual register of everything that has occurred through time. Unlike Cayce, he did not have to enter a self-induced trance to reach the information. It came to him as part of his conscious clairvoyant abilities.

In reading the Akashic Record, he too, connected with a time before we were human beings. Steiner called the stages of transformation from pure soul to human being the root races. But, instead of numbering three previous root races, he said there were four previous root races and human beings were the fifth.

Steiner's *Atlantis and Lemuria* describes the thought form type of root race as being predominantly Lemurian and the animal mixture root race as being predominantly Atlantean, as did Cayce. In this fascinating book, Steiner beautifully explains the mixing of our souls with the physical as the earth developed from a swirling mass of gases to our present planet of earth, water, and atmosphere.

Madame Helena Petrovna Blavatsky and Theosophy

Rudolph Steiner at one time joined with the Theosophists, an organization started by Madame Helena Petrovna Blavatsky. She is considered by many to be the originator of the New Age movement. Steiner separated from the Theosophists because they focused on the Eastern religions and he on Christianity. Theosophy literally means, "wisdom about God."

The Theosophists also believed in a transition from Light Beings to human beings through the root races. In fact, Steiner used the Theosophists' names of the root races in his descriptions of them. Steiner and the Theosophists agreed that humans are the fifth root race while Cayce said that the fifth root race is yet to come.

A prolific writer, Mme Blavatsky's masterpiece, *The Secret Doctrine*, which comprises two huge volumes, is the compilation of much of her knowledge of the religious, philosophical, and hidden metaphysical concepts she learned during her two years in Tibet. *The Secret Doctrine* includes such beliefs as karma, reincarnation, and the root races.

She talks about the first root race as being a sexless shadow and the second, an asexual form. Her writings weave through complicated phrases of great detail, for example, that the early second root race were the "Fathers of the 'Sweat-born;'" while the later second root race were the "Sweat-born."

Continuing in Volume Two of *The Secret Doctrine*, she says that Adam was androgynous, as was discussed in Chapter Nine, "Who Was Eve?" She explains the fruit of the tree of the knowledge of good and evil as having to taste the bitter fruit of the personal experience of pain and suffering. She also says that the Sphinx was androgynous.

She says that true sexual union did not occur until the later third root race and calls the fourth root race the Atlantean. She, like Cayce, says that some of the Atlanteans were giants.

I find this very interesting since, during one of my seminars, a Native American approached me and told me that he had memories of his time in Atlantis. He said that he remembered me in my scientist body. Evidently, I was about twelve feet tall.

Chapter Fourteen

SERPENTS, ROOT RACES, AND MYTHS

The Atlantean Serpents and the Root Races

You may be wondering how the Atlantean serpent transportation system worked. Let me do my best to explain it in terms of the root races based on my understanding of it through my trance memories.

To begin, the Atlanteans who used the serpent for transportation were those third root race beings who could still go in and out of matter. At the same time in Atlantis there were also those third root race beings who were stuck in mixtures of different kinds of animals. They could not use the serpent transportation system since they could not pull their Light Bodies out of the physical.

In my experience, when it came time to leave for safety lands, my soul essence pulled out of the pixie-faced frog being and I fell into the mouth of the serpent. Next, I flew through space as a spinning glowing ball—the semi-solid encapsulated Light Being.

Why did I not just fly through space without the thrust provided by the serpent? Looking back on my regressed memories, I can only surmise that there must have been some mass to me even though I looked like a glowing fiery ball. Why else would I call myself "semi-solid" or "encapsulated?" I was still a Light Being, but the process of becoming entrapped in the physical must have made me denser than a Light Being free of the physical.

Whatever the reason, it seems to me that I needed the thrust of the serpent's strike capability to achieve the momentum required to fly from Atlantis to Egypt. Today, of course, we use jet engines and solid rocket boosters, but today, we are much denser.

Why did I not get killed when I fell into the serpent's mouth? Because third root race beings did not die. The first three root races did not die. Only human beings experience the life/death/-life reincarnation cycle. In all of the previous root races, we could pull our soul essence out of the physical at will . . . that is, except for those who were permanently enmeshed with matter.

That was the big problem. Because their souls were permanently enmeshed with matter, their souls could not get free.

It may seem as if those who were permanently enmeshed with matter were the only ones who were in danger of being lost forever on earth. Actually, those who could still go in and out of matter were also caught in the physical and could not get free of the earth. They just were not permanently enmeshed with matter.

The Myths and Legends of Ancient Cultures

The mystics and psychics are not the only ones aware of our souls' experiences through the root races. Many ancient cultures also preserve a memory of different worlds in which there were different creatures. Although the ancient cultures do not call the various creatures in the previous worlds the root races, nonetheless their stories can help us to consider that our souls may have inhabited different physical bodies in the distant past.

In the rest of this chapter, I will discuss the root races as they were remembered by ancient peoples. These stories were handed down through the generations to become myths and legends.

For example, earlier we discussed the feathered serpent and the descending god of the ancient Maya. Do you know that they also believe in a succession of five creations of the earth leading up to our present humanity? According to Frank Waters in *Mexico Mystique,* the ancient Maya believed that the Creator made a series of unique types of beings on earth. Human beings are the corn people, probably because the ancient Maya ate corn.

Frank Waters also wrote *The Book of the Hopi,* in which he says that the Hopi believe that four successive worlds were created. Each of the first three perished because the people stopped living by the laws of Creation. We are presently in the fourth world and are warned to keep singing praises to the Creator lest our world be destroyed also.

In *The Supergods: They Came on a Mission to Save Mankind,* Maurice M. Cotterell shows the many similar characteristics shared by four of earth's modern-day religions: Buddhism, Brahminism/Hinduism, Christianity and what he calls Pacalism, which is based on the beliefs of the ancient Maya.

Like the Maya and the Hopi, the Hindus believe there have been previous worlds. In the Hindu tradition, there are three previous worlds in which earth's inhabitants are different creatures.

In the early Hindu philosophies, a belief existed in the transmigration of souls between animals and humans, which parallels the idea of third root race human and animal mixtures. In addition, the early Hindus believed that the sun or solar disc was the ancient ancestor of humanity, which sounds like the glowing solar discs of the original Light Being first root race.

Old Testament Mythology

We have already discussed some aspects of the Old Testament creation story in Chapter Nine, "Who Was Eve?" In this section I will compare that story with the root races concept.

To begin, in Genesis we are told that man and woman are made in the image of the Creator, which would mean that man and woman are light, energy, power, and vastly creative. There is no mention, yet, in the Old Testament of a man or a woman made of clay or of the physical—only light. I believe these early creations refer to the Light Being form of our souls or the first root race.

It is not until the second chapter of Genesis that Adam is made out of the dust of the earth. As discussed earlier, this second creation sounds like the creation of an androgynous physical being, similar to the third root race beings, since Adam originally contains both male and female within him. It makes sense that Adam would be androgynous at first since the soul is made in the image of the Creator and therefore contains all.

It is in this second chapter of Genesis that God decides to end the man's loneliness. The Creator makes a woman out of the man's rib, separating the androgynous Adam into a male and female.

When Adam and Eve eat of the tree of the knowledge of good and evil, they must leave the Garden of Eden, which is, in my opinion, the blissful state of the Light Being. They are no longer immortal, will die, and are now fourth root race human beings.

Ancient Mayan Mysticism

During my third and most recent visit to Yucatan, in January 2008, I interviewed Santiago Dominguez, a modern-day Maya whose family has lived for generations close to Uxmal. He told me the story, handed down to him from his grandparents, of the witch. She, like Adam, was lonely. Therefore, she took an egg and hatched out of it a dwarf who became her companion. The dwarf is a sorcerer, likely an Atlantean, who made Uxmal in one night.

This sounds very much like an Adam and Eve creation story except that the original androgynous being is portrayed as a female instead of a male. Both the witch and the dwarf appear to be powerful Atlantean gods. The egg is their Light Being form.

Incidentally, the Cayce readings say that Atlanteans also brought records of their civilization and their technological knowledge to Yucatan as well as to the Hall of Records in Giza as described in Chapter Six, "The Atlanteans and the Great Pyramid." The Atlantean records in the Yucatan are examined in greater detail in *When We Were Gods*.

The Maya also have a mother goddess whose name is Ixchel.

Islam and the Djinn

Most people have heard of the stories in *One Thousand and One Nights*, which include tales of genies, magic lanterns, and flying carpets, one of which is "Aladdin's Lamp" recently made popular in Disney's *Aladdin*.

These stories are based on Arabian myths that existed prior to and separate from Islam. However, the stories about the djinn, also spelled jinn, are common to both pre-Arabic myth and Islam. In fact, to many Muslims, the djinn are not considered mythological creatures at all, but are real.

Some people believe that the genie in Aladdin's lamp is derived from the djinn. In the Islamic holy book, the Koran, also spelled Qur'an, it is written that the djinn were created by God, as were men. However, humans were made from clay whereas the djinn were made from a smokeless flame of fire.

The djinn sound very much like second root race beings, or as I described them, wisps-of-smoke. They can push into matter and can therefore assume the form of animals, humans, and human/-animal mixtures—third root races beings.

Interestingly, Islam believes that each of us has our own djinn. Therefore, I wonder if the second root race being, the thought form, is still always with us. Could it be that the second root race thought form projects into the human body?

Based on the following Cayce reading, it appears that this is so. I came upon the following reading excerpt while preparing a lecture called, "Edgar Cayce on Psychic Development."

"When there is a manifestation of a psychic force . . . there is then the rolling back . . . that mental trained individual consciousness - has been rolled aside, or rolled back, and there is then a visioning - To what? That as from the beginning, a projection OF that form that assumed its position or condition in the earth . . ., rather its THOUGHT body . . ." (364-10)

As I understand this reading, Cayce is saying that when we have a psychic experience, the mentally-trained physical consciousness is rolled aside to reveal the thought form body. And, it is this thought form body that manifests our psychic experiences by knowing more than the senses of the physical body. As mentioned earlier, the thought form is the second root race.

Chinese Gods and Goddesses

Like so many other cultures, the ancient Chinese people also have their gods and goddesses. One of them is Ch'ang O, the goddess of the moon. Some believe she was transformed into a three-legged frog. There it is again—the transformation—so typical of a third root race being . . . and also a frog goddess.

Nu Kua, another mythological goddess, has sometimes been described as possessing both sexes, a characteristic of the androgynous third root race Atlanteans before the separation into the sexes. Like third root races beings, she is also a mixture of human and animal, either depicted as having the body of a serpent and the head of an ox, or the body of a serpent with a human head, with or without ox horns.

She is supposed to have created human beings, male and female, and to have invented marriage. In some legends, she is separated into the first humans: Nu, the male, and Kua, the female. This gender separation legend is similar to the Adam and Eve story, only with a female the first androgynous being like the witch in Uxmal. If you remember, the sexes separated during the third root race Atlantean time according to the psychics.

Finally, there is the great Chinese dragon. Although it can fly, it usually does not have wings. With the characteristic of other third root race beings, it is a mixture of animals: a snake body, fish scales, deer antlers, eagle talons, and the face of a gilin, which is another Chinese mythical beast having a face like a deer and a fire-covered body.

Since, with dragons, we are talking about mythological serpents, you also might find it interesting to know that the Chinese have their own version of the Virgin Mary called Kwan Yin or Gwan Yin. Like the Christian Mary who originally came from the androgynous Adam, Kwan Yin is considered by some to be neither male nor female and some Buddhist schools refer to Kwan Yin as either male or female interchangeably.

Originally depicted as the young Buddha when he was a prince, he is sometimes portrayed with chest-revealing clothing and a mustache. More recently, Kwan Yin, who is known as a goddess, is also depicted as a lovely young woman, sometimes on top of a dragon with a bird, possibly a flying serpent memory.

Jewish Mysticism

The Jewish religion is the foundation of both the Christian religion and Islam. Therefore, Jewish mystical and mythological traditions that predate Christianity and Islam also provide a foundation for all three religions.

In the Talmud, which is the most important compilation of oral interpretations of the Jewish holy book, the Torah, there is an understanding that the soul at some time became attached to the body, which sounds similar to the story of the Light Beings who became enmeshed in matter. The Talmud also contains stories of reincarnation and hints that there is more information about creation but it is secret.

Jewish mysticism is called Kabala. There are many interpretations of the information in the Kabala. One explanation has to do with original Beings of Light, similar to the first root race.

You May Have Memories of the Root Races

In summary, the myths and legends of people throughout the earth, many of them isolated from each other, all have many similarities. They say that in our far distant past there were combinations of humans and animals, that there were gods and goddesses with a close connection with the Creator, and that there were beings who could transform into animals and humans.

Many also believe that there were different kinds of beings in previous worlds on earth, and that the original beings on earth were pure light or suns and more like God.

After reviewing the many mythological and mystical traditions of so many ancient and contemporary cultures, as well as the root race stories of the psychics, I concluded that my memories of this very long-ago time in our souls' past were likely a recollection of real developments in our collective souls' histories.

I wondered if other people might also have these kinds of memories. In the seminars and retreats I led, I discovered that many people who had been drawn to the topic of Atlantis, also had memories of their experiences in previous root races.

Sometimes they did not realize what these memories represented until I shared my story. Then they would have one of those "ah-hah" moments. They might begin to share a significant dream they had had that they could not forget. As they learned more about the root races, their dream began to make sense to them for the first time.

Although the concepts presented in these chapters on the history of the soul may appear to be foreign to our conscious minds, in reality, our subconscious minds are replete with memories of these times.

You do not have to have dream memories of your experiences in the previous root races or go to a hypnotherapist for deep trance regression. You are likely connecting with memories of your experiences in previous root races when you find yourself drawn to various books and see certain movies.

That is why so many people resonate to the ability to communicate with the tree beings in J.R.R. Tolkien's *Lord of the Rings*. Remember, Cayce's trance source said that Atlantean bodies even partook of the vegetable kingdom.

In my seminars, I show participants how popular movies contain memories of the times when we were third root race beings.

J. R. R. Tolkien and the Lord of the Rings

For example, the *Lord of the Rings* is about the time when the immortal elves as third root race beings are leaving the earth. Who will remain? The human beings or fourth root race beings. The third root race beings such as Gandalf, the elves, the dwarves and their evil counterparts, Sauron, Sauroman and the Orcs, all have supernatural capabilities. Some of them can shape-change and can control their environment through their minds. These are all third root race capabilities. In addition, they are immortal. It is only human beings that know death.

J. K. Rowling and the Harry Potter Series

The fabulously successful Harry Potter books by J. K. Rowling are hotbeds of references to archetypal memories of the history of the soul on earth. Why else do you think the Harry Potter books and movies are so wildly popular? The images of giants, wizards, magic, invisibility, animal mixtures such as unicorns, all harken back to the third root race. They also promise the hope of the upcoming fifth root race, the more spiritually attuned individuals predicted to come after human beings.

Star Trek, Star Wars, Star Gate, and E.T.

Think of the perennially popular Star Trek. This is almost the root races story. Their purpose is to explore of the Universe, as is yours. They enter different worlds to study them and often have difficulty getting free again, just as we are all stuck on earth. To leave and enter, they need to be in a vibrational state, just as we need to be free of the physical to leave the solar system.

What about the Star Wars series? There you have wizards similar to the gods and goddesses. You also have mixtures of animals and humans, which come from other worlds.

In Stargate you have to go through a Star Gate associated with ancient Egypt if you want to go to other worlds. In my memories, I entered earth through a Star Gate.

And what about dear little E.T. who is so lonely for home?

If you resonate with these stories, it may very well be that the stories awaken you to your own memories of being a vibrational being who came to explore earth through a Star Gate. Your soul may also be yearning to go home.

The Golden Ones

In my first two books, I said that the Golden Ones were in the process of reincarnating now to help humanity through the difficult times ahead. These Golden Ones had chosen, during Atlantean times, to reincarnate again at the time when earth's inhabitants have the responsibility of highly advanced technology that is potentially self-annihilating, similar to Atlantis.

It could be that you are one of the Golden Ones, those who decided to incarnate now to be of help to the world. They will also help to bring in the fifth root race.

Immortality

I hope that by considering these examples from the myths and legends of ancient cultures, you will see that the real underlying story is the story of your immortality. The progression from purely spiritual being to a combination of spiritual and physical being shows that in your essence you are pure soul. You, at one time, were not blended with the physical. When that part of you that is physical dies, the true self, the soul, survives.

That is why I like the story of the root races so much—because it shows how we, who appear to be purely physical, could actually be immortal.

Having found these images in the pharaohs' tombs that validated my memories and also our immortality, I felt a great satisfaction in fulfilling my purpose. The rest of my visit to Egypt, I believed, would merely be superfluous to my real objective.

Little did I realize that the Holy Mother fits into the story of our souls' history on earth. As I did the research for this book, I felt astounded to discover that just as Jesus was and is intimately connected with leading us to freedom from the physical, so too is Mary. Like Jesus, she is here so that we may return to oneness with Spirit.

When I left for Egypt, I had not put any of this together. I only knew that I felt driven to go to the land of the pharaohs. I thought my main reason in going was to find confirmation of my Atlantean memories. Amazingly, in spite of everyone's warnings, everything kept working out. Because of a great many synchronicities, I was also going to a town forbidden to foreigners where apparitions of the Virgin Mary were appearing.

When I look back on it now, the situation was very similar to the experience with my first book. I was in the grip of something larger than myself. The universe was truly in charge.

PART III

ENCOUNTER WITH A GODDESS

Chapter Fifteen

THE TRAIN STATION AND THE POLICEMAN

Asyut's Historical Significance

No sooner had Peggy and I arrived back in Cairo than we were off to Asyut to see the apparition of the Virgin. We traveled on the train with Mohga, her son Marcos, her daughter Rena, and Rena's best friend Mary.

I felt breathless with all the amazing discoveries we had made. What would happen in Asyut? Would we be sent away because we were tourists? Would the apparition appear?

Asyut is a town with a population of about 400,000 situated on the Nile about 234 miles (376 kilometers) south of Cairo. The name, Asyut, comes from a hieroglyphic in two syllables, "sa wat," which means guardian of the road, since Asyut is on the edge of the frontier of Upper Egypt.

It also used to be a camel caravan destination from the Sudan. Today it is a carpet and pottery manufacturing center and the location of the third largest university in Egypt. In addition, the surrounding agricultural land produces quality cotton and grain. During the Greek occupation of Egypt, Asyut was called Lycopolis.

An interesting tidbit as far as Mary's appearance in Asyut goes: Asyut is supposed to be the most southerly place where Mary and Joseph traveled with the Baby Jesus when they lived in Egypt after fleeing the Holy Land to keep the baby safe from Herod. What a fitting place for Mary to appear exactly two thousand years later.

Train Travel

As we traveled on the train, I continued to display that one outstanding travel characteristic for which I am well known—the ability to fall asleep instantly. Peggy, on the other hand, sat with her eyes bright and shining—perhaps a little glazed over with fatigue—but nonetheless, with her eyes opened.

I knew her secret. She had managed to get an afternoon nap on the previous day when I had gone with the guide to the Temple of Karnak and the Temple of Luxor. While I shuffled through the amazing ruins in sauna-temperature heat snapping rolls of film, Peggy remained at the hotel with a mask over her eyes catching up on her sleep. Now Peggy managed to keep her eyes opened while I felt overwhelmed with exhaustion.

Although the train seats did not feel all that comfortable, I found my eyelids getting heavy. It became difficult to keep my head from falling forward. I assume I must have fallen fast asleep since Mohga, smiling her usual dimpled and impish grin, playfully kidded me about my sudden sleep states. Ho hum, we are all talented in some way or another.

The Asyut Train Station

Women in Mohajjaba and young men in military uniform.

When we arrived at the Asyut train station, for the first time, I saw Muslim women covered totally in fabric. So far, the Muslim women I had seen had had their hair covered in what looked like large kerchiefs, but their faces were visible.

These women at the Asyut train station even had their faces covered with only tiny slits for their eyes so they could see out. Hani tells me this is called Mohajjaba—when a woman is totally covered up. Her face cover is called Hejab in Egypt. In other Arab countries, it is called Borkoa.

Whereas the Muslim women I had seen in Cairo wore different colored outfits, the women with their faces covered were totally dressed in black. I do not know how people in these women's communities can tell them apart because they look exactly the same in their black outfits. Perhaps their families know them by their height, posture, and voices.

I believe they take the face covering off when they are home. They would have to. How else could they cook safely? Then, when they go out of the house, they don their full-face covering just as many of us who wear Western garb don better-looking clothes when we leave the house instead of the casual work clothes we usually wear in the home.

While we waited on the train platform for Mohga's Asyut cousins to meet us, a group of fit young men in military uniform passed through the crowd. They wore eye-catching white dress uniforms with black peaked caps. As do all men in uniform, they looked attractive and full of life. Their faces shone with self-confidence. Because they were in dress uniform, rather than combat uniform, I assumed they must have been heading out to a military academy rather than to fight somewhere.

When I think back to my experience at the train station, I realize that Peggy and I were the only foreigners I saw there.

We waited on the train platform for Wahid (Wa HEED), who is Marcos' and Rena's cousin, to pick us up. Wahid is Hani and Mohga's nephew, the oldest son of their sister, Nahid (NA head). Sadly Nahid, who was as warm and welcoming as Mohga, has passed away since this 2000 visit.

When Wahid arrived, I enjoyed seeing the happy reunion of cousins. Wahid went to get his car. The rest of us walked through the train station, a large open classical train station with a ceiling that towered high above us. I loved the play of light shining in through high ornate windows, sending beams of sunlight glistening through the shaded cavernous space.

I took out my camera to take photographs but Mohga reminded me that tourists were not allowed in Asyut and that taking photographs would bring attention to me. I slid the little point-and-shoot camera into my pants pocket. Because of the ban on tourists, I had packed my 35mm professional camera in my suitcase.

An Irresistible Photo Opportunity

My finger itched to push on the shutter. My way of relating to the world often involves a camera. My work as a photojournalist has always depended upon my talent for taking pictures. I have won awards for my photographs. It gives me great pleasure to produce images that I can share with others.

I have never been in a place where I could not take pictures. Even in a monastery in France, a cathedral in Mexico, and a hospital in Nicaragua, I have taken photographs.

However, here in Asyut, Mohga was telling me I had to curb my desire to record the serenity and beauty of the train station.

I managed to resist the temptation partly because I realized that, unlike the loading platform which thronged with people, the empty tiled walls and polished floor inside the train station would reverberate with the click of the camera shutter.

We walked through the train station, the sound of our feet echoing off the walls, and stepped through the large front doors to wait on the steps for Wahid to pick us up.

While we waited, I watched two cabs parked by the curb, one a modern-day automobile, the other a horse and buggy. This was potentially a picture that could say more than a thousand words about the juxtaposition of the old with the new in Egypt. I had to take a picture so I could remember this wonderful place that few other Westerners can visit.

I touched the outside of my pants feeling the tiny point-and-shoot camera nestled within my pocket.

Quickly, I pulled out the little camera from my pants pocket. I lifted it to my eye and pressed the shutter. Click.

Two cabs, each from a different era in Asyut.

Trouble with the Law in Asyut

Immediately, a policeman wheeled around and stared at us. He had been directing traffic on the street in front of the train station with his back to us. I had not notice him before. His brow furrowed as he scanned our group.

Wow! I thought. *Mohga's tourist agent cousin was right. Tourists really are not allowed in Asyut!*

I kept still and held the little camera by my side, trying to act nonchalant as my heartbeat accelerated. *Who me, take a picture? Never!* The policeman slowly turned back to face traffic.

I let out the breath I did not know I had been holding. He was not going to approach us.

Then I did something that baffles me to this day. I do not know why I did this. Perhaps I was experiencing culture shock. I know I was suffering from lack of sleep. My rational mind was turned off. Perhaps I just could not make the mental switch, for the first time in my life, to refrain from taking pictures. Maybe after years of clicking the shutter, it had become a habit. Like a dog that salivates whenever it hears the dinner bell, I take a picture whenever I see something wonderful, interesting, or beautiful.

Even though the policeman had heard the sound of the shutter when I took the first photo, I now believed that he would never hear the click of the shutter while encircled by the commotion of the street sounds. I must have been half asleep because I told myself he could not possibly hear the tiny sound of the camera's shutter. He stood in a sea of cars and horse-drawn carriages. The sound of motors and wheels on the pavement surrounded him. While he directed traffic, a man spoke to him. Surely the commotion of cars, horses, buggies, and people talking would mask the tiny sound of the camera shutter.

Swiftly, I pulled the little camera out of my pocket and snapped the shutter. Click.

The policeman in Asyut.

He wheeled around again! How could he hear such a tiny sound from so far away in the middle of all those distractions!

Fortunately, I had already lowered my arm, holding the little camera behind the fabric of my trousers. I had not expected this. It had never happened to me before in my life. Usually, I am expected to take as many pictures as possible.

After all the days and nights of hardly any sleep, my mind began to wake up. I could see it was time for me to learn something new . . . and fast!

The policeman scanned our group again. His eyes fixed on me.

How did he know it was me? Did I have a guilty look on my face? I held my breath and tried desperately to look nonchalant while my heart beat like the percussion section of a marching band.

He glowered. For an instant I feared a reprimand or worse yet, to be banished from Asyut. I saw the policeman's eyes scan Mohga, her family, and Peggy . . . and then back to me again.

I believe he figured out the situation. Peggy and I were not tourists. We were guests of Egyptian citizens. I felt relieved. He would not arrest me or force me to leave on a train all by myself.

The policeman turned back to the street to his duty directing traffic. I tucked the little camera in my fanny pack and felt immense relief. I also felt grateful that I had not embarrassed Mohga and her family after all they had done for me and Peggy.

Our Asyut Hosts

Mohga's sister and her family lived in a typical Egyptian apartment building, about four or five stories tall. The whole family lived vertically within the same building. Members of the family occupied different apartments positioned one on top of each other. A street-level door opened to an inside stairway, which rose to the doorway of each individual apartment overhead.

Wahid's mother Nahid and his father Refaat (REF aat) occupied the bottom apartment. Wahid lived with them. His family also included his delightful wife Mervat (MER vat), and their two charming young sons, Kerolos (Ke ro LOS) and Beshoi (Be SHOI), named for Coptic Saints.

Wahid and Mervat

In an apartment above them, Wahid's brother, Hani's namesake, lived with his lovely young wife, Sally. They were very much in love and expecting their first child. I recently learned from Hani that the baby was named Mary, not surprisingly since she was born during the Virgin's appearance in Asyut.

A Scrumptious, Sumptuous Feast

Nahid made us a lovely multi-course meal of Egyptian treats. I always love to eat foods from different nations. As one plateful after another of hors d'oeuvre-sized delicacies passed before me, I must admit, I helped myself to a heaping plateful of the tidbits and ate the whole lot.

As the day progressed, more and more people poured into the downstairs apartment. Many came to see Mohga, who had grown up in Asyut, and her family. Visitors also greeted the women from the United States. However, I noticed that something else was up.

To my great surprise, I learned that we were all going to a wedding. As nighttime fell and the welcome cool of the evening revitalized the city, we headed out in Wahid's car to the wedding. We drove through residential streets with three- and four-story apartment buildings on both sides of a narrow road. It reminded me of Brussels or Paris.

As it had been in Cairo, my first real look at the city of Asyut occurred at night. But Asyut at night felt very different from Cairo. Cairo was lights, noise, and bustle. Asyut, on the other hand, felt still, quiet, and dark. Of course, Cairo is the largest city in Africa. And Asyut, although it is a good-sized town, is not the sprawling megalopolis that is Cairo.

As we drove along, all of us in the car were in a jolly mood. We had eaten well. The Asyut branch of Mohga and Hani's family had welcomed us warmly. I felt full of good spirits. When Wahid stopped and parked the car, we piled out. Rena, Mary, and Marcos stepped out of another car.

The Wedding at Saint Mark's Cathedral

We were at a church, actually a cathedral. It towered over us and was located at the corner of a number of very narrow streets in the old section of Asyut. Unlike the church Peggy and I had visited with Mohga and Gad in Cairo, this place of worship did not have a surrounding green area. In fact, the stairs leading up to its open front doors rose right from the sidewalk.

Peggy and I followed Mohga up the tall cement steps to the two doorways of the church. Light streamed out of the doorways into the dark of the night. We stood outside peering into the lighted interior of the church. It was a large sanctuary filled to capacity with wedding guests, dressed in their best finery, sitting in rows of pews. The nuptial ceremony proceeded within.

Mohga pointed out to Peggy and me that in the Coptic Church, men sit on the left side of the sanctuary and women sit on the right. I also saw that inspirationally produced paintings called icons decorated the walls. The figures in the paintings looked like saints staring down at us. In spite of the serene paintings on the walls, the church looked happy and festive within.

As we watched and waited, a number of people strayed outside, perhaps to cool off or maybe because they knew Mohga would be arriving late. They greeted her and her family as if they were relatives or old friends and conversed in low tones.

Unexpected Forces at Work

It appeared as if the ceremony would soon be ending because more people came outside to say "Hello" to Mohga. I found myself warmly greeted by many people. Speaking in low tones, so as not to interfere with the wedding ceremony, someone introduced me to someone else who introduced me to someone else. People took my arm and led me forward. I was now fully in the sanctuary.

People continued to lead me forward. They were friendly and welcoming. I appreciated their kind acknowledgement of me but I had no idea why they were bringing me into the sanctuary.

I hoped I was not making a mistake carrying my camera in full view. I had unpacked it in anticipation of taking photographs under cover of darkness if the Virgin appeared.

Now, I was in an aisle along the outside left wall of the church being pushed and prodded forward. Numerous people sitting in the ends seats of the pews gestured to my camera. They smiled and nodded their heads eagerly as if they were expecting me to do something.

I looked up at the altar and saw that the ceremony still continued. Most of the congregation remained in their pews.

People continued to hand me from one person to another, until I found myself right at the front of the sanctuary across from the happy couple and the priest.

Slowly I turned around to face the congregation. The whole of the sanctuary stretched before me. What was I doing here? It felt like a dream scenario. I felt close to panic. Many people sitting at the side of the sanctuary where I stood smiled at me.

My confused brain could manage only one thought: that I should have worn a dress like all the other women instead of my cotton pantsuits. I felt extremely awkward.

A number of people in the front pews made gestures as if they were lifting a camera to their eyes and taking a photograph. They smiled at me and whispered in Arabic. Some also whispered in English. They told me to take pictures.

I did not know what to do. Only a few hours earlier, I had almost had an encounter with the law by taking two photographs. Now, everyone was telling me to take pictures.

I looked around for Mohga to get direction from her but could not find her in the sea of strangers smiling up at me.

If I took a photo, would a policeman leap up out of the congregation and arrest me? Did they assume, because my camera hung around my neck, that I wanted to take pictures? Actually, I just carried my camera around my neck so I would not lose it.

I did not know what to do so I did what I would normally do at a wedding. I murmured to the people in the front seats close to me that the bride looked so beautiful.

They agreed but continued to encourage me to take pictures. They definitely assumed that I was there to take photographs. Did they think I was the wedding photographer? I scanned the sanctuary, especially probing along the walls and the far corners for a man in uniform. I saw none. Where was Mohga? If only I could get an "OK," from her. But I could only see people smiling and gesturing at me.

I felt as confused as a little child who is trying to make sense of his or her world. *First they tell me it is bad to take pictures. Now, they're telling me I'm supposed to take pictures. If I take a picture will I get in trouble? What should I do?*

Then, I noticed that a man videotaped the event. Maybe it would be all right to take pictures after all.

I turned toward the bride, groom, and priest. My hands found the familiar form of my camera. With an automatic motion borne of years of practice, I took the lens cap off, put it in the pocket of my pants, and lifted the camera up to my eye.

No footsteps echoed toward me. I looked through the viewfinder, centered the image, adjusted the focus, and pushed on the shutter. "Click." The flash blazed throughout the sanctuary.

Unaware that I had been holding my breath, I released it slowly and turned toward the congregation expecting to see a policeman striding toward me. Instead, I only saw all the people in the front pews glowing with joy and smiling widely, perhaps in the hopes of being included in the next picture. I seemed to be getting favorable feedback. Mohga had not rushed forward and pulled me to the back of the sanctuary.

I took a couple more pictures. The flash blazed through the sanctuary again. Everyone seemed to be happy. Their faces shone with delight and gratitude. I took a few more pictures. It seemed to be the right thing to do. They seemed to like it. I felt happy and encouraged.

Wedding Photographer

Soon I was in my element. I know how to take wedding pictures—record everything and make everyone look as good as possible. The fact is that there is nothing I like better than happy, beautiful people and this bride and groom fit the bill. The bride had blue-black hair fastened on the top of her head with a couple of curls hanging down to frame her lovely face. She also had slanted black almond-shaped eyes, a creamy complexion, a cupid's bow mouth, and a petite figure. You could tell she adored the groom, who was also gorgeous with his black hair and glistening dark eyes.

I also like anything interesting. What a beautiful, wonderful place to photograph. I loved the sanctuary with the serene icons on the walls. The priest looked so different than our priests do, with his long black beard, long black outfit, and hat.

The Bride, Groom, and Priest.   **The icon of Jesus blesses the happy couple.**

At the time I did not realize it, but this was the same cathedral on top of which the apparition was supposed to appear later that night.

The ceremony over, I scurried to the back of the sanctuary to get photos of the happy couple as they drifted down the aisle. Now I was having fun, doing my best to photograph them with the icon of Jesus blessing them forever in the photograph.

Now at the back doors I saw a car appear from one of the dark and narrow streets. When it came closer I recognized the ribbon and flower decorations of a newlywed car. Amid good wishes and rice, the happy newlyweds got into the car and were sped away.

There followed much good natured greetings by people happy to see Mohga and the members of her family. I must have done the right thing because Mohga seemed pleased with me. After a while, Wahid appeared in his car again and picked us up.

Chapter Sixteen

NIGHTTIME PILGRIMAGE

Second Thoughts

We were now on our way to see the apparition of the Virgin Mary. The time was about midnight but I felt neither tired nor excited. So much had happened—from discovering the images in the pharaohs' tombs that validated my memories of Atlantis to a close encounter with an Asyut policeman to an unexpected avocation as a wedding photographer. I now felt numb and worn out.

If I had only had the time to do some research into apparitions of the Blessed Virgin Mary, I might have found something to help me understand the heightened expectations of the people sitting in the car with me. If I had done my homework, I would have discovered that the apparitions are usually seen only by visionaries and that only very occasionally do many people see them—usually in countries in which the Eastern Orthodox Church predominates, such as in Egypt. As I said earlier, the Copt Orthodox Church is part of the Eastern Orthodox tradition, the first Christian Church. The Roman Catholic Church separated from it.

In addition, there are also times when the crowds may not see the apparition, but they see other phenomenon, such as the sun spinning or falling to the earth.

In any event, this was a case when ignorance was not bliss. Suddenly, as we sped through the dark streets of Asyut with Wahid at the wheel, I began to feel apprehension building in me. What had I gotten myself into? I hardly knew these people and now they were taking me to some kind of unusual religious event in a town where the police would not even allow a person to trip a camera shutter!

Although I did not feel it, I must have also been totally exhausted. Since our arrival in Egypt, I had hardly had a full night's sleep. Peggy and I had arrived in Cairo from Luxor at four in the morning. Now, we had been awake all day and it was well past midnight.

On the Way to the Apparition Site

I have to admit that I was starting to feel afraid. Could I change my mind and go home now? Or maybe Wahid could drop me off at his parents' place and I could wait there until everyone else came back from their encounter with the apparition—whatever that was.

However, when I thought of returning to Wahid's home, I noticed with surprised that I felt envious that others would see whatever there was to see. I decided I did not want to miss it.

Wahid parked by the side of a road and we all got out—his wife, his two sons, Mohga, Peggy, and me. Rena, Mary, and Marcos also arrived.

Once we got out of the car, we began to walk. I followed Mohga through narrow alleyways. The buildings on either side of the dark alley rose the usual three, four, or five stories high. Balconies hung over the alley, sometimes with laundry hanging from railings. I saw no plants in pots or even weeds growing up through the hard, dry dirt upon which we walked in the night.

We kept walking and walking. Hundreds of people swarmed around us, all of them trudging in the same direction. I saw men, women, and children, some in Muslim finery, some in Western clothes, some in gallabias with and without turbans.

However, except for Peggy, I did not see another foreigner among them. Everyone who tramped down the dark, narrow streets of Asyut with us was Egyptian. However, I did not feel out of place because no one seemed to notice us. They did not stare or point or gesture toward us.

It must have been about one in the morning by now. Many more strangers streamed through the alleyway with us. They poured in from side streets, all striding purposefully and, for the most part, silently. We too marched along without speaking.

Occasionally, we passed stairs leading down to the door of a basement apartment. As we passed yet another below-ground-level entrance to an apartment, I suddenly realized that someone could grab me and drag me down into one of the dark basements and no one would ever know what became of me.

Who would look for me? Who would care? My family would care but they lived far, far away and could not speak Arabic. They would have no idea where to even start to look for me.

"No!" to Foreigners

Fortunately, at the time, I did not know that Asyut had been designated as out-of-bounds for all foreigners, not only tourists. The town had received that designation, with a few other towns along the Nile, because it was a hotbed of Islamic fundamentalism. In fact, Asyut had been known as a center of Islamic terrorism, where attacks had targeted Christians and tourists for 25 years.

In a recent telephone discussion with Peggy, she said that Mohga told us that recent violence had to do with an unfortunate clash between Muslim fanatics and a number of Christian teenagers. The six youngsters had been killed because they refused to convert to Islam.

Perhaps I had been distracted at the time Mohga told us this. I did spend a lot of my time either looking through the viewfinder of my camera or searching for photo opportunities. Perhaps I did not hear what Mohga said because I was already so distracted with all the new sights, sounds, and aromas in this amazing country, as well as with my need to fulfill my purpose in visiting the pharaohs' tombs. Maybe I simply did not care since we were going to Asyut anyway. Maybe, at some deep subconscious level, I knew I was in the stream of whatever I was meant to do so I simply drifted along with the current.

Whether or Not to Take Revenge

I have learned since coming home that, following the brutal murder of the six Christian teenagers, one group of Asyut Copts prepared to take revenge against the terrorists, but another level-headed group talked them out of it.

Everyone agreed that the Holy Mother had manifested as a special gift to affirm the righteousness of the decision not to take revenge and also to calm down apprehensions and encourage peace among neighbors of all faiths.

As a result of Mary's appearance, Asyut now was at peace. However, because of the previous tensions between Christians and Muslims, even after the apparition brought peace to the town, the government would not let any foreigners into the city for fear of a return to terrorism.

More Reasons for Apprehension

I also did not know that 58 tourists had been massacred in Luxor in 1997. After this terrible incident the authorities decided that foreigners were not allowed in Asyut, and a few other designated towns, because of the threat of violence. This is probably the incident that had influenced my husband's decision not to come with me.

Furthermore, I also did not know that during the first few days of the apparition's appearance in mid-August, security forces had been called into Asyut. The authorities must have feared that if crowds of people descended on the apparition site, hostilities would ensue.

According to newspaper accounts displayed on the internet and listed in the "Online Resources" section of the Bibliography, authorities at first evacuated the heavily populated inner city, where the apparition appeared, between 10:00 p.m. and 6:00 a.m., the times when the apparition usually occurred. To quell panic, the newspaper articles reported that the tales of apparitions were rumors—likely the result of hallucinations.

But, no matter how the authorities tried to control the crowds, the news spread throughout Egypt and people came in droves, as I personally experienced. Happily, in spite of the authorities' misgivings, no hostilities occurred.

Now, when I look back on it, I wonder if the young men dressed in military uniform at the train station had arrived in Asyut to help with crowd control.

As I said, in 2000 as I trudged through the narrow alleyways of Asyut in the middle of the night, I was unaware of just how potentially dangerous a situation existed in that city at that time.

Nonetheless, I did feel some fear. I was in a foreign country where most of the population did not speak my language, eat the kind of food I ate, or even wear the same kind of clothes I wore. I only knew a handful of people—Mohga and her family—and them, only for a couple of days. And, it was the deepest part of the night.

At times like this, when my mind feels confused and negative emotions appear to be taking over, I often turn to my connection with Spirit. I checked in with my inner knowing. Did I have a gut feeling of some impending danger? No, I felt amazingly safe and protected with Mohga and her family. Did I feel I was being misled? Was it a mistake to visit the apparition site? No, I felt certain, with each step I took, that I traveled in the right direction.

I decided to go with my gut feeling of rightness and safety rather than my mental construct of reasons to be anxious. And anyway, what could I do? I was on my way to see the apparition, like it or not, ready or not. I had no way of finding the route back to Wahid's car, his parent's apartment building, or the train station. Simply, there was no going back now.

Throngs of People

I walked blindly on. There was no use wondering or worrying. I was on an adventure. This was no time for fearful fantasies. I would have to trust Mohga and make sure to keep her in sight like a duckling waddling after its mother. I truly felt like a child, totally at the mercy of the world around me.

Even more people joined the throngs of humanity flowing forward like a mountain stream cascading to a river flowing to the sea. They came from side streets, Copts and Muslims alike. I could tell the Copt women because they wore outfits that included pants, like Rena, or dresses, like Mohga, without head coverings. The Muslim women always wore a scarf over their heads.

It turns out that Muslims also revere the Virgin Mary as the mother of Jesus, who is considered a prophet in the Islamic faith. Of course, all the women walked with men.

We all moved in the same direction—the place where the apparition of the Blessed Virgin Mary had been occurring for the last couple of months.

I wondered if I would see it. What would it look like? Would it appear this night? Would I be disappointed?

Preview of the Apparition

Before we had left Wahid's apartment, he had shown us a videotape he had taken on previous visits to the site. It showed us what to expect.

He also wanted us to know that sometimes the Virgin did not appear and that she might not appear that night. I guess he felt that if Mary did not appear that night, we would at least have seen her on the screen of his television set.

This was the end of September 2000. The apparitions had started on August 17th, so Wahid and his family had had a number of opportunities to view and videotape the event.

On the screen of their television set, we saw a nighttime scene that included two steeples of a church—the same church where the wedding had taken place. Wahid and Mervat explained that it was their church.

With my eyes focused on the television screen in their apartment, I saw that for a number of minutes, the scene did not change. Occasionally the person holding the camera became distracted while talking to people, so the camera whisked around and pointed away from the church into the night sky or down at crowds of people in a lighted square.

As the tape rolled along with the lens of the camera focused on the steeples of the church most of the time, I was beginning to wonder if I had missed the apparition.

Suddenly bright flashes of light appeared on the church drenching the steeples in blazing light. All along, while watching the video, I could hear the hum, snatches of conversation, and rustlings of a formidable crowd in the background. However, when the flashes appeared, a roar of excitement accompanied the scene.

The flashes built to a crescendo and then stopped. Those of us watching the videotape waited as scenes of the steeples, now in darkness again, continued on the television screen. Then, the flashes blazed anew, built to a crescendo, and then stopped again. This sequence occurred a number of times.

Then suddenly, a column of light appeared in the center of the screen. It looked almost as if the church steeple glowed with a cap of neon.

Wahid said that when the apparition appeared, the light was blinding. He could hardly look at it because it was so bright. Fortunately, his video camera automatically adjusted for the brightness.

So, this is what the apparition looked like—a column of light. I studied the image on the television screen. I did not know that when visionaries, as opposed to crowds of people, saw the Virgin Mary, they saw her as a human being, with real human attributes, rather than a column of light as she had been appearing in Asyut. I also did not know that when crowds of people saw the Virgin, she often appeared as a Being of Light or as a glowing form.

Because I did not have any preconceived ideas of what an apparition of the Virgin Mary should look like, a Being of Light seemed reasonable to me. After all, I had seen Beings of Light in my hypnosis sessions as I had described in Chapter Twelve, "Light Beings in the Pharaoh's Tomb."

Besides experiencing myself as a Light Being, I had also seen huge angelic Beings of Light. They were the Archangels Michael and Gabriel, and also Christ in His spiritual form. When the three spiritual guardians first appeared in my trance states, they looked like Tibetan lamas, with shaved heads and wearing ochre robes with hoods that hung over their foreheads. However, after a year of hypnosis sessions, I would usually see them in their real form—gigantic Beings of Light.

Therefore, it made sense to me that the Virgin Mary could also appear in her spiritual form, that is to say, a glowing Being of Light. I have since read that even when the visionaries see Mary in a human form, they describe her as glowing more brightly than the sun. Hence, it seems Mary always appears in a luminous form whether or not she also looks like a human being.

When I examined the Being of Light on the television screen further, I could see an outline that looked as if she carried something in her arms, which I assumed must be the Baby Jesus.

As I watched the image, I could see it move. I saw her turning slightly from side to side. She turned away from me and then slowly back again. Sometimes, she bent forward. Other times, she straightened. At times, I could also see the features of a face in the bright glow.

It also appeared that a companion accompanied her. I have since read that the people in Asyut assumed the Virgin's companion must be a monk. The companion often appeared as a faint glow beside her. At other times, the companion glowed as brightly as she did but was always smaller than she was.

When the videotaped preview ended, I felt grateful that Wahid had thought to show us what to expect. Probably he wanted us to be especially ready for the extreme brilliance of the apparition when it appeared.

While watching the videotape, someone said that people had also seen birds flying in the nighttime and that the birds appeared to be lit with lights.

I appreciated the videotaped preview but as soon as I heard about the brightly lit birds, my skepticism reappeared. If you remember, even though my memories of Atlantis were as real as memories from this lifetime, I could not believe that what I had seen could be real. Only when I saw the stone carvings in the Yucatan did I begin to accept that I might have tapped into some primordial archetypal memory in my hypnosis sessions.

A Skeptic's Reaction

In any case, knowing my reaction to my own memories of Atlantis, it was no wonder that one of my first reactions to Wahid's videotape was skepticism.

Birds flying in the night? Impossible. Birds, unless they are night birds such as owls, find a safe place to perch and stay there until the sun comes up.

Furthermore, it bothered me that the apparition occurred specifically at the Coptic Church. An uneasy thought arose in my mind. It said: *Why hadn't the apparition occurred in a field, as it had in Fatima, or in a cave, as it had in Lourdes, or somewhere neutral? Why the Coptic Church in a country besieged with problems of religious intolerance?*

At the time, I did not know that Mary often appears near or on top of churches. She frequently floats over the rooftop. Sometimes she manifests inside the church. There have also been a number of times when a statue of the Virgin Mary in a church began to weep tears—occasionally tears of oil and occasionally tears of blood.

Someone in the living room made the comment in English how wonderful it was that the Virgin had come to the Copts in Egypt, especially at a time when the Muslims were making things so difficult for the Copts.

Wasn't that a nifty coincidence? I thought. *The Virgin appears just when the population needs her. It's got to be something set up by the church to increase the numbers of their congregation.*

At the time, I did not know that the Holy Mother often appears at times when her people need her. Of course, during my visit to Egypt, I did not yet know that Mary had appeared thousands of times to many visionaries throughout the world, or that she had often visited during times of difficulty either to warn, protect, or to support her people.

Someone else said how fortunate the Egyptians were that the Virgin had appeared several years earlier at another Coptic Church.

My mind clutched at that statement. I did not like the coincidence. I began to wonder if the Asyut apparition could be manmade. Had the priests created the apparition? Had they taken the same light-show equipment they had used at the previous apparition site and moved it to Asyut and quietly, behind-the-scenes and at night . . . so no one would suspect . . . set up their electronic light-show machine to create the present "apparition?"

Unfortunately, I did not know that the previous apparition had occurred in 1968 in Zeitun, a suburb of Cairo. It happened so long ago that even if the priests had used electronic equipment to create the 1968 phenomenon, their equipment would be sorely out of date by 2000.

Furthermore, I was unaware that Mary had looked more like a glowing human being than a column of light when she appeared in Zeitun. Therefore, even if both of the apparitions had been manmade, the priests could not have used the same equipment in both instances.

Neither did I know that Mary looks different wherever she appears. Visionaries have seen her with hair color ranging from blonde to black. She has had eyes that are blue, golden, and brown. Even her skin color has ranged from a creamy complexion to olive colored to brown. Moreover, she often takes on the characteristics of the country in which she appears, for example, in China, she looked Chinese, and in Venezuela, she looked to be of Latin descent. It is said that Mary appears in whatever way is most comfortable for her viewers to see her.

But, in 2000, sitting in Wahid's parents' living room, I knew very little about apparitions of the Virgin Mary. I only knew that I felt grateful to have the opportunity to experience Mary's appearance in Asyut, and I especially did not want to show any disrespect to my gracious hosts.

Therefore, I shoved the skeptical thoughts out of my mind determined to keep as open a mind as possible. I also felt guilty because I had begun to doubt the authenticity of the apparition. Everyone around me, including Peggy, seemed so joyful and sincere.

Peggy had even gone to see Mary in the place that started with an "M," which I discovered, once I started to do research at home, was called Medjugorje, Bosnia.

I did believe the unusual situation of the children in Fatima. After all, Mary's prediction that two of them would die at a young age came true. I also believed that something of a phenomenal nature had truly occurred in Lourdes, because people had received miraculous healings at the spring created as a result of the Virgin's visitation.

I reasoned that if other people had experienced something phenomenal and miraculous, why not me? Why shouldn't my life arrange itself in such a way that I should see something miraculous as well?

Therefore, as I trekked along with the throngs of people in the narrow alleyways of Asyut, I approached the apparition with a feeling of both skepticism and eager anticipation.

The Dark Stairway

Finally we came to a ground floor doorway at the bottom of a typical four-story apartment building. The door opened and a number of people greeted us. Although I could not understand what the people said because they spoke in Arabic, by the tone of their voices, they sounded warm, welcoming, and happy to see us. Mohga and Wahid exchanged words with them, and we were ushered in.

Again, because I could not understand Arabic, I did not really know what was going on. Looking back on it, I wonder why I did not ask Mohga or any of her family members who walked with us. Maybe I had come to the realization that it did not matter whether I knew the details of the situation. Maybe I was too tired. The fact was, I was going to follow this group and do whatever they did and see whatever they saw because there was nothing else I could do.

I followed everyone through the doorway. Inside the building, it was darker than it was in the alley. I expected that there would be artificial lights on the other side of the door, as there usually are inside a building in the United States. But there was no light whatsoever. Unable to see, I followed behind the person in front of me. We began to climb stairs. It was pitch dark on the stairway. I followed the crowd of people, who all seemed to know each other, up the stairway. They all chatted amiably with each other in Arabic. We continued to climb in the dark. I let my feet see for me and held onto the railing so I would not trip or fall.

After a while, my eyes began to adjust to the darkness. I discovered that some parts of the outer wall opened up like a balcony. The sky looked a dark gray color from the muted lights made by the city below the balcony.

It turned out that we were in a stairwell made of cement that occasionally opened, at about chest level, to the outside. These openings were lined with cement pillars that I supposed supported the floors above us. Whenever we came to a higher story, we walked across a dark landing that contained a door to the apartment at that level.

I felt happy that I could catch my breath whenever we came to one of these landings. Although my camera bag, lenses, and film had not felt heavy as we traipsed through the alleyways, it became heavier the higher I climbed.

I had lost track of Mohga and could only assume that she was somewhere ahead of me on the stairs. We climbed and climbed and climbed, alternately stomping through complete darkness and then coming out into a level area dimly lit by the dark gray sky of the city, only to march right back into the blackness of the stairwell.

Chapter Seventeen

MARY APPEARS IN ASYUT

On the Roof

After we climbed about four stories, we emerged onto a flat open area. It was the roof. Someone had placed fold-up chairs in rows for us. Our hosts expected so many people that the chairs had been arranged with an aisle down the middle.

To my surprise, about 35 people already milled around on the rooftop. People continued to arrive until there were easily 50 individuals. They included children, teenagers, adults, and the elderly. I felt comfortable in this mix of ages because I had grown up in a large extended family where everyone of all ages was always included.

I especially liked to see the children. Wahid and Mervat's two little boys enjoyed Mohga's company so much. She talked to them with animation, played games with them so they would not become bored, and held them on her lap when they became tired. The little boys also enjoyed Peggy's company and her lovely, easy way of relating to children.

The building on which we stood turned out to be a corner building. When I looked over one side of the roof, I could see the alley in which we had walked.

Throngs of people continued to pour into the square. Amazingly, a car arrived, moving very slowly. It looked like a boulder in a stream surrounded by a flowing torrent of people. I thought the driver of the car down below me had to be mentally deranged to drive in such a narrow area.

The alleyway opened up into a commercial square. The bright, slightly greenish neon lights of storefronts blazed. I could see that the merchants took full advantage of the myriads of people attracted to the event. I assume they provided chilled drinks, snacks, and commemorative trinkets.

As I looked down from the rooftop, a few more cars slowly pushed through the crowds and parked in the lighted square. I realized, then, that the drivers were not insane. The alleyway had to be a very narrow European-style street—not an alley.

Saint Mark's Cathedral is located in the midst of the old part of town. The streets are the narrow streets of an old town with deep historical roots reaching to long before automobiles came on the scene.

A Rich Experience

Four stories up, only a faint light, reflected from the street, illuminated the balconies and rooftops. When I looked across the lighted area to the other buildings that surrounded the square, I at first saw five or six people sitting on a balcony. Attached to the balcony, there were three metal rods that provided a clothesline. Laundry hung on the rods.

As I continued to look across the lighted square, I saw dim shadows of people filling each balcony and rooftop. Hundreds, perhaps thousands, of people waited for the apparition. At the same time, the lighted square no longer teemed with people.

Because the streets were so narrow in this part of Asyut, the only way you could easily see the apparition, which usually appeared on top of the roof of Saint Mark's Cathedral, was on the high balconies and rooftops of the surrounding apartment buildings. The crowds of people must have left the lighted square and gone to the balconies and rooftops.

Someone had certainly been kind enough to invite all of us to the top of their flat roof. I believe it was a friend or relative of Wahid's. Beyond the rooftops, the steeples of the church rose into the night sky. We, and hundreds of other people, at about two o'clock in the morning, sat in excellent vantage points on rooftops and balconies in hopes of seeing the apparition of the Virgin Mary.

Newspaper reports, which I discovered while doing research for this book, say that, in total, over two million people viewed the apparition. Evidently pilgrims even slept in the streets in the hopes of catching a glimpse of the miraculous event.

The people who lived in the area—Christians and Muslims alike—graciously opened their doors to people who wanted to see the apparition, especially the sick and the elderly.

On our rooftop, Mervat fed her sons the sandwiches she had previously prepared. After the boys finished eating, they ran off to tail their father, follow some other adult male on the rooftop, play with other youngsters, or visit with Mohga and Peggy.

Mervat turned to me and reminded me that sometimes the apparition did not appear. I told her that I felt comfortable should that happen. In fact, I told her, whether I saw the apparition of the Virgin or not, I loved that I could experience being with her and her family and friends.

I meant it. This experience on the rooftop in the middle of the night is one of my most precious memories of Egypt. It meant so much to me because I had the opportunity to be with all these people in a real setting, sharing with them a real event rather than seeing Egypt only as a tourist.

My experience in Asyut and with Mohga's family in Cairo is so much more valuable to me than to have been cooped up with a bunch of Americans on a cruise ship in the Nile or on a bus. Here, in Asyut especially, I shared the real Egypt with real Egyptians. It was truly one of those rich experiences in life that happen very infrequently and for which I feel deeply grateful.

The Phenomena Begin

As I began to walk to the corner I had chosen to set up my camera, a brilliant white flash of light lit the church steeples. It was blinding. Then another flash occurred. It appeared to emanate from inside the steeple. And then another flash electrified the night sky. It seemed to emanate from the other side of the steeple. A number of brilliant flashes followed. The blazing light played on the steeples of the church as if coming from different directions.

As soon as the first flash occurred, everyone who had been milling about on the rooftop—eating, talking, playing, and resting—rushed to stand against the cement wall exactly at the spot where I hoped to put my camera. I could not even get to the wall, never mind find a place to set up my camera.

Wahid came to my rescue and offered me the use of his videotape camera tripod. I felt delighted that the mount fit the base of my camera. Next, Wahid asked the people crowded along the wall to give me some room to place the tripod. They did not argue or fuss, but graciously and politely moved away for me. It warmed my heart to see how kind everyone was. For the rest of the night, I had a clear spot to take photographs of the church.

Throughout the rest of the night, brilliant flashes of light lit the church at irregular intervals. They blazed on and off. They flashed with a radiant white light similar to lightning except the sky was clear and there were no lightning bolts or thunder. Where were the flashes coming from?

Sometimes the flashes came in groups and sometimes they came individually. Then a long stretch of time would occur in which the church remained dark.

When the flashes occurred, the crowds of people on the rooftops and balconies roared with delight. During the times when the church and the steeples remained dark, I could see people milling around and talking on the tops of the buildings surrounding us.

However, when the flashes began to occur in quick succession, yells and bellows rose like waves into the night air from all the people on the balconies and rooftops.

As the night wore on, the crowds of people became more and more restless. Some groups of people began to chant prayers. Out of the cadences of the chanting, a single female voice would rise above the other voices to proclaim that poignant high-pitched and plaintiff cry that many Middle Eastern people use in times of great emotion and great devotion.

Waves of voices rose as the flashes became more and more frequent. This time, when the flashes stopped, the chanting and poignant calls increased. I felt as if people around me called to the Holy Mother, encouraging her to appear. The flashes returned, coming even more frequently. At the same time, the chanting and calling increased as well.

The air itself reverberated with electricity. The heightened expectation, the communal excitement, and, I would imagine, the anxiety of what the apparition's appearance could mean to each of us, permeated our bodies, minds, and souls.

Beleaguered with Skepticism

At first, my skepticism returned. The whole scene seemed almost surreal. Except for large sporting events or huge outdoor rock concerts, I had never been in a situation in which so many people participated together in a heightened emotional state. But this experience was not centered on entertainment. It centered on religious zeal.

As the emotion built, my mind looked for ways to understand what I was seeing and feeling. I also wondered if the chants, prayers, and poignant cries helped the apparition to occur.

I remembered a friend telling me about an experience he had had when Rolling Thunder, a Native American medicine man, had conducted a healing in an auditorium of hundreds of people.

Rolling Thunder had asked the crowd to sing, which they did. However, he kept encouraging them to sing with more conviction. He said that he could not perform the healing successfully unless his surroundings reverberated with the appropriate energy. Therefore, the people in the auditorium needed to lift their energies higher.

Finally, when the roomful of people's voices soared, he began his healing ceremony. He performed a psychic operation in which he actually removed an offending tumor from within a sick person without cutting the person open.

I wondered if the apparition worked on the same principle. Did Mary appear when the surrounding energy was right for her? No one had asked the people to chant. No one had told them to pray. Yet, the fervor with which they poured out their devotion seemed to electrify the very air we breathed.

At the same time, I continued to ponder the authenticity of the flashes. I could not help but wonder if the priests had come to Asyut six months earlier while no one suspected what they were doing. Had they planted large electrical lights at strategic places around the town? Did they now electrically manipulate these lights from a remote location, so no one would know the priests were associated with the phenomenon?

My skeptical theory explained the flashes, but it did not explain how the flashes could be so blindingly bright. I had never seen a spotlight that bright.

Still, I hoped my photographs would show a large light trained on the steeples of the church. Since the flashes came from the right, the left, from above, and from the side, I figured that surely someone in the town, perhaps not a Copt, would have noticed the huge spotlights set up around the church. Even if the priests only took the spotlights out after dark, before the crowds arrived, surely someone in one of the four-story apartment buildings that hemmed in the church would have noticed.

I have since read that both Egyptian and British journalists tried to find a source for the brilliant flashes without success.

While I struggled with the dilemma of how the priests managed to stow the spotlights so that they created flashes unobtrusively, another problem emerged.

Glowing Birds

People on the rooftops where we sat gasped in unison as a flock of what appeared to be pigeons flew up over our building in the night. The birds hovered right over the rooftop where we sat without flapping their wings—a flock of about four or five of them. I tried to turn my camera on Wahid's tripod up to the sky to photograph them but they were gone.

Because I fiddled with my camera and the tripod, I did not notice where the birds came from. Peggy told me later that a brilliant light would flash out in the dark sky. Then a white dove would suddenly fly out of that light. It would circle around the church high in the sky in huge circles and then disappear behind some building never to return. She especially enjoyed one glowing bird that circled low over our heads for a minute or two before disappearing behind another building.

I must have been adjusting my camera when this low-flying bird appeared. However, I did see when a group of about two or three arrived—flying high over the rooftop. I tried again to move the camera, but failed to photograph the glowing birds because the camera was attached to the tripod and awkward to maneuver.

The birds appeared to have little lights on the undersides of their wings. People who had seen the Virgin had told me how glowing birds, which they thought were doves, would appear in the night. As you know, I had dismissed their reports as fanciful.

In newspaper articles which I have read on the internet since then (the web site addresses of which I have listed in the Online Resources section of the Bibliography) I read that one onlooker said the chest of the doves glowed as if lit up. Other witnesses said the whole birds glowed. At one link, there are photographs of the glowing birds. Everyone agreed they did not flap their wings.

To me, it looked as if the birds had little lights glowing in their armpits. I had an explanation for that. The priests must have fit the birds with little harnesses that included the lights and a little battery pack. I figured that if naturalists could fit birds with tracking devices, the priests could just as easily fit pigeons and doves with light packs.

An irreverent image came to my mind of a couple of patriarchs in black robes and long beards fitting the harnesses onto the little feathered backs. In my mind, the priests worked stealthily in a stone-walled room in the dirt-floored basement of the church, a scheming look on their faces like Fagan in the Charles Dickens classic *Oliver Twist*.

Running Out of Logical Explanations

While I contemplated the possibility of such a gigantic ruse, I also felt afraid that the flashes and the lights on the birds might actually be real, but supernatural, phenomena. I could see that my attempts at logical explanations were becoming ridiculous.

I thought I felt comfortable with the idea of the appearance of the Virgin in an apparition form. However, another part of me felt terrified at seeing such a blazing spectacle as I had seen on Wahid's videotaped television image.

He had said the light was so bright it was blinding. He had had to hold his hand up in front of his eyes to protect his eyes.

What if I fell on my knees in supplication? What if I began to cry, the tears pouring down my face? What if I made a spectacle of myself?

Looking back on that night, I can see that my fears were reasonable considering my unfamiliar surroundings and that I might be on the brink of something miraculous. Already, I was running out of rational explanations for the brilliant lightning-like flashes and the lights on the birds.

Throughout that night, as the flashes of blinding light illuminated the steeples of the church and the people around me chanted, prayed, and called out with that poignant sound typical of the Middle East, I kept taking photographs.

Could It Be Real?

But at the same time, an inner unease began to grow in me. What if it was real? What if the priests had not set up a light show ahead of time? What if the flashes I saw were not manmade?

Then, who could have made them? If not who, what could have made them? How were they made? Where were they coming from? They definitely were not lightning. There was not a cloud in the sky. If they were not lightning, what were they?

Why did I feel the way I did, on the verge of tears? Why did the air feel as if it was charged with electricity? Why did I feel so energized? Was it a mass hallucination? Was I feeling a crowd effect?

I had certainly never felt this way at a rock concert where even more people attended. I had never felt this way at any other meeting of peoples before, whether at an entertainment event, or a religious event. It was certainly powerful.

There have been many times that I have looked back on this event. In doing so, I have mused how those of us who live in technologically advanced countries are so used to all kinds of light phenomena—from neon store signs to laser lights at grocery check out stands to the tiny laser lights we hold under our palms in the mouse controls we use to direct the cursors on our computers.

We have gigantic spotlights that light up the night sky, crisscrossing in dramatic patterns. In fact, the downtown streets of many of our big cities glow so brightly that nighttime photographs from space show the blaze of our large cities.

We go to the movies and see phenomenal special effects. Space ships speed through space. Light sabers flare. Planets explode. Schoolchildren fly on broomsticks. Wands flip and multi-headed monsters appear. Ghosts hover. Unicorns glow in the night.

We have seen everything. There is not much that amazes us. It is not like we are people who need to get into the house before nightfall. We do not depend on the glow of a fire to light our nights. We just flick on a switch and it is daytime in the house. We are not like Thomas Jefferson who had to have his evening meal by three in the afternoon during the winter so the serving staff could clean up before dark.

We have a scientific explanation for everything and anything. Or do we?

All I knew as I stood on that rooftop surrounded by praying, chanting people in the dark hours of the morning was that something amazing was happening. I could not explain it. It did not make sense.

And so, all I could do was to live in the moment and click the shutter of my camera. In all, I took two rolls of 36 exposure film—a total of 72 pictures.

I began to have strange feelings as if the Virgin communicated with me. She seemed to expect something of me.

I felt afraid. My hypnosis sessions had opened me up to an amazing understanding of existence that had changed my life. Now I had a new occupation where I wrote books and gave seminars. It had been earth shattering to make these changes.

I felt as if Mary scrutinized me. She felt powerful. She seemed to delve into the depths of me. There was a feeling as if I fell short of her expectations. The feeling intensified. She had tasks for me. What if she gave me another ridiculous task like visiting a grotto? What if she insisted I join the throngs of people, many of whom were much better qualified than me, who were trying to open a secret room in a pyramid? Could I deny her any request?

I did not want to change. I had had enough of change.

At one time, as the flashes increased, I heard someone say in English that they saw someone on the roof of the church.

Hah! I thought. *The priests are lifting the electronic device that creates the apparition up on to the roof.*

Then someone said, "No, there is no one there."

Still, the seed had been planted in my mind. I decided I now knew how the priests did it. They had constructed a figure made of neon. They brought it out onto the roof while the crowd was distracted by the flashes of light. In the periods of darkness, the priests worked with stealth. I knew that at the proper time, they would suddenly turn on the electric current connected to the neon statue and we would all believe we had seen a miracle.

I waited with anticipation to see the neon spectacle, unsure of how I would explain it if the glowing figure moved or, heaven forbid, floated.

The flashes continued to build in intensity. Around me, from the surrounding rooftops, the people chanted with increasing vigor. That plaintiff female call soared above the chanting voices.

The feeling that I may fall on my knees and pray or that I was about to cry . . . or even faint . . . became intense. The sense that Mary was there with me terrified me. In my mind's eye I could see her glowing form fly over to me.

This couldn't be happening to me, I thought. *I have to control myself—think of something else, concentrate on my photographs.*

If something appears, it can't really be the Virgin Mary in spirit form. It has to be a manmade phenomenon. It can't be real!

True Confessions

The reality is that I grew up in a largely Atheistic household.

When my first book, *The Golden Ones*, was published, because it described my experience with a vision of the Jesus, and my past life memories of being in the Holy Land when the Master walked the earth, I felt I had to tell my family beforehand.

One by one I took my loved ones aside to tell them. It was like "coming out of the closet" to admit to my family members that I believed in God and in an afterlife.

"That's OK," one of my brothers told me. "We love you anyway. Actually, we've suspected for some time."

I really do appreciate that my family loves me anyway. Basically, I believe that whether my family believes in God or not, their souls . . . and everyone else's . . . will continue to live after they die. Many of my family members believe that no matter how much I believe in an afterlife, when I die . . . and everyone else dies . . . there will be nothing. And, we're OK with it and love each other anyway and even talk with each other about our differing views.

My grandparents came out of Russia and the Ukraine during the time of the Czars. They were peasants . . . serfs . . . owned people with masters. They came to the new world for freedom.

The church had been extremely corrupt in their homeland so when they came here, many of them forsook the oppressive religion of their childhood. As a result, I grew up in a family that ranged from interested nonbelievers to outright atheists.

We occasionally went to church, especially at Christmas and Easter. We attended church banquets, but at home there were no prayers, no devotions, and no belief. We had many discussions about philosophy, religion, and human nature but there was nothing in my childhood that made me feel either punished by a vengeful God . . . or protected by a loving God.

On the other hand, the members of my family were open-minded about religion. They had the viewpoint that Jesus had to have been a wonderful teacher and healer—why else would He be remembered thousands of years later. However, they believed that all the supernatural stories of, for example, Jesus leaving on a cloud, were the result of the powerful clergy preying upon ignorant, superstitious minds.

The good thing about this kind of childhood is that I was never made to feel afraid that if I did not do what the church said, I would have to go to Hell or to suffer Fire and Brimstone. I was good enough just the way I was. There would basically be no Hell to torment me. And, since my family was open-minded, if I wanted to believe it, there was no proof, but there just might be a heaven.

Another advantage of this kind of upbringing is that I did not grow up with a preconceived dogma explaining what religious texts were supposed to mean. I believe that my ability to see the myths of ancient peoples, including the Christian story, from a new perspective—in terms of the history of the soul through the root races—came from my free-thinking childhood.

In addition, I was allowed to explore religious beliefs on my own. Because of their open-mindedness, my family allowed me to attend the once-a-week religion classes provided in the public schools in Canada. My desire to hear God's voice started there.

One week, when I was in grade two or three, I learned about young David who prayed to God and then heard God's reply. I really wanted God to talk to me, too. Therefore, when I came home from school, I entered my parent's bedroom, closed the door, sank down on my knees and prayed. I waited but heard no reply. When I came out of the bedroom, my Dad asked me, "What were you doing in there?"

I told my father about the lesson in school and my experiment when God did not speak to me. "Now you know," he told me.

In recalling this story, I realize that my quest to hear God's voice started long ago in my childhood and has been fulfilled as described in *When We Were Gods*.

My grandfather set the tone for my family's lack of religious belief. On those few occasions when my family did go to church, for example, at Christmas or Easter, my grandfather who never went to church would be sure to tell me, "Don't believe a word they [in church] told you."

So there you have it. Although my family prided themselves on their open-mindedness, they "knew" that the silly stories of God speaking from a cloud, "This is my Son, my Chosen; listen to him!" (Luke 9:35) were stories written by ignorant, superstitious people who were uneducated and full of fear. They felt that people who believed these stories were preyed upon by the church.

My first books dealt with personal experiences that revealed that we are truly spiritual beings who are immortal. It also explained how the Christ Consciousness fits into the ancient myths about the root races that became the basis of our religions.

Therefore, it was now a big step for me to consider that not only are we spiritual, immortal beings, but it may be that there truly are supernatural beings out there who are deeply concerned with our welfare.

In other words, I was now confronting my childhood training that said that if you believed in the supernatural, you must be an ignorant, superstitious person.

What if Mary really did appear? What if she floated, or in some other way made it obvious that she was not a manmade light show created by the priests?

In my first book I described how I dealt with my unusual experiences by fearing I might be crazy. What an easy out! However, in Asyut, I would not be able to say I was crazy because everyone else would see Mary also. Would that mean we were all crazy? Would we all be superstitious, ignorant people? Would it mean we had been duped by the priests? Were our minds being controlled? Were we hallucinating? All of us?

What was creating those brilliant flashes? Why were they coming from so many different directions? Why wasn't there any lightning in the sky? How could birds be lit up like that? There had to be a natural explanation for it all. Or, were we all having a mass hallucination?

Of course, while standing on the rooftop, feeling as if Mary talked with me, shaking with fear that she might actually appear, and that I might make a spectacle of myself I was not thinking any of this through. I was just a quivering emotional mess.

What would I do if she appeared?

It couldn't possibly be real because my Dad had told me it couldn't be. And my grandfather made sure that I would always remember, "Don't believe a word they tell you."

Time to Leave

All of a sudden everyone on the rooftop began making movements as if they were leaving. They gathered sandwich wrappings into their picnic baskets, collected their purses, and called to their children. The men folded up the metal chairs and placed them in a stack against the outside wall of the roof.

What? I thought. *But we haven't seen the apparition yet!* Mohga confirmed my fears. We were leaving. She explained that the apparition, if it appeared, usually occurred by five in the morning and it was past that time.

I felt bewildered and angry. Couldn't we stay until daybreak? At the time, I did not realize how much I wanted to see the apparition. I only knew that I felt full of conflicting emotions.

Also, I knew that Wahid and Mervat's little boys needed to get to bed. It was way past their bedtimes. Everyone had been so kind to make this opportunity possible. And, I really had no choice in the matter. As Wahid said, sometimes she appeared and other times she did not.

Back to the Apartment

I filed down the dark stairway with everyone else and shuffled through the alleyways to the prearranged place where Wahid picked us up in his car. Once back at Wahid's parents' apartment, I sat on the couch in the muted light of the living room.

Rena's friend, Mary, kept me company. We whispered so as not to wake up Wahid's parents who had not come with us. They slept in an adjacent bedroom.

The next thing I knew, someone tapped my shoulder. My mouth felt funny. I could feel rough fabric against my lips and teeth. *Where am I?* I thought. *What's going on?* I opened my eyes. Glancing up, I saw Mervat's kind face staring down at me. I was lying with my mouth open against the rough upholstery fabric of the living room sofa. I realized what had probably happened. In mid-sentence, while talking with Mary, I must have fallen asleep while sitting up and keeled over. *How embarrassing!*

Mervat offered me the bed she shared with Wahid so I could sleep lying down instead of with my face on the sofa. She said that she and Wahid did not mind sleeping with their sons for the night.

I know I did not express my gratitude enough for the wonderful sacrifices they made on my behalf because I fell asleep almost before I took my shoes off and as soon as I sat on their bed.

I did not know that while I slept, the young people in the group—Rena, Mary, Marcos, and their cousins—went up on the rooftop of the apartment building. Although they were now further away from the church, they did see the apparition.

I slept right through it!

That's right. It was one of the biggest events of my life, but where was I? Asleep!

It turned out that Peggy had slept through the apparition as well. In the morning, when she found out, she talked with Rena, Mary, and Marcos who were in the kitchen eating breakfast. She wanted to know if they had really seen it.

"Yes," they replied. It really did happen. They told us that it really was a brilliant figure of light blazing in the night.

"That's good enough for me," Peggy said. I admired her equanimity. I, on the other hand, felt disappointed that I had missed it. In retrospect, I wish I had asked to stay another night. But our train tickets were booked, and at the time, I still struggled with the conviction that the apparition might actually be a manmade electronic light show.

When we talked on the telephone recently, Peggy said that she felt like the Apostles when Jesus faced his imminent Crucifixion at Gethsemane. Afraid, he had asked the Apostles to stay up and pray with him. But they fell asleep. He asked them three times but they fell asleep three times.

I had felt so drowsy, it almost felt like the fairytale story of Sleeping Beauty when her whole kingdom is put into a sleep for a hundred years until she wakes up. I felt as if some irresistible force had put me to sleep.

Perhaps I had to sleep because that was the only way I could handle the possibility that the Holy Mother might actually appear. Perhaps the Apostles kept falling asleep when Jesus faced his imminent death because they just could not bear it either.

When I think back to that very special time in Asyut, I am overwhelmed with appreciation for the risk Mohga and her family took with Peggy and me. Mohga could have decided not to take us to Asyut as soon as she learned from her travel agent cousin that tourists were not allowed in that city. But she kept her word to us, and I am so grateful. It truly was an experience of a lifetime.

When I left Asyut, I knew I had been profoundly changed by the events of the night before. Something had touched me to my core. I also felt confused and a little shaken. It has taken me years to fully appreciate the wonderful experience that came my way seemingly out of nowhere.

Today, I still ponder the amazing flashes I saw and the feeling of expectancy and electricity I felt that night. Although I did not see Mary, I most certainly felt her. She felt most amazingly powerful, good, perfect, all-knowing, and kind but also keenly and sharply full of an expectation that I do something that is worthwhile with my life. She demanded it of me.

I feel very blessed to have stood in the midst of her energy. There was an aspect of it that is beyond my comprehension and beyond my ability to convey. All I can say is that she resonated in my deepest depths with a part of me I did not even know existed.

As I left Asyut, I did not expect that there would be more to my encounter with Mary. However, as I reveal in the next chapter, I would soon discover that the Holy Mother had more in store for my unbelieving mind to confront.

Chapter Eighteen

DID MARY PROVIDE PROTECTION?

Leaving Cairo

When we returned to Cairo, Peggy and I moved to Mena House so I could get early morning photographs of the Sphinx and Great Pyramid. Early morning and late afternoon light are good for photography in the tropics or during the hazy days of summer. Because Peggy left a day before me, I had one full day to devote to photographing these ancient marvels, a lifetime dream come true.

After taking my photos, the next morning, I awoke at 1:00 a.m. to make my flight, which was scheduled to leave at 2:55 a.m. By now I was getting used to being awake most of the time and at different times of the day and night . . . and carrying on in spite of exhaustion. One in the morning? No problem.

As previously arranged with the front desk, a taxi-driver picked me up at Mena House and dropped me off at Cairo International Airport. Again, I flew Lufhansa.

My flight arrangements had been made a day before I left the U.S. because of changes in my husband's schedule. It was a last minute flight. Therefore, my connection was out of the way in Frankfurt, Germany, followed by a long layover in the airport while I waited for my flight to Barcelona.

Knowing my husband well, I had called home the day before and told my daughter that I definitely was flying to Barcelona the next day. I knew that John would not be absolutely sure about the time or even the day I would be arriving in Barcelona. Likely the paper on which I had written my flight information had become misplaced among his papers. Because I felt nervous about being totally alone in Barcelona, a non-English-speaking country, where no one would be waiting for me if John did not turn up, I felt that the telephone call home was a very necessary expense.

I had a considerable amount of time in the Frankfurt airport to gather my thoughts. I sat down at one of the tables, wrote down some notes about my experiences in Egypt on the notepad I always carried with me, and thought about my upcoming reunion with John. Even though I had been disappointed that he had decided not to come with me, I looked forward to seeing him again.

When the plane landed, I moseyed along with the other people from my flight. We followed the exit and baggage symbols down numerous hallways, made a number of turns, showed our passports a couple of times, and finally arrived at a large room containing four baggage kiosks. Unfortunately, none of the baggage kiosks produced baggage from our flight.

Lost in the Barcelona Airport

Somehow I had become lost in the Barcelona airport. In fact, I discovered that I had somehow ended up in the wrong terminal. I had no idea where I was and no one around me spoke English. Eventually, I found someone who could help me.

I found my luggage. It was in a dark corner office in a special section for misplaced baggage. I went through customs and had my passport stamped. Ahead of me, I saw a wall of gray doors. Through the cracks between the doors, I could see brilliant sunshine, which made ribbons of light on the dark floor.

This was it—the end of the line. When I opened the doors, I would leave the secured area of the Barcelona airport. It was now over an hour and a half since my plane had landed. Would John be waiting for me on the other side of the gray doors? Or, had he left the airport believing he had come to pick me up on the wrong day?

My backpack weighed heavily on my shoulders as I pulled forward my two wheeled suitcases and opened the doors. Bright sunlight streamed in through glass floor-to-ceiling windows. Silhouettes of people sitting in chairs lined the bottom of the windows.

I walked into a roped off area where, I imagine, passengers are expected to step out to be greeted by loved ones. Because I had become separated from the other people on my flight, I was the only one standing there. Blinded by the brilliance of the sunlight after the dark interior of the building, I squinted, hoping to see John's familiar form silhouetted in the blazing sunlight.

I saw only one person stand up and walk toward me. It was a tall, husky man—John! He was there! I felt like we were in one of those commercials where the man and woman come running toward each other in slow motion. People around us sighed as we grasped each other in our arms and embraced.

"I thought I had lost you," he murmured in my ear. He held me in his arms and kissed me. More sighing followed all around us.

I tell you, after all our disagreements over my going off to Egypt alone, I could see that the both of us had rethought our opinions of the other. I had missed him so much. I could see that the feeling was mutual.

He grabbed one of my wheeled suitcases as we headed toward the exit doors. "I thought I got the wrong day," he told me. "I had almost given up waiting."

"Did you call home?"

"Yeah," he said.

I gave him a squeeze, thankful that I knew him well enough to know that he might fear he remembered the day wrong. I also felt grateful that my intuition must have known I would be late and that he would need assurance he had come on the correct day.

He hugged me with one arm as he pulled my wheeled suitcase with his other arm. "I was afraid you got caught in the riot."

"What?" I said.

"The riot."

"The riot?" I said. "What riot?"

"The one in Cairo."

I stopped walking and looked up at him. We were now out in the parking lot. Sunlight streamed down on us. The fragrance of earth and flowers surrounded me.

"Wait a minute, John. What are you talking about?"

"Israel just declared war on Palestine. There has been widespread rioting in Cairo."

My mouth dropped open. "Are you kidding? When?"

"Today. Now."

He explained that he had been watching the British Broadcasting Corporation television station in his hotel room while he waited for the right time to pick me up at the airport. News of the war and the riots in Cairo cycled throughout the day.

"You're kidding," I said.

"When did your flight leave?" he asked me.

"At 2:55 a.m."

"Amazing," he said. "You got out just in time. The riots started at daybreak."

"After I was in the air," I said with incredulity.

I learned later that Egyptian tour guides preparing to lead groups from the United States and Canada had been notified that their tours had been cancelled. No one could get into Egypt for weeks after the rioting.

And, to think, I had been there, safe and sound, and left at exactly the right moment.

While writing this book, I looked online for documentation of the rioting in Cairo and found none. I also could not find documentation supporting a declaration of war by Israel. However, I did find information saying that peace talks had been in progress at the time. Perhaps declarations of war had been threatened during the peace talks.

I did find archived articles by the *London Times*. One article, dated Monday, October 2, 2000, said that Israeli troops had killed a ten-year-old boy the day before, which was the day I flew out of Cairo. Evidently, his death was the 28th Muslim fatality in only four days. He was also the third child killed in that short time. I can see why people in Egypt would be outraged.

In Barcelona, John and I drove to the hotel. He turned to me and asked me if I had had any problems with violence.

"No," I told him. "None at all. My travel in Egypt was fantastic. Wherever I went and whatever I did—everyone I met—everything about Egypt was wonderful, friendly, and helpful."

Then he told me about his experience in Barcelona. It turned out that John had been assaulted in the subway by pickpockets. Fortunately, he had managed to hold on to his wallet and scare his assailants away.

How ironic, we both agreed. He had feared to go to Egypt because of violence. Instead, he stayed in Barcelona where he thought he would be safe and had been assaulted. I had gone to Egypt, naively unafraid that all would be well in spite of the warnings of violence, and had experienced only safety.

Photographs of the Flashes in Asyut

I could hardly wait to get home to develop my film. I feared the photographs taken in the pharaohs' tombs in the Valley of the Kings would not turn out because of the low lighting.

Even though I work with a marvelous professional film lab in Hampton, Virginia, I feared the professionals at the lab would not be able to push process the film adequately to produce viable images. To my great relief, the photographs turned out good enough—not great because of the low light, but enough photos turned out that I could use them to illustrate Chapter Eleven, "Winged Serpents in the Pharaohs' Tombs," and Chapter Twelve, "Light Beings in the Pharaoh's Tomb." The photographs were also good enough to show in slide presentations during my speeches. I felt elated and very grateful for the fine work done in the lab.

On the other hand, I did not expect any problems with the pictures taken of the flashes leading up to the apparition of the Virgin in Asyut. For those of you experienced in nighttime photography using film, I had taken 72 exposures with the aperture of the camera lens set at f8, the exposure on bulb. I had used a cable release and had taken exposures from a second to ten minutes. My film was ASA 200. Because I did not know the intensity of the flashes, I simply left the film opened to light and closed the shutter after a flash would occur. If the flashes were very bright, they would show on the film after one flash.

Just in case the flashes were not that bright—I had no way of knowing, but they looked like lightning and I had photographed lightning successfully many times before—I also left the shutter open long enough so that many flashes in a row would be recorded in the same exposure. In Asyut, numerous flashes often occurred in the same place in rapid succession. That way, if the flashes were not as bright, the repeated light in the same place would register on the emulsion of the film. I left the lens open to light for up to ten minutes whenever a series of flashes occurred.

I knew my techniques would work because I had had numerous nighttime photo shoots of aircraft at NASA. One of the photos I had taken this way won an honorable mention at a prestigious national photography contest. I knew what I was doing.

When I picked up my photographs at the lab, I saw that every one of my nighttime photographs of Asyut had turned out. In the pictures, I could see the domes of the church, the people on the rooftops, and the blazing lights of the city. Some of the photographs which had been exposed the shortest length of time only showed the city lights. I knew that if the city lights turned out, the flashes would turn out, because the flashes were much, much brighter. Other photographs, which had been exposed the longest time, showed the church steeples almost as brightly as if the photograph had been taken in daylight.

To my great surprise, I saw no lightning-like flashes in any of the photographs. Not even a hint of one. Even in the longest exposed images, where I knew there had been multiple flashes in quick succession, nothing registered on the emulsion of the film. Nothing! Of 72 exposures, not a single flash appeared! You could see everything else in the photograph—church, people, rooftops, and city lights—but not a single hint of a lightning-like flash.

I felt so shocked that I put the transparencies away and could not look at them. I had never before taken photographs where the image was technically correct but parts of the photo were missing.

It would be like taking a picture of houses on a street and, when you picked up your photographs from the lab, everything in the picture would be in the picture—the trees, the street, the sidewalk, the children playing—but there would be no houses.

It took me about a week before I could take the photos out and look at the images again. By now, the shock was sufficiently behind me that I could examine the photos thoroughly and objectively for any hint of a flash. I did find one image of a tiny flash from someone's flash camera from across the square. However, my examination of my slides did not reveal even a hint of the multitude of blinding flashes I had seen against the church coming from many directions that amazing night in Asyut.

There was no explanation for it. Here was a great mystery! When I told people about it, they said that you could not photograph apparitions of the Virgin Mary. I had never heard of that. I told them that I had seen the images of the flashes and the apparition on Wahid's videotape.

"Ah, yes," they said, "but that was on videotape. It's a different medium—electronic. You were using emulsion-based film."

I did some research on the internet and found nothing about difficulty photographing the Virgin. Maybe I did not look at the right web sites. I did see images of apparitions, including the apparition at Asyut. There were also photos of the apparition, which had appeared in 1968, at Zeitun, a suburb of Cairo.

Someone was obviously taking photographs of the apparitions. Or, were these photos taken from videotape? Actually, one photograph of the Asyut apparition was accompanied by a caption saying that it was taken with a camera without a flash. That would definitely not be a video camera.

It has occurred to me since doing research into the apparitions of the Virgin that when people say you cannot photograph the apparitions, they must mean the kind of apparitions that only the visionaries can see. In that case, there is nothing for participants to see or to photograph.

In this short exposure, for one flash, only the city lights of the lighted square are visible on the left.

This is a longer exposure for a couple of flashes. The translucent image of a person on the balcony on the right occurred when the person moved in this longer exposure.

A long exposure, in which there were many flashes. The shutter of the camera remained opened so long that the sky looks almost as light as day. The city lights blaze on the left, but there is no sign of any flashes.

However, in Asyut, everyone could see the apparition and its accompanying flashes, and also photograph them. Someone in the U.S. suggested that perhaps the flashes were so faint that they did not turn up on my film. Impossible. The lights of the city, which were much dimmer than the flashes, registered even in the shortest exposures.

There is simply no explanation for 72 photographs showing the people on the balconies and rooftops, the city lights, the church steeples . . . but no ethereal flashes.

Ah, so you have noticed my use of the word, "ethereal." After spending numerous pages describing the flashes as a manmade light show, I am suddenly calling them "ethereal."

Ah hah!

The truth is that until I received my photographs from the lab, I still held on to the notion that I had perhaps seen an electronic light show put on by the priests. Now I knew that it had to be something else. If it had been a manmade light show I would have captured the images on my film, just as I had captured the images of airplanes in my nighttime photographs at NASA. If it had been a natural event, like the lightning I had photographed previously, the images would have turned out also.

There had to be another explanation, and, I had to admit, the only other explanation had to be that I had actually viewed a supernatural event.

The flashes should have looked like this. These are photographs made from the videotaped images taken by Wahid's video camera.

As you can see in the images from Wahid's videotape below, the flashes were so brilliant that they wiped out everything else in the electronic image. They were truly blazing.

At the time, I did not know that I was not the only one who had reservations about the authenticity of the Asyut phenomena. While doing research for this book, I discovered that to allay conjecture that the Asyut apparition had been produced electronically, the city of Asyut had turned off all the electricity in the neighborhood of Saint Mark's Cathedral one night.

Photographs by Wahid Refaat Sedra

Lightning-like flashes blazed from all directions illuminating the steeples of St. Mark's Cathedral. Note the unusual image bottom left. If manmade spotlights had illuminated the steeples, the top part of the steeples would have also been blazing with light in this image.

The flashes and the apparition still appeared. That meant that the flashes I saw were actually part of the apparition. It also meant that the flashes and the apparition were not a manmade light show. They were real supernatural events.

Wow! I had seen something real that was unfathomable. It was not special effects, as in a movie. It was not a hoax, as in a Halloween haunted house. It was not magic, as in sleight of hand. It was something real, and it was more than natural. It was supernatural.

I have read that Mary manifests in whatever way a person can best understand her. If I had seen her on the roof of St. Mark's Cathedral, I would have either assumed the priests had made a neon image that they placed on the rooftop . . . or fainted.

The universe must have known that only photographs would convince me. There is simply no scientific explanation for everything else registering on the silver emulsion of my film except the flashes.

Here is how the apparition looked. Again, the image is a photograph from Wahid's videotape. I have labeled it so you can understand the image better.

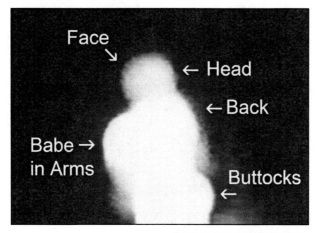

Photograph by Wahid Refaat Sedra

One view of the apparition of the Virgin Mary as she appeared in Asyut in September 2000.

If you remember, I said that it made sense that she could appear as a Light Being since I had seen the archangels, including the Christ, in their Light Body form during my hypnosis sessions.

For apparitions to be accredited by the church, they need to fulfill certain criteria. Usually these criteria are quite stringent and take a long time because the church dignitaries cannot see the apparition. They have to take the word of the visionaries.

However, in Asyut, the dignitaries of the church could see the apparition with their own eyes. Therefore, the accreditation process proceeded rapidly. Mary's appearance has been accredited by the Orthodox Pope H. H. Shenouda III, Patriarch of Alexandria.

Here are more images from Wahid's videotape. The images show how the apparition moved and changed and also the companion that sometimes accompanied her.

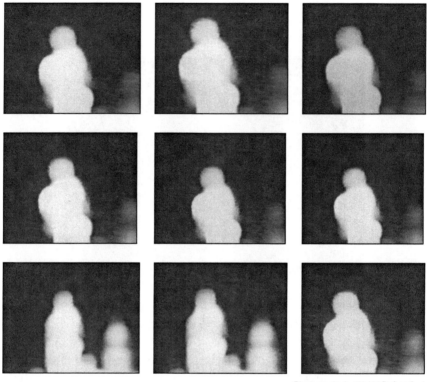

Photographs by Wahid Refaat Sedra

Numerous views of the Marian apparition in Asyut showing movement of the figure and including various aspects of her companion.

Chapter Nineteen

BLESSED AMONG WOMEN

What Is an Apparition of the Virgin Mary?

According to Roy Abraham Varghese, author of *God Sent: A History of the Accredited Apparitions of Mary,* apparitions of the Virgin Mary are God reaching out to mankind in a form that humanity can understand. Since Mary has already been the emissary of God by bringing forth His Son, she carries on as a handmaid of the divine by continuing to bring the spiritual into our lives.

How often has Mary appeared? I have discovered that, according to Joan Ashton in *Mother of All Nations: The Visitations of the Blessed Virgin Mary and Her Message for Today,* she has appeared at least 21,000 times in the past one thousand years.

Most of the time only one, or at the most, only a handful of visionaries can see her. For example in Lourdes, France, only one person, a young peasant girl called Bernadette Soubirous, saw a beautiful glowing woman appear in a cave in 1858. Similarly, only three peasant children could see the lady dressed in white who shone more brightly than the sun when she appeared in a hilly region of Fatima, Portugal, in 1917.

It is relatively unusual that two million people would be able to see her, as was the case in Asyut.

Prophecies

Mary frequently makes prophecies, which come true. For example, during her manifestation in Amsterdam, Holland, on March 25, 1945, she predicted the end of World War II. The visionary Ida Peerdeman, a forty-year-old single woman who lived with her sisters, saw a beautiful woman step out of a glowing cloud in the living room of the house the sisters shared. No one else could see the luminous woman.

During this Amsterdam manifestation, the Blessed Virgin called herself the Mother of All Nations or the Mother of All Peoples. The Dutch word Mary used can be translated into English as either "nations" or "peoples." In any case, Mary wanted it known that she considers herself the mother of everyone—in every country and every religion—on earth.

Some of her prophecies in Amsterdam, as they had been in Fatima, were apocalyptic in nature—having to do with the end of the world as we know it. She predicted a time of peace after the Second World War followed by another great catastrophe.

Between 1961 and 1965, she also appeared in Garabandal, Spain, to four girls aged 12 to 13 and made predictions of a terrible chastisement by fire. Also in Akita, Japan, during Mary's visits from 1973 to 1981, the visionary Sister Agnes Sasagawa heard Mary say that a terrible punishment of fire would fall from the sky and obliterate much of humanity.

As a counterpart to these dire predictions, Mary also tells us how to avert the calamitous future she sees us heading towards by returning to an appreciation of God's prominence in our lives.

Warnings and Hope

Mary often tempers her messages of warning with suggestions of what to do to turn away the calamities she sees forthcoming. For example, in her 1846 appearance to two peasant children in La Salette, France, she included the admonition that the local people needed to mend their ways. Unless they returned to spiritual devotion, the population's staple crops of potatoes, walnuts, and grapes would fail that year and children would die trembling in their parents' arms. As it turned out, the crops did fail and thousands of children died of cholera, trembling as they passed away, just as Mary had predicted.

Fortunately, she also comes to bring hope. A few years later, in 1871, she appeared again in France during a war between that country and Prussia. At the time, the Prussian army had swept through France. They had overrun Paris and were now approaching Brittany, the northwestern corner of France, which included the village of Pontmain. The people of the village prayed for the safe return of thirty-eight of their young men who were fighting the war against the Prussians.

Late in the afternoon of January 17, the Virgin Mary appeared to six youngsters. During this manifestation she did not speak but words appeared on a scroll she held. The words said that her Son, Jesus, had allowed himself to be moved, meaning that the prayers of the people would be granted.

At the same time as the Virgin appeared to the children, the Prussian army mysteriously stopped in their tracks. Some of the soldiers said they could see an image of the Virgin in the sky. The Prussian commander, General Schmidt, said that his army could not proceed because the Holy Mother protected Brittany. He could not go forward.

As it turned out, all thirty-eight of the young men who had fought in that war came home to Pontmain unscathed.

Solar Phenomena

As I said earlier, usually only one or, at most, a handful of visionaries can see her during the appearances when Mary speaks. Nonetheless, there are also instances when thousands of onlookers who flock to the event can also see flashes of light, as I did in Asyut.

At other times, they also see solar phenomena, often during the time the visionaries are communicating with the apparition. A young man I met while traveling in Costa Rica told me how he had been part of the crowds in Cincinnati, Ohio, USA, when a visionary communicated with Mary. Unfortunately, I did not think to ask the man what year these apparitions occurred or the name of the visionary. However, there are postings on the internet about Sister Mildred Mary Neuzil who saw various apparitions, including the Virgin Mary, in and near the city of Cincinnati, Ohio from 1938 until her death in 2000. The young man told me that although he could not see Mary, he did see the sun become a gray disc so he could look at it without hurting his eyes. Then, the sun spun around and "danced" in the sky.

These solar phenomena have occurred at other times when Mary has appeared, for example, in Fatima, Portugal, in 1917, in Kerizinen, France in 1953 , in San Damiano, Italy, in 1964, and in Lipa, Philippines, in 1948 and 1949.

Photographing Apparitions of the Virgin Mary

I also learned of an interesting corollary to my inability to photograph the phenomena in Asyut. In *The Great Apparitions of Mary: An Examination of Twenty-two Supranormal Appearances*, the author Ingo Swann describes a visitation of Mary in Bayside, Queens, New York City, in 1970.

Veronica Leuken, the visionary, was the only one who could see Mary. However, Mary told Veronica to tell the thousands of on-lookers who flocked to the event to take Polaroid pictures, pointing their cameras where they saw nothing. Amazingly, images appeared on many of the Polaroid films, including one of the Virgin on top of the nearby Church of St. Robert Bellarmine.

In my Asyut experience, my camera did not record what I, and thousands of others, could see. In Bayside, Queens, New York City, the camera recorded what no one but the visionary could see.

First Appearance

The Blessed Virgin's first appearance occurred when she was still alive. In A.D. 40, the Apostle James the Greater saw her while he was in Saragossa, Spain. At the same time she was still living in the Holy Land, an example of bilocation—being in two places at once.

She is presently appearing in a number of places. Notable among them is a small Bosnian village called Medjugorje—the place that started with an "M" that Peggy had visited.

In Medjugorje, six visionaries began to see Mary in 1981. True to her usual way of appearing to bring hope during times of trouble, Mary manifested in Bosnia during a very bloody war, considered to be the worst European atrocities since World War II. However, even though fighting surrounded Medjugorje, the town remained safe, evidence of the Virgin's protection.

At times, her appearances have had profound effects on the nation she visits. In 1531, when she appeared in Guadalupe, Mexico, her manifestation influenced the lives of 8,000 indigenous Aztecs. As a result of her visitation, the nation turned away from the ritual human sacrifice of their religion to the Christian religion.

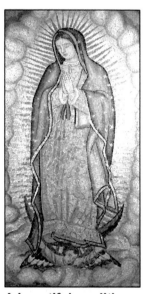

Juan Diego, the 57-year-old visionary, found her image on the inside of his cape when he brought flowers to the local bishop. The bishop had asked for a sign from Mary of her authenticity. The flowers turned out to be Castilian roses, which had not yet been imported to the New World from Spain.

A beautiful rendition of the Guadalupe Virgin on display at the Mary Queen of the Universe Shrine in Orlando, Florida

No one knows how the image appeared on Juan Diego's cape. He said it looked like the woman whom he had seen floating on the hilltop. In effect, Mary had left her image on the inside of his cape.

The image shows a young woman with a slender and serene face who appears to be in the early stages of pregnancy. Her skin color has somewhat of a bronze cast so that many people believe she looks as if she is Aztec, as was Juan Diego.

Over the years, the original image on the cape has been embellished. For example, a black outline and rays were added plus the moon has been painted under her feet.

In his native tongue, Juan Diego's cape is known as a tilma. It is made of cactus fibers and normally disintegrates in about 20 years—100 years for sure. However, more than 470 years later, in the 21st century, Juan Diego's tilma and its miraculous image of the Virgin still exists intact and is on display under glass in the Old Basilica of Guadalupe in Mexico City.

Experts who have studied the image on the tilma say that the colors that make up the picture do not penetrate the fibers of the tilma as would ordinary paints. In addition, because the image appears on the irregular surface of the woven cactus fibers, one would expect the picture to look uneven, but it does not.

As I said earlier, Mary's image on Juan Diego's Tilma has Aztec features. That Mary looks as if she comes from the same heritage as the visionary is not unusual. In Dong Lu, China, she looked Chinese. In Walsingham, England, she looked Anglo-Saxon. When she appeared in Kibeho, Rwanda, she did not have white skin. Mary appears in whatever way it is the most comfortable for her visionaries to see her.

Miraculous Healings

Mary's visitations are often accompanied by miraculous cures. Sometimes she leaves behind healing springs, as she did in Lourdes, France. Or, an existing body of water starts to have miraculous curative powers as did a pond in Vailankanni, India, in the sixteenth century.

In Asyut, too, a number of people reported miraculous healings. Many of the cures were documented and investigated, such as the cure of a prolapsed disc, the total healing of multiple fractures of the spine and shoulder, the cure of a person with facial paralysis, as well as a person who was healed of bleeding piles.

During one visit of the Virgin in 1982, a visionary in Damascus, Syria, had the bizarre experience of oil seeping from her fingers. Myrna Nazzour had first seen Mary while praying for a relative who lay on the brink of death. When another relative praying at the deathbed rubbed the oil seeping from Myrna's fingers onto the dying woman, the terminally ill woman made a full recovery.

Miraculous cures also occurred in Banneux, Belgium when Mary appeared in January, 1933. In the dark of a cold winter evening, Mary led the visionary, a girl of 12, out of her yard, across the road, and to a small spring that flowed beside the road. The Virgin told the girl that the spring had been set aside for the Holy Mother, and it would be used to heal the sick of all nations.

During this visitation, Mary called herself the Virgin of the Poor, especially significant in 1933 since the world was going through the Great Depression. As a result of her appearance in Banneux, nine religious orders have built hospitals for the poor in the area.

Mother of All Peoples

As far as I can tell from my research, Mary has manifested on all of the continents except Antarctica. People of many nations, of many racial backgrounds, and of many religions—including atheists—have seen her. Over and over again, she makes it clear that she is here for all people, all nations, and all religions.

Here is a great story from *Mary's Message to the World* by Annie Kirkwood, a visionary living in the state of Texas, USA. Annie was a practical nurse. She knew that people who heard voices in their heads could be losing their mind. Therefore, when she started to hear Mary speaking to her, she wanted the voice to stop. She also could not believe Mary would speak to her since Annie was not Roman Catholic.

Therefore, Annie told Mary that the Holy Mother had made a mistake. Annie had a close friend who was Roman Catholic. Annie told Mary to speak to her Roman Catholic friend instead. However, Mary persisted and continued to give messages to Annie to share with the world. This went on for a number of days. Each time, Annie would tell Mary she had made a mistake—that Mary needed to talk to Annie's Roman Catholic friend instead.

One day, when Mary spoke to Annie, Annie again told the Holy Mother that she was making a mistake and that Annie was not Catholic. Mary replied that she was not Roman Catholic either. You probably know that Mary was actually Jewish.

Here is another wonderful story about Mary's universal motherhood for all people on earth. In Medjugorje, Bosnia, the visionaries, who were Christians, asked the Virgin to reveal to them the holiest person in the town. Mary replied that a good example of a person living a holy life was an elderly Muslim lady.

Over and over again, Mary makes it clear that she cares for all people on earth and that all people are equally important to her. For example, people of all faiths saw her during her appearance in Egypt, mentioned earlier. She manifested in a suburb of Cairo called Zeitun, which used to be the ancient city of Mataria. The Copt Orthodox Church over which Mary appeared in Zeitun is supposed to be built at the location where Mary, Joseph, and Baby Jesus lived during their exile in Egypt after they fled from Herod.

During the Virgin's 1968 visitation in Zeitun, approximately 250,000 people of all faiths . . . including those with no religious belief . . . saw the glowing figure that floated over the rooftop of Saint Mary's Church. Unlike Asyut, anyone could visit Zeitun, even foreigners.

At first mechanics at a garage across the street from the church thought a nun was about to commit suicide. A crowd formed when emergency vehicles appeared. However, the supposed nun disappeared. Mary reappeared a week later and continued her appearances for a number of months afterward, usually floating on top of the church. Sometimes, she appeared on one side of the roof. Then, she disappeared and suddenly appeared on the other side of the roof.

So many people came to see her in Zeitun that the garage where the mechanics first saw her had to be torn down to make a parking lot.

The Zeitun apparition is an example of one of her appearances where she is silent but seen by thousands. When approximately two million people saw her in Asyut, she was also silent. Crowds of people also saw her in Knock, Ireland in 1879, in Tilly-sur-Seulles, France in 1896, in Mantara, Lebanon in 1908 and 1911, as well as in Dong Lu, China in 1990 and then again in 1995.

Her Protection

Often, when many people can see the Holy Mother, she manifests at a time of great difficulty to give people hope and assurance of her protection. She frequently appears preceding or following a very difficult time in a group of peoples' lives.

For example, her 1968 Zeitun appearance occurred during a time of great turmoil in Egypt. In the same way, her 2000 appearance in Asyut occurred during a time of great unrest because of the threat of war in the Middle East. The people in Asyut in particular had suffered with terrorist attacks for 25 years.

When she appears to visionaries and speaks, she often makes predictions and offers advice to help the people. In 1981, when she manifested in Kibeho, Rwanda, she exhorted the visionaries to leave the country before further escalation of that country's brutal civil war. Many who did not leave were killed.

She also appeared to a visionary in Hrushiv, Ukraine in 1914, just before that country became overrun by the Bolsheviks. During her 1914 manifestation in Ukraine, she made predictions that the Ukrainian people would undergo terrible miseries but their anguish would be over by the end of the century. In 1987, she appeared in Hrushiv again, this time, one year after the terrible Chernobyl nuclear disaster in which so many Ukrainian people were contaminated with nuclear fallout. During her 1987 visitation she thanked the Ukrainian people for enduring all their suffering without losing their faith and promised them that their afflictions were over. She predicted they would become free of Soviet rule. They gained their freedom within a couple of years.

Graces to Give Us

For me, the best part of Mary's appearances on earth is her insistence that she has graces to give us. In Roy Abraham Varghese's beautiful book *God Sent*, the author details many apparitions of the Virgin Mary. I especially enjoyed reading about her appearance in Rue du Bac, Paris, France, in 1830, when she made it clear that it is one of her purposes to give us graces.

During this visit, the visionary saw Mary wearing jeweled rings. Rays of beautiful light streamed from some of the gems. Mary told the visionary, a novitiate nun named Catherine Laboure, that the reason light did not stream from all of her jewels was because these gems represented the graces she has to give us, but which we have not requested. She wanted us to ask her for her graces.

Furthermore, Mary has also said that when we pray, we often do not ask for the kind of graces she can give. Too often we ask for things we want, like a car or wealth, rather than qualities of the soul such as patience, strength, love, wisdom, or joy, which she can easily grant.

She also said that we should pray to her when we are troubled with what we consider to be trivial issues. Evidently, she wants to help us with the smallest difficulties in our lives.

Suffering and Sorrows

The question is: If Mary wants so much to give us her graces, why does she not heal all of us? Why do we have to suffer? There is no person on earth that has not endured some kind of loss. No one is free of imperfection or sorrow.

Because of the healings in Mary's presence and the healing springs that have appeared as a result of her manifestations, you would think that her purpose would be to heal us all.

I also wondered why the visionaries were not healed of afflictions. Even though the visionaries often experienced ecstasy during her appearances, they also sometimes suffered with diseases and even died at an early age.

As I said earlier, during her appearances in Fatima, Portugal, Mary told two of the three young visionaries that the two youngest would die soon. And, they did . . . of complications of the terrible influenza that swept through the world between 1918 and 1920. Before their passing, the two young peasant children who were under the age of ten said that they no longer feared death because they knew Mary would be waiting for them.

Bernadette Soubirous, the visionary in Lourdes, France, also knew about suffering. She had always been a sickly child suffering with asthma, the after effects of a bout with cholera. Considering that she had been so blessed to see the Holy Mother, you would expect that she would be cured of her asthma. However, even though many others were healed at the spring that appeared as a result of Mary's instructions to Bernadette, the young seer never benefited from the spring's healing powers herself. She died at the age of 32. Mary had told her that she could not make Bernadette happy in this world, but only in the next.

During her appearance in Cuena, Ecuador, from 1988 to 1990, she said those who are sick have been chosen by God to suffer on all of our behalf for our redemption.

She also reminds the seers that she, Mary, endured great suffering as did her son, Jesus. The implication is that it is part of the human condition to suffer.

The Rose

Paradoxically, the need for our suffering brings us to the subject of the rose. It is the most beautiful of flowers in both its appearance and fragrance, but at the same time, it is covered with hurtful thorns, representing our suffering and the sorrows of life.

Mary is often associated with the rose. Her special set of prayers are counted on a set of beads called a Rosary, which refers to a rose garden.

During some of her appearances, the fragrance of roses accompanies her manifestations, as it did in Naju, South Korea in 1985. Sometimes, visionaries become aware of a rose perfume before she appears as did Veronica Leuken in Bayside, Queens, New York City, in 1970.

Occasionally, rose petals float around her, as they did in San Damiano, Italy in 1964, at the same time as the visionaries saw and talked with her.

Mary's emblem, the Rose.

She has also worn a golden rose on the top of each foot as she did in Banneux, Belgium in 1933 or appeared with pink roses surrounding her feet as in Necedah, Wisconsin, USA in 1949.

The bush on which she floated in the cave when Bernadette Soubirous saw her in Lourdes, France, was a wild rose bush.

Earlier I mentioned the famous 1531 Mexican apparition of the Virgin in Guadalupe, Mexico. Here is more of the story. When the visionary Juan Diego obeyed Mary's insistence that he go to the bishop to describe Mary's manifestation, the bishop demanded a sign of her authenticity. After all, Juan Diego was just a peasant. What did he know?

Juan Diego felt discouraged. He did not know what to give the bishop to show that Mary's appearance was real. He decided to stay away from the place where he had originally seen the lovely 14-year-old girl who said she was the Mother of God.

However, she appeared to him again. He told her to find some-one else to do her bidding, preferably someone who had greater influence with the bishop. She told him to climb back up Tepeyac Hill, where he had first seen her. To his surprise, he saw the desert hilltop covered in blooming roses—even though it was December and the middle of winter.

He gathered these roses up in his cloak and presented them to the bishop. As mentioned earlier, when the bishop saw the roses, he recognized the roses as being a variety that did not exist in the New World—Castillian roses. He was convinced.

Personal Visions of Mary

The more I delved into research on the apparitions of the Virgin Mary, the more fascinated I became. I discovered that people have not only seen apparitions of her, but also visions. In *Visions of Mary: An Inspiring, Unforgettable Collection of Mary's*

Extraordinary Encounters with Ordinary People throughout History, the author Peter Eicher describes encounters with Mary through the centuries. Many who saw visions of Mary dedicated their lives to her and became saints.

An apparition is different from a vision in that you see an apparition with your eyes opened and a vision with your eyes closed.

Whereas *Visions of Mary* describes encounters with Mary in the past, G. Scott Sparrow's lovely book *Blessed Among Women: Encounters with Mary and her Message,* describes both the author's own contacts with Mary as well as those of many other contemporary people.

As I wrote this book, I discussed it with others. To my surprise and delight, I discovered that a number of people in my own circle of friends and acquaintances have seen either apparitions or visions of Mary in their lives today. These people felt they had been blessed by their association with Mary.

One woman told me how she had been on the brink of suicide when Mary appeared to her and told her that although her life seemed unbearable at the time, the woman had a good and fulfilling life ahead of her. With tears of gratitude, the woman did not end her life. As Mary predicted, the woman did have a good and fulfilling life.

Another woman told me she had been healed of cancer. Still another woman said that she received guidance from a presence she knew to be Mary who appeared to be sitting in the passenger seat of her car.

A staunch Atheist told me that on his wedding night many years ago, he dreamt of a woman floating above him. She wore a veil and a long robe, carried a huge cross, and told him not to marry his betrothed. He could also see the apparition floating above him when he woke up in the night. In the end, he married the next day anyway, suffered with years of unhappiness, and finally divorced his wife.

Blessed Among Women

I found the topic of Mary and her manifestations so interesting that I have been reading and researching about apparitions and visions. I find the concept that she is blessed among women especially captivating.

In addition, I love that she over and over again proclaims that she considers herself to be mother of all peoples on this planet. Most heartening, she declares herself to be co-advocate with Jesus and acts as an ambassador of peace giving instructions as to how we may finally bring about a lasting peace on earth.

Therefore, I wondered, who is Mary that she can make these claims? Is she merely the mother of Jesus or is she much more than that . . . a goddess in her own right?

             *   *   *

On the next three pages, please find maps showing apparition sites in the Americas, Europe, Africa, Asia, and Australia, including an enlarged map of Europe. These maps show some of the thousands of locations where Mary has appeared. Many of the apparitions at these sites have been officially accredited by the Roman or Orthodox Churches. Some are in the process of accreditation. Some are included for your information.

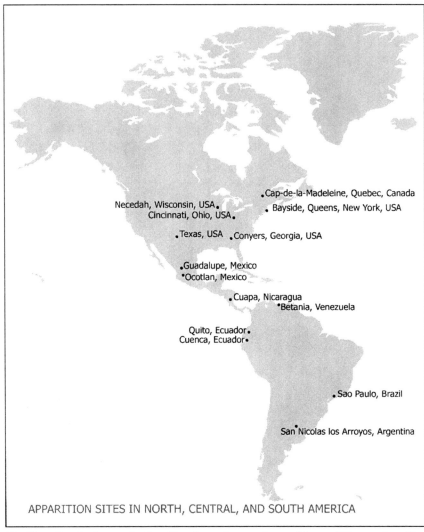

APPARITION SITES IN NORTH, CENTRAL, AND SOUTH AMERICA

North, Central, and South American Apparition Sites. On the following page, please find a map of Europe, Africa, Asia, and Australia, and, following that, an enlarged map of Europe. These maps show some of the thousands of locations where Mary has appeared. Many of these apparitions have been officially accredited by the Roman or Orthodox Churches. Some are in the process of accreditation. Some are included for your information.

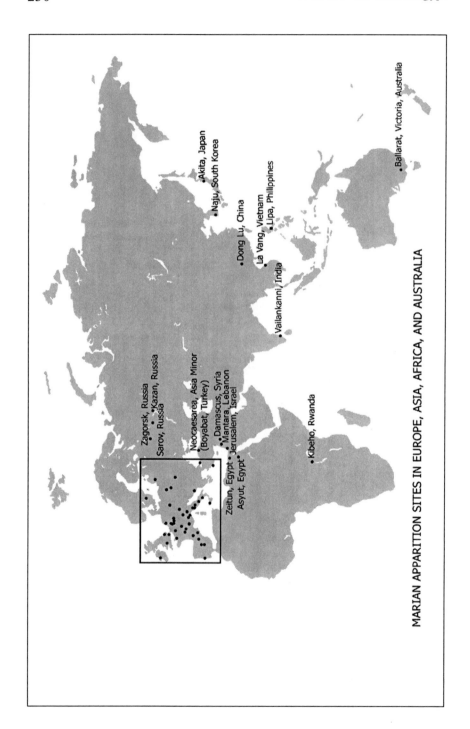

MARIAN APPARITION SITES IN EUROPE, ASIA, AFRICA, AND AUSTRALIA

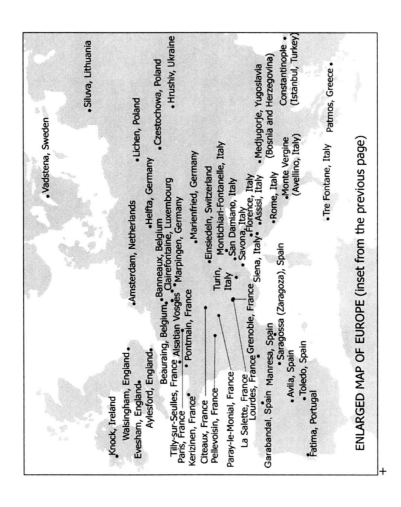

ENLARGED MAP OF EUROPE (inset from the previous page)

Knock, Ireland
Walsingham, England
Evesham, England
Aylesford, England
Tilly-sur-Seulles, France
Paris, France
Kerizinen, France
Citeaux, France
Pellevoisin, France
Paray-le-Monial, France
La Salette, France
Lourdes, France
Garabandal, Spain
Fatima, Portugal
Toledo, Spain
Avila, Spain
Manresa, Spain
Saragossa (Zaragoza), Spain
Grenoble, France
Siena, Italy
Turin, Italy
Beauraing, Belgium
Banneaux, Belgium
Alsatian Vosges
Clairefontaine, Luxembourg
Marpingen, Germany
Amsterdam, Netherlands
Heffta, Germany
Marienfried, Germany
Einsiedeln, Switzerland
Montichiari-Fontanelle, Italy
San Damiano, Italy
Savona, Italy
Florence, Italy
Assisi, Italy
Rome, Italy
Monte Vergine (Avellino, Italy)
Tre Fontane, Italy
Medjugorje, Yugoslavia (Bosnia and Herzegovina)
Lichen, Poland
Czestochowa, Poland
Hrushiv, Ukraine
Vadstena, Sweden
Siluva, Lithuania
Constantinople (Istanbul, Turkey)
Patmos, Greece

The magnificent statue of Mary with Baby Jesus, a photo of
which is on the cover of *Arrival the Gods in Egypt,* was sculpted
by Jill Burkee. It illuminates the sanctuary of the Mary Queen
of the Universe Shrine in Orlando, Florida.

PART IV

GODS OF THE PAST AND PRESENT

Chapter Twenty

TWIN SOULS AND SERPENT GODS

Who Is Mary?

In numerous of her appearances, Mary calls herself co-advocate, co-redeemer, and co-mediator with Jesus. Furthermore, during her Amsterdam, Netherlands appearance from 1945 to 1984, she told the visionary Ida Peerdeman that she, Mary, had become united to her Son and that she had always been united with Him.

It sounds as if Mary is saying that she and Jesus are one. If she calls herself co-advocate, co-redeemer, and co-mediator, it also sounds as if Mary is saying that she has equal status with her Son to act as an intermediary upon our behalf. How can this be?

As I said earlier in Chapter Nine, "Who Was Eve?" Mary calls herself the New Eve. In the same chapter, I showed how Eve and Adam came from the same androgynous individual.

I would like to go into a deeper examination of how it could be that Mary calls herself co-advocate, co-redeemer, and co-mediator with Jesus.

To do so, I would like to again consult the insightful trance readings of America's great psychic, Edgar Cayce. He interjects a unique concept into our understanding of Mary's relationship with the Christ Consciousness. In reading 5749-8 Edgar Cayce says:

"In the beginning Mary was the twin soul of the Master in the entrance into the earth!" (5749-8)

What is a twin soul? Many mystics and researchers believe we all have a twin soul. I wrote about twin souls in *When We Were Gods*:

> "A twin soul is a person whose connection with you is at a deep soul level. Some sources say that the twin soul is actually one soul split into a male and a female half. Other sources say the twin is a separate soul but has chosen to take the same path with your soul right from the beginning.
>
> Whatever the origin, the basis of a twin soul relationship is supposed to be one of mutual helpfulness. Although there might be some smoothing of rough edges, karmically speaking, in a twin soul relationship, the two souls carry a feeling of having come home to each other."

In another trance reading, Cayce also gave a description of two twin souls who had found each other in this lifetime. The following reading gives a beautiful explanation:

> "For we find in the beginning that they, these two (which we shall speak of as 'they' until separated), were as one in mind, soul, spirit, body; and in the first earth's plane as the voice over many waters, when the glory of the Father's giving of the earth's indwelling of man was both male and female in one." (288-6)

Cayce is saying that the two individuals in the above reading were also one—"both male and female in one," an androgynous being. Since this reading was given for two regular human beings (actually Edgar Cayce and his secretary who was his twin soul) rather than spiritual giants like Mary and Jesus, I deduce that the twin soul relationship can be common to all of us.

In further explaining the relationship between Mary and Jesus, Cayce simply said that:

"They were one soul so far as the earth is concerned." (5749-8)

Mary is not so much the female half and Jesus the male half, but more that they are both duplicates of the same soul. One manifests as a female and the other as a male. Therefore, since Mary and Jesus were one soul, it makes sense that Mary would have equal status with Jesus and that she could act as intermediary on our behalf, as does Jesus.

The Separation of the Souls into Twins

As I said in Chapter Fourteen, "Serpents, Root Races, and Myths," the Old Testament describes the separation of Adam into male and female, thereby inferring that Adam was originally androgynous and had both sexes within him.

It makes sense that our first experience in the physical would be as androgynous beings since the soul is made in the image of the Creator and the Creator is all things: both male and female.

In Chapter Ten, "Scariest Memory of Atlantis," I noted that many of the Atlanteans or third root race beings were androgynous as well. I described my own memory of being an androgynous human/animal mixture, the pixie-faced frog being. I also referred to Shirley MacLaine's *The Camino* in which she writes about her Atlantean memories of being androgynous and her experience of being separated into a male and a female.

Twin Soul Gods and Goddesses in Ancient Egypt

I believe that the brother/sister gods and goddesses of ancient Egyptian mythology who were also husbands and wives were twin souls. In one of my past life regression sessions, I relived a reunion with my twin soul. I wrote about it in Chapter Twenty-one, of *When We Were Gods*.

The experience occurred in ancient Egypt during the time Atlanteans came to those safety lands. My twin soul Amon and I communicated telepathically at the construction site of the Great Pyramid.

He and I had just had a disagreement. Upon the resolution of the difficulty, to show our unending love for each other, I leapt into his arms and we melted into each other . . . literally. Although we were no longer one soul as we had been in the beginning, now that we were separated into male and female twin souls, we could literally melt into each other. This was possible because we were less tightly bound to the physical than we are now.

Isn't that what we are all looking for—that melting experience—in our personal relationships? Unfortunately, now that we are in human bodies, the most we can hope for is a deeply emotional union.

An example of a twin soul relationship from actual ancient Egyptian mythology is the story of Tefnut, the goddess of clouds and moisture who is the sister and wife of Shu, the god of the atmosphere and dry winds.

You can see how they could be two sides of the same soul since they represent such interactive characteristics. It is not surprising that legends say that Tefnut and Shu were two halves of the same soul.

Tefnut is often depicted with a lion head and human-type body, one of the third root race Atlantean human/animal mixtures.

Modern-day researchers assume that these brother/sister unions among the gods and goddesses had to be incestuous. However, modern-day researchers tend to think of us as human animals rather than as souls. Therefore they do not consider that the ancient Egyptian people, who kept these legends of our beginnings alive, might have been referring to the souls we really are rather than the human beings we only temporarily find ourselves to be.

I believe that, especially since we are dealing with the ancient Egyptian gods and goddesses, the legends about brother/sister, husband/wife pairs, were really about souls in one of the previous root races. The pairs were actually recently separated twin souls similar to Adam and Eve.

According to legend, Tefnut and Shu had children, Nut and Geb. They appear to be another twin soul brother/sister, husband/wife pair. Nut is the sky goddess and her husband/-

brother is the earth god Geb who causes earthquakes when he laughs.

Tefnut and Shu formed a dynasty of twin souls. Their children Nut and Geb were the parents of another twin soul pair Isis and Osiris. Isis was the ancient Egyptian mother goddess. Some equate Isis with the divine mother. She was married to her brother Osiris, the god of the underworld.

To continue with the dynasty, Tefnut and Shu were also the parents of a younger daughter Nephthys, the goddess of death. Nephthys was another third root race individual depicted as a falcon or a woman with falcon's wings. She was also in a twin soul relationship with her brother/husband Set, who was the god of chaos and destruction.

Ra, the creator and sun god, is father of both Tefnut and Shu so you can see how all of these gods are descended from the Creator. In addition, since Ra is often depicted as a solar disc—a Light Being—you can see the progression from Light Being to twin soul animal mixtures.

Horus and the Serpents

The ancient Egyptians venerated many gods and goddesses. Among them, an interesting legend refers to Horus, who is described sometimes as the son of Ra and at other times as the son of the twin soul sister/brother, wife/husband pair Isis and Osiris.

Many legends surround Horus. He is the god of kings. Like Ra, Horus is often called a sun god. He specifically rules the East and the sunrise.

In one myth, Horus is trying to find and crush the followers of Set, the god of chaos and destruction. Horus in the form of a glowing winged disc pursues Set's followers.

Wait a minute. I saw myself as a glowing disc flying through space in my hypnosis sessions. In Chapter Thirteen, "Psychics, Mystics, and the Root Races," I called myself a Light Being and described the Light Being as one of the earliest root races. Could Horus be a first root race Light Being?

In the myth, Horus is helped by two serpents. That is another similarity with my Atlantean memories: serpent transportation.

Horus is the glowing disc. He has wings, which means that he's flying. And, he is flying with the help of two serpents. This sounds exactly like my memories of a first root race Light Being in Atlantis. This brings us to an examination of two ancient Egyptian serpent goddesses and the use of serpent transportation.

Good Serpents in Egyptian Mythology

In the ancient Egyptian pantheon of gods and goddesses, there are both good and bad serpents. Two marvelously good serpents are Wadjet and Nekhbet, both of them goddesses.

Wadjet, a cobra goddess, fulfills the typical characteristics of the mythological serpent gods of Atlantis in that she has wings, can fly, and also carries a solar disc or Light Being in her coils. In fact, she is one of the serpents carrying the semi-solid encapsulated Light Being through the stars on the ceiling of Thothmose III's tomb on page 136, a color image of which is on the back cover.

It was her job to protect the pharaoh, ready to strike deadly venom into anyone who threatened him. Because her image symbolically guards the pharaoh by her position on his headdress, pictured on page 127, her presence shows that the pharaoh has been chosen by the gods to be supreme.

Wadjet ruled Lower Egypt, including the delta area where the River Nile emptied into the Mediterranean Sea. She is usually depicted as a woman-headed cobra or a winged cobra, and occasionally as a lion-headed woman with the cobra on her crown—a definite third root race being.

Her counterpart, Nekhbet, ruled Upper Egypt or the high land where the Nile entered the country. Nekhbet is portrayed as a cobra especially when she is shown in concert with Wadjet, as in the bottom half of the photograph on the opposite page. However, she is also portrayed in her form as a vulture goddess as in the top half of the same photo. Again, she is one of those beings from our past who could work in agreement with the natural world to exist in different forms—another third root race characteristic.

The photograph, below, shows more of the image on page 136, which was painted on the ceiling of Thothmose III's tomb. Nekhbet, in her vulture form, is portrayed in the top half of the picture and Wadjet and Nekhbet in their dual serpent forms carry Horus or Ra in his Light form through the stars.

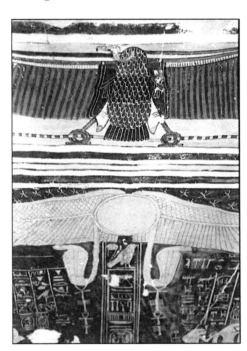

Nekhbet in her vulture form astride an image of Nekhbet in her serpent form with Wadjet. The two serpent goddesses carry Horus or Ra (depending upon which legend you are consulting), as a glowing disc, through the stars. The image is painted on the ceiling of the tomb of Thothmose III.

The Uraeus

It turns out that the image of a serpent, of a glowing ball, and indications of flight capability are common symbols in the mythology of many ancient cultures, not only the Egyptian.

In his fascinating book, *The Encircled Serpent: a Study of Serpent Symbolism in All Countries and Ages,* M. Oldfield Howey shows that the symbol of the serpent carrying the sun is universal throughout the world.

Whether the serpent turns up in the solar disc of Ra in ancient Egypt, the heraldic dragon of the Druids, the feathered serpent of the Maya, or the serpent/dragon of the Chinese, the symbol often contains the same characteristics:

- a serpent or dragon,
- a solar disc, a glowing egg, fire, or a human, and
- wings or feathers

The uraeus occurs when the solar disc or glowing egg is encircled by the serpent, as in the images on pages 132 and 134. It can also occur when the serpent encircles a human's head, for example, when the serpent Ka decorates the pharaoh's headdress, its body encircling the pharaoh's head as on page 127.

When the image is in the form of a uraeus, or the form of a flying serpent with an egg, glowing ball, fire, or human, these mythological serpents represent the same creature: the powerful Atlantean serpent gods in our previous root races.

Most of the serpents have wings or feathers to show their ability to fly. In addition, they all carry or hold a solar disc, a glowing egg, or have a human or fire in their mouth. All of these symbols that they carry, either in their appendages or in their mouths, represent the soul caught in the physical either in its Light Being form—the solar disc, glowing egg, or fire—or in its human form when the soul body connects with a physical being,

A Dragon with a "Cosmic Egg" Light Being.

represented by the human in the mouths of the Mayan feathered serpents.

I especially like the dragon with its cosmic egg as a representation of the serpent and the first root race Light Being. There are many legends about dragons, and many mythological dragons throughout the world. These include those with or without wings, with or without cosmic eggs, good or evil, and fire breathing.

The dragon is so powerful because it represents one of the third root race serpents. The great cosmic egg from which the world emerges is one of us—you, me, everyone of us—in our pure soul form, when we were no longer free enough of the physical to leave earth, but when we were still free enough of matter to separate into our Light Being soul self.

Why else do you think so many of us are fascinated with dragons? On an unconscious level, our souls resonate with memories of that time when we were not so tightly bound in the physical as we are now. Our unconscious minds remember that time long ago when we traveled by dragon power.

From Saint Patrick's routing of the serpents in Ireland to the story of Archangel Michael slaying the dragon, the underlying theme of *Encircled Serpent* is that ancient peoples worshiped serpents but that Christianity wiped out serpent-worship.

The serpents the ancients worshipped are the powerful serpent gods from Atlantean third root race times.

Good and Bad Serpents among the Egyptian Gods

Among the ancient Egyptian gods and goddesses, there are good serpents such, as Wadjet and Nekhbet, and bad serpents. Mehen is another good serpent. He is a protector of the creator sun god Ra. Myth says that Mehen ensures that Ra, as the sun, will appear every morning at the horizon.

Mehen has to protect Ra from Apep, an evil serpent known as the destroyer, lord of the darkness. Every night Apep tries to destroy Ra. Fortunately, Mehen triumphs so that the sun rises every morning except on the days when there is a solar eclipse.

Ancient Egyptian priests of Ra despised Apep, who ruled a multitude of demons that tormented humanity. Every year the priests held a ritual when they would make an effigy of Apep, pray that all the evil in Egypt would go into the effigy, and then they would crush, beat, coat with mud, and eventually burn the effigy. By this ritual, they felt they could restrain Apep's evil for one more year.

With this evil serpent that controlled the darkness, we come to the evil serpent in the Garden of Eden. The story of the serpent in the Garden of Eden is also a description of our experiences in that long-ago time when we were not yet entrapped in the physical.

The Evil Serpent and Mary

Set, the god of destruction, was one of the twin soul gods married to his twin soul sister Nephthys who ruled death. In later Egyptian history Set became associated with the evil serpent god Apep so that they became a composite god known as Apep-Set.

It does not really matter whether the evil serpent in the Garden of Eden was Apep, Set, or Apep-Set. What does matter is that this serpent is described in Genesis 3:1 as being more "subtle" than any other wild beast that God had made. This serpent is obviously not one of our present-day snakes because it speaks—communicating so effectively, cunningly, and "subtly" that it confuses Eve. It is actually one of the Atlantean serpent gods.

If you remember, Adam and Eve were newly separated twin souls who existed during the time of the previous root races. They were not yet human beings because they were still immortal.

The evil serpent cleverly convinces Eve to partake of the fruit of the tree of the knowledge of good and evil assuring Eve that, "You will not die."

Well, the serpent lied. As you know, by partaking of the fruit of the tree of the knowledge of good and evil, Adam and Eve are faced with death.

Of course, as soon as Adam and Eve eat the fruit, they know they have made a terrible mistake because they immediately feel shame. Then, they are kicked out of the Garden of Eden and are no longer immortal.

Adam and Eve must now toil for their food and Eve will have to go through the hard work of birthing to bring human beings into the world. Prior to this time, they were not entrapped in the physical and therefore did not have to eat to survive or to produce offspring like an animal. In addition, they are now going to die.

With this transition, they are no longer immortals of the first, second, or third root race. They are now fully in the fourth root race—human beings.

In the next chapter, we will examine the progression of the Master Soul, Christ, through the root races.

Chapter Twenty-one

AMILIUS AND ATLANTIS

The Time before Adam and Eve

Going back to the time before Adam and Eve requires an examination of the past lives of the Master Soul, the Christ Consciousness who became Jesus. Author Glenn Sanderfur describes Cayce's story of the past lives of Jesus in his book, *The Lives of the Master: the Rest of the Jesus Story.* Cayce's trance source said that the Christ Consciousness' pure soul, which was not yet connected with a human body, was called Amilius.

In *When We Were Gods*, I described my memories of Amilius during the time of being an Atlantean goddess:

> "Although I could not see him [because he was still entirely in spirit form], as always when I was in His presence, He was recognizable by the overwhelmingly powerful feeling of love that emanated from Him."

Amilius, since He was not yet in the physical, was the spiritual form of the Christ Consciousness. As a totally spiritual being, like the Light Beings we used to be before entering the physical, Amilius was neither male nor female. Another way of looking at this is to say that since he was the embodiment of the Creator on earth, he would be all things and therefore both male and female.

Amilius, as a spiritual being, decided to help those souls who had become entangled in matter by entering the physical to lead us out. By doing so, he took on death. Therefore, when Jesus says, "I died for you," he means more than the death on the cross. He means taking on the death of becoming human.

That is why, during his final incarnation as Jesus, He says that he is "The Way." He is the way out of the physical and back to the freedom of a Light Being and a citizen of the Universe.

When he entered the physical, Amilius was known as Adam. As we have seen already, at first Adam was undifferentiated sexually—containing both male and female—as were all first, second, and many third root race beings.

The story of Eve's creation is the story of Adam's separation into male and female twin souls known as Adam and Eve. This also means that Amilius became not only Adam when He entered the physical, but Amilius also became Eve. Therefore, Eve is also the embodiment of the Christ Consciousness in the physical.

In this reading on Atlantis, Edgar Cayce says:

". . . this Amilius—Adam, . . . discerned that from himself . . . could be drawn—*was* drawn—that [Eve] which made for the propagation *of* beings *in* the flesh . . ." (364-5)

Since Adam, after many incarnations in the earth, eventually overcame the physical during his lifetime as Jesus, the Savior is also known as the New Adam.

As Edgar Cayce says:

"Jesus . . . the first to know flesh, the first to purify it." (1158-5)

Eve, also, eventually becomes Mary. Therefore, Mary is also known as the New Eve.

You may find it interesting to learn that Cayce's trance source said that during various lifetimes, one of the twin souls may not incarnate but instead may hover over its twin from the spirit world as a Guardian Angel.

The Cayce readings present a chronological description of the male Christ twin's incarnations from Adam through Enoch, Melchizedek, Joseph of the coat of many colors, to Jesus. Unfortunately, the Cayce readings do not go through a chronology of the female Christ twin from Eve to Mary. Perhaps this occurred because no one thought to ask the "sleeping prophet" about Mary's previous incarnations or perhaps it occurred because during most of the male twin's incarnations from Adam to Jesus, the female twin did not incarnate in flesh but hovered nearby as Christ's Guardian Angel.

Obedience and the Christ Consciousness

The Biblical story emphasizes obedience to God's will. Jesus is tempted three times before He comes into his glory. He also struggles on Gethsemane when He asks that "this cup pass from me." After all, he is a young man of only 33 years who is just starting his work as a teacher and healer. Nonetheless, he resolves, to follow God's will (Matthew 26:39).

Mary, the female receptive twin of the Christ spirit, is obedient from the beginning of that lifetime in the Holy Land. She not only accepts the angel Gabriel's pronouncement that she will bear a child through union with the Holy Spirit, but also she is the one who tells Jesus when it is time for him to begin his work.

At the wedding feast of Cana, Jesus tells his mother that it is not yet time for him to begin his work (John 2:4-5). She disagrees and tells the servants to follow her son's instructions. Mary knows it is time for him to show his abilities so that his disciples will believe in him. Jesus follows his mother's instructions and turns the water into wine (John 2:11).

It is vital to an understanding of the root races to examine why the quality of obedience is so important. The Biblical story is *not* about whether or not we will live after we die. We will. We are souls. We are infinite and eternal by definition. Our real bodies are spirit bodies. Our natural, permanent form is spirit. This present form, the human form or the mix with the physical, is temporary.

The Biblical story is actually about our soul's entrapment in the physical and how to become free of it. Over the generations and millennia of human habitation on earth, the original story of our soul's entrapment in the physical has become distorted based on our perception of who we really are. Because we are now in the life/death/life reincarnation cycle, during our incarnations (while we are alive) we believe that we are merely an advanced animal.

Because many of us only relate to the human animal our soul temporarily inhabits, we believe there can be nothing after death.

In addition, many of us have come to make sense of the Biblical myths by believing the story has to do with maintaining obedience to a certain religion so we can go to heaven.

We have missed the point. The original story is about our soul's fall into the physical. The original purpose of our religions was to help us live a life that brought us closer to freedom from the physical and a return to the pure soul Light Beings we really are.

Many people live very soulful lives without even setting foot in a place of worship. Others may be deeply involved in the outer trappings of organized religion but may only see its power, pomp, and influence, not being aware of religions' real purpose.

Whatever our formal relationship with organized religion may or may not be, our deep inner goal is to maintain obedience to an alignment with our soul. Heaven is the bliss of the pure soul, the Light Being, when unencumbered by the physical. We long for it.

During my hypnosis sessions, I relived my own encasement in the physical. When I realized I could no longer go "home" to the world of light and vibration, I wailed in sorrow. I wonder if, on a deep spiritual level, our souls continue to grieve our entrapment.

A Problem of Will

In my memories of my own personal "fall" from a pure soul and citizen of the universe, I remember throwing off the quality of humility. I did this so I could disregard my mission, which was exploration. As a totally vibrational Light Being, I wanted to stop and savor some of the energy systems I encountered instead of merely noting them and continuing on my journey.

This memory is described in greater detail in *When We Were Gods*. Suffice it to say, the problem was my will . . . and your will, and everyone else's will. Because our souls have free will, we can choose to do something other than our spiritual purpose. However, there are consequences.

The big consequence was the fall into the physical. Without humility, our souls could not resist the pull of the physical's enticing vibrations. Once we were in the physical, we played with the earth vibrations, mixing with them and experimenting with the energies.

Unfortunately, the more we played with the physical vibrations on earth, the tighter we mixed with them, until we feared we would never be free to roam the universe again. We might remain lost from our true home, the universe, and alienated from our true selves, Light Beings made in the image of the Creator.

If you have read *When We Were Gods*, you know that one of the reasons we, as souls, entered the human being/reincarnation cycle was because we had "hit bottom" in Atlantis.

Souls had played with the physical without considering consequences. Many could no longer free themselves from matter. In addition, even those souls that could still go in and out of matter, could not free themselves from the sphere of the earth to return to the freedom of exploring the universe. We were stuck.

Turning the Will Around with Suffering

The advantage of a human body and the reincarnation cycle is that we now suffer and die. Suffering and death don't sound like an advantage to you? Well, these experiences are opportunities as far as your soul is concerned. There is nothing like grief, sorrow, regret, and a finite end to each lifetime to turn our wills around toward the spiritual.

Some people interpret the Bible, because it extols the virtues of suffering, to mean that we need to torture ourselves or to submit to abusive relationships. However, the original story behind the Biblical story is the story of our soul's entrapment in the physical. To be a human being that dies, grieves, hurts, suffers, and becomes ill, is enough suffering for a soul made in the image of the Creator that normally lives in bliss and is a citizen of the Universe.

You could say that the human condition is the spiritual equivalent of detoxification from an addiction. It was an addiction to the physical that might sever our ties with our souls forever.

When we were in Atlantis, while living in our addiction, many of us believed we had infinite power over the physical. Therefore, we did not consider that we might be hurting others or ourselves or that we might be stuck in the physical forever.

The problem of willfulness is the story in Genesis. The rest of the Bible describes lessons in obedience. The Biblical story is really about our souls becoming caught in the physical and showing us the things we must do to become free again. By entering and overcoming the life/death/life reincarnation cycle, the Christ Consciousness showed us the way to freedom from the physical.

Interestingly, Kwan Yin, described earlier in Chapter Thirteen, "Psychics, Mystics, and the Root Races," is the Chinese equivalent of the Christ Consciousness. As mentioned earlier, Kwan Yin is like Adam in that she is sometimes considered male and at other times female or both interchangeably. Another similarity is the Buddhist legend saying that Kwan Yin vowed she would not rest until she had freed all human beings from the reincarnation cycle.

In the same way, Jesus assures us that we will be free of the life/death/life reincarnation cycle when we follow his example.

Now that we are discussing freedom from the reincarnation cycle, this brings us to the immaculate conception. It shows the soul's ability to be less tightly bound by the physical.

Mary and the Immaculate Conception

To begin, the Cayce readings say that the immaculate conception is a natural law. Here is the reading given by Cayce in 1937:

> "It's like many proclaiming today that the Master was immaculately conceived; they say "Impossible!" They say that it isn't in compliance with the natural law. It IS a natural law," (5749-8)

And, before you assume Cayce's trance source had to be mistaken, let me bring to your attention two news items on the internet. The first article, by James Owens, writing for the *National Geographic News* on December 20, 2006, reports the "virgin birth" of two female Komodo dragons in two British zoos. Owens says that DNA testing confirms what the zookeeper knew: the mothers had not been near a male for years. Furthermore, the babies are not clones of their mothers. They are all males.

Until these two Komodo dragons, in two different zoos, gave birth to viable clutches of eggs, scientists thought that immaculate conceptions in higher vertebrates were extremely rare. Previously they had only noticed immaculate conceptions in simpler animals such as aphids, snails, and zooplankton.

Immaculate conceptions have also been observed in pythons, turkeys, and certain fish. A September 26, 2002 online *National Geographic News* article by Hillary Mayell reports a "virgin birth" in a Detroit zoo shark. The scientific term for an immaculate conception is called parthenogenetic reproduction.

What about humans and immaculate conceptions? The Cayce reading quoted above continues:

"It IS a natural law. . . . Then, that there has been an encasement was a beginning. Then there must be an end when this must be or may be broken . . . then the Master AS the son; but the ONLY begotten of the Father in the flesh AS a son OF an immaculately conceived daughter!" (5749-8)

Cayce is saying that since the soul at one time became encased in matter during the previous root races there could also be a time when the encasement in the physical would end.

At the time when the soul would free itself from its "encasement" in matter, which is the story of Jesus and His triumph over death, the soul would incarnate from an immaculate conception since the original encasement occurred as a result of the projection of mind into matter. To be able to get free of the life/death/life reincarnation cycle, both the mother and the child would have to have that same ability of mind over matter as to be conceived immaculately.

The same reading confirms that Mary was also immaculately conceived. This section of the reading was in a question (Q)/ answer (A) format:

> "15. (Q) Neither Mary nor Jesus, then, had a human father? (A) Neither Mary nor Jesus had a human father. They were one SOUL so far as the earth is concerned; because [else] she would not be incarnated in flesh, you see." (5749-8)

A further explanation of immaculate conception occurs in reading 5749-7 in which Cayce says that the immaculate concepttion results when both the physical and mental are so attuned to spirit that spirit can create an immaculate conception. He also says that previous incarnations of the Christ as Enoch and Melchizedek were by immaculate conception.

Since Jesus is "The Way" out of the physical, I wonder if conception immaculately might become more common in the future. Therefore, I am curious to see what else Cayce's trance source says about it. In reading 2072-3 he says that the mother's body would have to be near to perfect in coordination. In addition, on the mental and spiritual level, the mother would have to have high mental and spiritual aspirations, desires, and purposes.

The Virgin Birth and the Fifth Root Race

If you find the immaculate conception too strange to accept, get ready for something even more challenging: the virgin birth.

As in the articles above, "virgin birth" is often used interchangeably with "immaculate conception" referring to a conception without the services of a male.

However, a true virgin birth is a very different concept. It refers to an immaculate conception followed by a birth in which the baby is born without going through the birth canal so that the mother gives birth and remains a virgin.

A virgin birth is a miracle. It is a miracle adhered to and believed in by the Roman Catholic Church. Church doctrine says that the influence of the Holy Spirit, which caused the immaculate conception, continued to the birth. The baby, who was a light unto the world, could pass through the natural physical barriers of Mary's body without injuring them.

Not surprisingly, this is one type of birth that appears to be so inconceivable as to appear ludicrous. Nonetheless, it is not so unbelievable if you have seen images of the upcoming fifth root race which appeared in my hypnosis sessions.

Cayce mentions the fifth root race twice in his readings. But, he does not reveal what they will be like. We only know to expect them after our present root race, the fourth. He says they will need to be fed, and that the Atlantean Hall of Records, which can be entered from a passageway at the right forepaw of the Sphinx, will likely be opened after the fifth root race begins.

As I described in *When We Were Gods*, in my hypnosis sessions, I had seen a baby born that was supposed to be a member of the fifth root race. It could appear and disappear. I called it a Casper the Ghost baby. Just as the second and third root race were not as tightly bound to the physical as we are, the fifth root race will also be less tightly bound to the physical.

I saw a fifth root race baby in its mother's arms. Then, it disappeared. The mother became alarmed as if something terrible had happened. She was distressed because she thought she had lost her baby. Then, the infant suddenly reappeared.

If Jesus is truly "The Way," there is a good chance that he embodied many of the characteristics of the fifth root race. That would include the ability to appear and disappear. After all, He did amazing things like walk on water. After his resurrection, He also appeared in a room where all the doors and windows were locked.

Is it possible, then, that even as a baby, Jesus had the ability to appear and disappear as I had seen the fifth root race babies do in my hypnosis sessions?

I found support for this assertion in an unusual little book called, *The Banned Book of Mary: How Her Story Was*

Suppressed by the Church and Hidden in Art for Centuries by Ronald F. Hock. The author contends that he has seen a papyrus manuscript called, in English, the *Infancy Gospel of James*. It is protected by security guards in the Bodmer Library and Museum located in Cologny, a pastoral lakeside village just outside Geneva, Switzerland. The Bodmer Library also contains the oldest known copy of the Gospel of Luke, dated at around 200 A.D.

Hock contends that since Saint Anne, the mother of Mary, is not mentioned in the Christian Bible, the *Infancy Gospel of James* must have been known by artists and scholars such as Leonardo da Vinci since da Vinci painted "The Virgin with Child and Saint Anne," which now hangs in the Louvre in Paris.

The *Infancy Gospel of James* also describes the birth of Jesus saying that he was born in a cave on the way to Bethlehem. When Mary told Joseph the baby was about to be born, Joseph found the cave to give her privacy. Joseph left Mary in the cave and went to find a midwife. However, as he and the midwife approached the cave, a cloud covered the entrance of the cave.

After the cloud disappeared, an intense light, so bright that Joseph and the midwife could not bear to look at it, shone out from the cave. When the light faded, they went in the cave and saw a baby in Mary's arms nursing at her breast.

This first midwife told another one named Salome that a virgin birth had just occurred. Salome did not believe her and insisted on examining the mother to prove that Mary was not a virgin.

However, when Salome attempted to insert her fingers in Mary's birth canal, the hand began to burn being engulfed by flames. Only when Salome prayed for forgiveness for her unbelief was her hand restored to her.

Very interesting, is all that I can say.

Mary and the Serpent

Let us get back to Mary and the very interesting stories about her in the Bible. Mary is traditionally association with the serpent— first, in the Garden of Eden when she is seduced by the serpent, and secondly when it is prophesied that she will crush the serpent's head. I believe the serpent, whose head she crushes, is actually a powerful Atlantean serpent. As I mentioned earlier, many pre-Christian religions have deified the serpent.

In addition, since the Jewish religion has many of the elements of the Ancient Egyptian religion, it is likely that Apep is the serpent that Mary crushes because Apep sounds very much like Satan. Since later in Egyptian history Apep becomes associated with Set, the god of destruction, some researchers equate the serpent in the Garden of Eden with Set or the Apep-Set mixture. Interestingly, Set, is often depicted as a human/animal mixture. He has an unknown animal's head, horns, and a long forked tail, very similar to the traditional image of Satan.

Therefore, it might be that the story of Mary crushing the head of the serpent refers to a particular evil Atlantean serpent god. However, whether a particular god or not, the idea behind the serpent god is that it represents the third root race Atlanteans and the willfulness of our souls. We played with our energies without considering the consequences to ourselves or others.

If you remember, it is Apep that attempts to swallow the solar disc. I believe this is a reference to our Light Being essence being swallowed permanently by the physical so that we can no longer get free.

Mary Crushes the Head of the Serpent

When Mary appeared in Rue du Bac, Paris, France, in 1830, the visionary Catherine Laboure, a young novitiate nun, saw the Virgin with her foot crushing the serpent's head. It was a green serpent with yellow spots.

In Chapter Nineteen, "Blessed Among Women," I described Mary's appearance in Rue du Bac when the she told the visionary that she had graces to give us but that we are not asking for all the graces available to us.

During that appearance, Mary asked that a medal be struck with the words in gold letters (in French), "O MARY CONCEIVED WITHOUT SIN, PRAY FOR US WHO HAVE RECOURSE TO THEE." Mary said that those who wore the medal would receive great graces.

Above, a close up of the Miraculous Medal showing Mary's foot crushing the serpent's head.

Left, a wall-size representation of the Miraculous Medal, on display at St. Mary's Cathedral in Washington, D.C.

In 1831, the director general of the Sisters of Charity, the order to which Catherine belonged, ordered the medal manufactured. Many who wore it reported healings and miracles. It became known as the Miraculous Medal. You can still get a Miraculous Medal if you visit Rue du Bac.

On August 15, 1951 during one of Mary's appearances in Amsterdam, Holland, she said that she had accomplished what she had set out to do: She had crushed the snake with her foot. By this she referred to her incarnation as Mary when her Son overcame death and so freed the twin soul pair of the physical.

By crushing the head of the serpent, the Light Being is freed of the bondage of the life/death/life reincarnation cycle. The soul is set free of the physical.

In the ancient Egyptian myth, Apep continually tries to destroy what modern researchers believe is a solar disc. However, as we have seen, the solar disc likely represents the Light Being that we all are in our pure soul form. Therefore, the light that Apep attempts to destroy is not really the sun but the light of our souls, keeping us "lost" and encased in matter forever.

The cyclical release of the Light Being soul by the powerful good serpent Mehen could also refer to the reincarnation cycle. During a lifetime, we are engulfed by the serpent. In between lives, our souls are free of matter. By crushing the serpent's head, Mary frees us of the reincarnation cycle and death.

In other words, the Consciousness entered the physical to show us the way out. The final turning point is the life/death/ life reincarnation cycle. We followed the Christ Consciousness into the human race to turn our wills around. It took immense faith that by doing so we would be freed of the physical.

Through their lifetimes as Jesus and Mary, they fulfilled their promise to us. They showed us that through the human experience, our wills could be turned around and we could become free of the physical.

However, although Mary and Jesus are free of the physical they have not left us forever. They came into the physical to lead us to freedom. Therefore, they continue to appear to us to provide encouragement and to keep us on "The Way."

Mary is the most active, appearing over and over again in apparition form to people all over the world. She often says that she holds back her son's arm from causing us great suffering.

This makes it seems as if God is a vindictive God. The common interpretation of the emphasis on suffering in the Bible is that unless we do God's will, we will be punished.

The reality is that the greatest punishment is the one we have inflicted on ourselves—by becoming caught, potentially forever, in the physical. Since most of us have little connection with our souls—and many more of us do not even believe we have a soul, never mind that we really *are* a soul—we do not understand how the suffering of being human is an advantage to our souls.

Suffering seems to be the only thing that turns our wills around. When we become in danger of separating ourselves permanently from our souls, our wills can always be tweaked back to striving toward our divine heritage through various calamities.

Would it not be easier to simply do God's will?

The Transition from Atlantean to Human

In this chapter, I have shown why Eve has been associated with the serpent. In addition, I have shown why she would crush the head of the serpent in terms of the history of the soul through the root races.

I have also shown how the spiritual form of the Christ Consciousness, called Amilius during Atlantean times, entered the physical to lead us out and that he became the twin soul pair of Adam and Eve.

In one hypnosis session, I recalled my memories of the Christ Consciousness as Amilius entering a newly created human baby. He was the first to become human. The hypnotherapist asked, "How did you feed the baby?" Since there had been no mother to suckle the baby, it was an interesting question to ask.

The Amenhotep II image of a man suckling a breast that is part of a tree.

I replied that we fed the baby on the nectar of flowers. This pronouncement, like many of the things I said while hypnotized, seemed outlandish to my waking mind. You can imagine my amazement when I saw, in Amenhotep II's tomb, an image that beautifully illustrated this Atlantean memory.

It is a typical Amenhotep II stick-figure image. In it, a man suckles a breast that appears to be attached to a tree limb. The man also holds an arm that looks as if it is part of the tree. The image seems to say that the man is being nourished by the tree.

The man, breast, and arm look as if they could have been added to the drawing at a later time. Perhaps they are ancient graffiti. Nonetheless, I include this photograph as a curiosity because it coincides with the information that turned up in my hypnosis sessions.

Chapter Twenty-two

MARY FOR YOU

What Happened to Mary?

If Mary is so powerful and a twin soul of the Son of God, what happened to her? In the Protestant religions she barely exists. Her role is only as a humble vehicle for Jesus to enter the world—and this, in spite of being mentioned in the New Testament more than any other character except for Jesus.

A March 21, 2005 *Time Magazine* article entitled, "Hail, Mary," quotes Princeton scripture specialist Beverley Gaventa as saying that not only is Mary seldom mentioned in Protestant sermons, but also there are hardly any academic articles on Mary. In comparison, there are a plethora of essays on Doubting Thomas.

Unlike the Protestant religions, Mary is highly revered in the Roman Catholic religion. The Roman religion began to separate from the original Christian church, now known as the Orthodox

In an icon, Baby Jesus is always portrayed with adult proportions to signify his stature as the Son of God.

Church, in the 9th century. In the Orthodox Church, Mary is known as the Theotokos or the Mother of God. In this way, she is elevated to godhood as is her Son.

By the way, you may be interested to know that religious statues are not allowed in the Orthodox religion. However, they do use icons, which are considered a written prayer in visual form, not simply a sacred painting. Icons are often "written" by monks while fasting and in prayer.

Mary and Mary Magdalene

Today, there appears to be more interest in Mary Magdalene, who is hardly mentioned in the Bible, than there is in the Blessed Virgin Mary. However, in her delightful book, *The Holy Women Around Jesus,* author Carol Haenni, Ph.D., describes Edgar Cayce's reading 295-8, which is given for Mildred Davis, a cousin of Gladys Davis, Cayce's secretary of many years.

In the reading, Cayce says that in a previous lifetime, Mildred had been Mary Magdalene. Although Mildred was a good woman who came into her 20th century lifetime with the sole purpose of helping others, she was just that—a woman—not Jesus' wife or His twin soul. For your interest, Cayce describes Mary Magdalene as being five feet four inches tall and weighing 121 pounds with blue eyes and reddish hair.

Mary and the Protestant Reformation

What happened to Mary, the Mother of God? She has manifested throughout the world at least 21,000 times in the last millennium. She brings peace to a town in Egypt afflicted with 25 years of terrorism. Yet reports of her appearances only get front page news on supermarket tabloids. Hardly anyone in the West knows about her appearance in Asyut.

Why do the Protestant churches give her so little recognition? I turned to my trusty *Grolier Encyclopedia of Knowledge* to see if their entry on the Protestant Reformation might explain why Mary is not accorded appropriate honor in the Protestant churches. I only found corruption, nepotism, and financial excesses in the

Roman Catholic Church of the 1500s listed as the main causes of the Reformation. There is no reference to Mary at all.

I did find some interesting information in a book by Alan Axelrod called *Elizabeth I CEO*. This book describes one of the reasons the great Renaissance Queen of England, who reigned from 1558 to 1603, fashioned herself the "Virgin Queen."

Elizabeth I inherited a country on the verge of religious civil war. Her deceased father, the infamous Henry VIII, had plunged his country into Protestantism to be free of the Roman Catholic Pope who would not allow him to annul his first marriage because his wife had not produced a male heir.

Axelrod says that Elizabeth recognized that a weakness of Protestantism, as far as the emotional life of the people was concerned, was its diminishment of the role of the Blessed Virgin. Therefore, to quell religious unrest in England, and mollify both Protestants and Catholics, Elizabeth continued with the Church of England. However, she became the Virgin to her people. She never married saying she was married to England.

Elizabeth encouraged the naming of Virginia in her honor. Therefore, indirectly, Virginia is named for the Virgin Mary.

Because Elizabeth became head of the Church of England, which had previously been governed by Rome, Protestantism in England also had to do with the increased power of the state.

The March 21, 2005 article in *Time Magazine* called, "Hail, Mary," mentioned earlier, says that Martin Luther, instigator of the Protestant Reformation, actually liked the Holy Mother. Nonetheless, many Protestants turned away from her but not because of the doctrine of the Protestant church. Some Protestants wanted to dilute the power of mediators between them and God. Therefore, Mary lost favor. I assume that Jesus did not lose favor in the Protestant religions because he was considered to be God.

Mary also became less important simply because the Roman Catholic Church revered her and Protestants were rebelling against the Roman church.

What a loss! The *Time* article says Mary is currently growing in importance in many Protestant churches.

Mary for Today

The reality is that even though the Roman Catholic and Orthodox Churches revere Mary it does not mean that they own her. She, like her Son, exists separately from any religion, church, dogma, or creed. She simply is. She appeared to all those thousands of people . . . two million by some estimates . . . in Asyut and they included Christians, Muslims, people of other religions, and non-believers.

Mary is no respecter of persons. She chooses people of diverse faiths to be her visionaries. For example, even though she originally appeared to Catholic students at a convent school in Kibeho, Rwanda, from 1981 to 1989, she also appeared to an Atheist boy and a Muslim woman.

She is also the feminine embodiment of the Christ energy and is intimately concerned with our well-being. It is part of her purpose to be an advocate for us to the Christ Consciousness.

Destroyed by Lukewarmness

From 1988 to 1990, Mary appeared to Patricia Talbott, a sixteen-year-old high school girl embarking on a modeling career in Cuenca, Ecuador. In *God Sent*, Roy Abraham Varghese says that Mother Mary made predictions to Patricia of both natural catastrophes and those created by man in our future.

These apocalyptic prophecies are not new as I revealed in Chapter Nineteen, "Blessed Among Women." Cayce, too, predicts worldwide earth upheavals. However, in Chapter Nineteen, I also said that Mary gives us hope for the future.

In Cuenca, she told us, through Patricia, that we do not have to let what seems inevitable happen. We can change the future. Mary says that we are destroying ourselves through our lukewarmness.

This pronouncement rang a bell with me. As I describe in *When We Were Gods*, Jesus appeared to me in a vision. He told me that he had died for me, which I now understand that he had entered death by becoming human. He also said that my sin was that I was too wishy-washy—too "beige" or too conformist.

He was right. I have been afraid to say what I believe and to tell people about my experiences. At every step of the way, I have struggled with my fear of condemnation by others. What will people say? What will my family say? What will my friends say? What will my neighbors say? And, so on and on and on.

However, I have learned that there are many who have benefited from my writing. People come to hear me speak. They listen to my interviews on the radio. Therefore, bit by bit, I learn that as I erode my wishy-washiness, my authentic self is acceptable . . . and actually helps others.

Before, I survived. Now, I am coming alive. I have discovered that I like myself so much more because, little by little, I am showing the world who I really am instead of pretending I am something else. It feels good. And, to my surprise, I am accepted.

Among the people I meet, I see that they too struggle with being genuine in a confusing world in which it is sometimes difficult to even connect with our genuine selves.

Therefore, I am here to tell you that I really did see brilliant flashes of light coming from many directions on a cloudless night without any lightning in the sky or the sound of thunder.

As you have seen, my photographs of Asyut at night inexplicably showed everything . . . except the mysterious flashes.

I really did drink more than a glass of Cairo city water and did not get dysentery, although other Westerners have become sick from downing a few drops of the same liquid. Also, I have been susceptible to serious stomach upset in other foreign countries.

I really did leave Egypt with perfect timing so that I missed riots in Cairo at a time that was so dangerous for foreigners that even organized tours were turned back from the country.

My Egyptian hosts and their family and friends attest that they really did see the apparition of the Virgin Mary. I have a copy of their videotape showing the apparition they saw, photographs of which I have reproduced in these pages.

Moreover, I have explored to my satisfaction that the reason the Protestant religion, with which I grew up, did not revere Mary is not because she is unworthy of honor and worship. It is because of an ancient feud between religious factions.

What is more, I have seen that Cayce's trance source elevates Mary to the same level as Jesus saying that, as far as the earth is concerned, they are one soul.

Is this enough for me, skeptic and unbeliever that I am, to take Mary in my heart and trust in her ability to intercede on my behalf? Can I believe she can bring peace on earth?

Is it enough for you, gentle reader?

Peace to the Peacemakers

Mary often says that she will bring peace to the peacemakers. Until my experience in Asyut, I did not understand what she meant. To me, it seems to be a rhetorical statement. The peacemakers must be bringing the peace to themselves.

However, often when people do not retaliate against an aggressor, they become victimized. I now understand that Mary has the power to stop the aggressors from victimizing those who do not retaliate against wrongs visited upon them.

The Copts of Asyut believe the Holy Mother appeared in their town because they resisted seeking revenge against the violence perpetrated against them by fanatical terrorists. As a result of Mary's visit, the terrorist attacks have stopped. By making peace, the people of Asyut brought a greater peace to themselves.

When Mary appeared near the end of the Second World War in Amsterdam, Holland, in 1945, she proclaimed that it is her mission to bring true peace to the earth.

As I said earlier in Chapter Nineteen, "Blessed Among Women," in 1871, the sincere prayers of the people of Pontmain brought Mary to them. She ensured the safe return of their young men during a time of war.

Also, in 1990, Mary brought peace in Dong Lu, China. She kept the army of the aggressors from decimating innocent people.

In 1980, when she appeared in Cuapa, Nicaragua, Mary elaborated on her message of peace. Emphatically, she proclaimed that asking God to bring peace to us would not be enough.

Unlike her many other graces, to receive peace we must do more than ask. To receive peace, we need to make peace.

How do we make peace? She said that we have to become peacemaking people, learning how to forgive, to lay aside grudges, and to make ourselves peaceful through prayer if we want to bring a greater peace to the world.

In other words, we need to create peace within ourselves. If we do so, she will bring peace to the world around us.

Mary and You

As I wrote in *When We Were Gods*, not only are you actually a soul yearning to return to your natural light state, but also you are immortal, eternal . . . pure light and love.

Arrival of the Gods in Egypt shows you that you are not only immortal but also that you have spiritual help. There really are supernatural beings intimately concerned with your well-being.

Therefore, there is help in averting these cataclysmic disasters predicted by many and that Mary, herself, warns us about. She asks us to change our ways so that devastating earth upheavals will be forestalled.

Long, long ago, when you, as a soul, found yourself locked in the physical and in danger of remaining stuck forever, Amilius took on the arduous task of leading you out to freedom. He entered the physical for one reason only: to set you free. By doing so, he helped you when you were in danger of being lost on earth forever.

His voluntary entrance into the physical occurred during the time of the androgynous Atlantean mixtures. This time has been immortalized in the gargantuan statue, the Great Sphinx. During that time, when we were third root race mixtures, Amilius promised to show us a way out of our entrapment in the physical.

Amilius became the twin souls, Adam and Eve. They helped us by undertaking a new life form, the human race, to give us the opportunity to turn our wills around with the suffering of the life/death/life reincarnation cycle.

When earth upheavals began to destroy the homeland of Atlantis, the Atlanteans—mixtures, gods, and goddesses alike— found safety in Egypt. You may have been one of them.

When the gods and goddesses arrived in Egypt from Atlantis, they, and the mixtures, were on the downturn. Even though they were filled with the importance of their power over the physical, they were also very aware of their separation from their real light selves and their lack of freedom to travel the universe.

Thousands of years later, the Christ Consciousness incarnated during the time of our upturn. It was the time when we had grown some humility through our experiences as humans.

In their final earthly lifetimes, Mary and Jesus came again to Egypt, the land of safety. This time, they came to protect Baby Jesus. During this incarnation, they showed us the way out of the physical by overcoming death.

They continue, in spiritual form, to help us by interceding on our behalf with the Creative Forces. They show us they are here to help when they appear in visions and apparitions.

In the autumn of 2000, two millennia after the birth of Jesus, the Christ Consciousness returned to Egypt again, this time, in apparition form. How appropriate that Mary should appear in the safety lands on the anniversary of Jesus' birth.

She came to the land of the great Atlantean monuments, the Great Pyramids and the Great Sphinx . . . and also the home of the Hall of Records where Atlanteans had preserved their knowledge in the shelter of Egypt, so long ago.

In her manifestations, Mary says she wants to give you graces. She asks that you turn to her for help with even the trivial matters in your life. She offers her protection. She offers peace on earth.

The twin soul duo, who were once Mary and Jesus, the embodiment of the Christ Consciousness, are showing your soul the way out of the physical to end the deep loneliness, emptiness, and longing for "home" that seeps into your physical body from your soul.

Their mission is to show you "The Way" out of the physical. By doing so, they bless you. You may not believe in them, they may not be a part of your religious beliefs, but still, they bless you.

They have been blessing you for millennia.

They bless you now.

BIBLIOGRAPHY

Applegate, Melissa Littlefield. *The Egyptian Book of Life: Symbolism of Ancient Egyptian Temple and Tomb Art.* Deerfield Beach, Florida: Health Communications, 2000.

Arguelles, Jose, Ph. D. *The Mayan Factor: Path Beyond Technology.* Santa Fe, New Mexico: Bear & Company Publishing, 1987.

Ashton, Joan. *Mother of All Nations: The Visitations of the Blessed Virgin Mary and Her Message for Today.* New York: Harper & Row, 1989.

Axelrod, Alan. *Elizabeth I CEO: Strategic Lessons from the Leader Who Built an Empire.* New York: Prentice Hall Press, 2002.

Bauval, Robert, and Graham Hancock. *The Message of the Sphinx: A Quest for the Hidden Legacy of Mankind.* New York: Three Rivers Press, 1997.

Bauval, Robert, and Adrian Gilbert. *The Orion Mystery: Unlocking the Secrets of the Pyramids.* New York: Three Rivers Press, 1995.

Blavatsky, H. P. *The Secret Doctrine: The Synthesis of Science, Religion, and Philosophy, Volumes I and II.* Los Angeles: The Theosophy Company, 1888, 1964.

Budge, E. A. Wallis. *The Book of the Dead: The Papyrus of Ani in the British Museum.* Mineola, New York: Dover Publications, 1967.

Cayce, Edgar Evans. *Edgar Cayce on Atlantis.* New York: Paperback Library, 1968.

Cayce, Edgar Evans, Gail Cayce Schwartzer, and Douglas G. Richards. *Mysteries of Atlantis Revisited: An Edgar Cayce Guide.* New York: St. Martin's Paperbacks, 1988.

Cerminara, Gina. *Many Mansions: The Edgar Cayce Story on Reincarnation.* New York: A Signet Book, 1967.

Collins, Andrew. *Gateway to Atlantis: The Search for the Source of a Lost Civilization.* New York: Carroll & Graf Publishers, 2002.

Cornwell, John. *The Pontiff in Winter: Triumph and Conflict in the Reign of John Paul II.* New York: Doubleday, 2005.

Cotterell, Maurice M. *The Supergods: They Came on a Mission to Save Mankind.* London: HarperCollins, 1997.

Day, Peggy, and Susan Gale. *Edgar Cayce on the Indigo Children.* Virginia Beach, Virginia: A. R. E. Press, 2004.

Dickens, Charles. *Oliver Twist.* New York: Everyman's Library, 1992.

Dunn, Christopher. *Giza Power Plant: Technologies of Ancient Egypt.* Santa Fe, New Mexico: Bear & Company Publishing, 1988.

Eagle, Jonathan, and William Hutton. *Earth's Catastrophic Past and Future: A Scientific Analysis of Information Channeled by Edgar Cayce.* Boca Raton, Florida: 2004.

Editors. "Protestantism." *Grolier Encyclopedia of Knowledge.* 1941.

Editors. *Webster's Dictionary.* Ashland, Ohio: Landoll, 1993.

Eicher, Peter. *Visions of Mary: An Inspiring, Unforgettable Collection of Mary's Extraordinary Encounters with Ordinary People throughout History.* New York: Avon Books, 1996.

Haenni, Carol. *The Holy Women Around Jesus.* Virginia Beach, Virginia: A.R.E. Press, 2005.

Hancock, Graham. *Fingerprints of the Gods: The Evidence of Earth's Lost Civilization.* New York: Three Rivers Press, 1996.

Hancock, Graham, and Santha Faiia. *Heaven's Mirror: Quest for the Lost Civilization.* New York: Three Rivers Press, 1998.

Hawass, Zahi. *The Mysteries of Abu Simbel: Ramesses II and the Temples of the Rising Sun.* New York: The American University in Cairo, 2000.

Hock, Ronald F. *The Banned Book of Mary: How Her Story Was Suppressed by the Church and Hidden in Art for Centuries.* Berkeley, California: Ulysses Press, 2004.

Kirkwood, Annie. *Mary's Message to the World.* New York: Perigee, 1996.

Laughton, Timothy. *The Maya: Life, Myth, and Art.* New York: Stewart, Tabori, and Chang, 1998.

MacLaine, Shirley. *The Camino: A Journey of the Spirit.* New York: Pocket Books, 2000.

MacLean, Dorothy. *To Hear the Angels Sing: An Odyssey of Co-creation with the Devic Kingdom.* Barrington, Massachusetts: Lindisfarne Books, 1994.

Mayell, Hillary. "Shark Gives 'Virgin Birth' in Detroit." *National Geographic News. September 26, 2002.*

http://news.nationalgeographic.com/news/2002/09/0925_020925_virginsha rk.html

McDowell, Bart. *Ancient Egypt: Discovering its Splendors*. National Geographic Society, 1977.

Montgomery, Ruth. *The World Before: Arthur Ford and the Great Guides Reveal Earth's Secret Past and Future*. New York: Fawcett Crest, 1976.

_____. *The World to Come: The Guides' Long Awaited Predictions for the Dawning Age*. New York: Harmony Books, 1999.

Moody, Raymond, M.D., with Paul Perry. *Reunions: Visionary Encounters with Departed Loved Ones*. New York: Villard Books, 1993.

Newton, Michael, Ph. D. *Destiny of Souls: New Case Studies of Life Between Lives*. St. Paul, Minnesota: Llewellyn Publications, 2001.

Owens, James. "Virgin Birth Expected at Christmas—by Komodo Dragon." *National Geographic News. 20 December. 2006 http://news.nationalgeographic.com/news/2006/12/061220-virgin-dragons.html*

Raswan, Carl Reinhard. *Drinkers of the Wind*. New York: Farrar, Straus, Giroux, 1962.

Sanderfur, Glenn. *Lives of the Master: The Rest of the Jesus Story*. Virginia Beach, Virginia: A. R. E. Press, 1988.

Seleem, Ramses. *The Illustrated Egyptian Book of the Dead: A New Translation with Commentary*. New York: Sterling Publishing Company, 2001.

Siegel, Bernie S. *Love, Medicine, and Miracles: Lessons Learned about Self-Healing from a Surgeon's Experience with Exceptional Patients*. New York: Harper Paperbacks, 1990.

Smith, A. Robert, Ed. *The Lost Memoirs of Edgar Cayce: Life as a Seer*. Virginia Beach, Virginia: A. R. E. Press, 1997.

Sparrow, G. Scott. *Blessed Among Women: Encounters with Mary and her Message*. New York: Three Rivers Press, 1998

Sparrow, Lynn. *Reincarnation: Claiming Your Past, Creating Your Future*. New York: HarperCollins, 1988.

Steiner, Rudolf. *Atlantis and Lemuria*. Mokelumne Hill, California: Health Research, 1963.

Stern, Jess. *Edgar Cayce on the Millennium: The Famed Prophet Visualizes a Bright New World*. New York: Warner Books, 1998.

_____. *Edgar Cayce—The Sleeping Prophet*. New York: Bantam Books, 1967.

Sugrue, Thomas. *There is a River: The Story of Edgar Cayce*. Virginia Beach, Virginia: A. R. E. Press, 1945.

Swann, Ingo. *The Great Apparitions of Mary: An Examination of Twenty-Two Supranormal Appearances*. New York: Crossroad Publishing Company, 2000.

Taylor, Robert. *What the Bible Says About the End Times: Prophecies You Cannot Ignore*. Bacon Raton, Florida: Globe Digests, 2001.

Timms, Moira. *Beyond Prophecies and Predictions*. New York: Ballantine Books, 1996.

Tinsman, Jennifer Lingda. *Not My Gift: A Story of Divine Empowerment*. Mystic, Connecticut: CPS/Mystic Children's Studio, 1999.

Tompkins, Peter. *Mysteries of the Mexican Pyramids*. New York: HarperCollins, 1987.

_____. *Secrets of the Great Pyramid: Two Thousand Years of Adventure and Discoveries Surrounding the Mystery of the Great Pyramid of Cheops*. New York: Harper & Row, 1971.

Van Auken, John. *Ancient Egyptian Mysticism and Its Relevance Today*. Virginia Beach, Virginia: A. R. E. Press, 1999.

_____. "Weird Times: Ancient Human/Animal Mix." *Ancient Mysteries Newsletter September, 2005*.

Van Auken, John and Lora H. Little. *The Lost Hall of Records: Edgar Cayce's Forgotten Record of Human History in the Ancient Yucatan*. Memphis, Tennessee: Eagle Wing Books, 2000.

Van Biema, David. "Hail Mary." *Time Magazine*. March 21, 2005.

Varghese, Roy Abraham. *God-Sent: A History of the Accredited Apparitions of Mary*. New York: Crossroad Publishing Company, 2000.

Velikovsky, Immanuel. *Earth in Upheaval*. Garden City, New York: Doubleday, 1955.

_____. *Worlds in Collision*. New York: Pocket, 1984.

Waters, Frank. *Mexico Mystique: The Coming Sixth World of Consciousness*. Chicago: Swallow Press, 1975.

_____. *The Book of the Hopi*. New York: Ballantine Books, 1978.

West, John Anthony. *Serpent in the Sky: The High Wisdom of Ancient Egypt*. Wheaton, Illinois: Quest Books, 1993.

_____. *The Traveler's Key to Ancient Egypt: A Guide to the Sacred Places of Ancient Egypt*. Wheaton, Illinois: Quest Books, 1995.

ONLINE RESOURCES

Official web sites.
Bauval, Robert. www.robertbauval.co.uk/index.html
Cayce, Edgar and the Association for Research and Enlightenment,
 Edgar Cayce's A. R. E. http: www.edgarcayce.org
Copts in the United States. www.copts.com
Day, Peggy. www.placeoflight.net
Dunn, Christopher. www.gizapower.com
Gilbert, Adrian. www.adriangilbert.co.uk/docus/home.html
Hancock, Graham. www.grahamhancock.com/
Hawass, Dr. Zahi. http://guardians.net/hawass/
Operation Smile. www.operationsmile.org/
West, John Anthony. www.jawest.net

Ancient Egyptian Gods and Goddesses
Apep (god)
 http://www.touregypt.net/godsofegypt/apep.htm
Geb (god)
 http://ancienthistory.about.com/od/gebmyth/Geb.htm
Horus (god)
 http://touregypt.net/godsofegypt/horus.htm
Isis (goddess)
 http://en.wikipedia.org/wiki/Isis
Mehen (god)
 http://touregypt.net/godsofegypt/mehen.htm
Osiris (god)
 http://www.crystalinks.com/osiris.html
Nephthys (goddess)
 http://en.wikipedia.org/wiki/Nephthys
Ra (god)
 http://touregypt.net/godsofegypt/ra.htm
Set (god)
 http://socsci.colorado.edu/LAB/GODS/set.html
Shu (god)
 http://en.wikipedia.org/wiki/Shu_(Egyptian_deity)
Tefnut (goddess)
 http://www.crystalinks.com/tefnut.html
Wadjet (goddess)
 http://www.touregypt.net/featurestories/wadjeta.htm

Ancient Egyptian Mythology
Serpent symbolizing the Ka of the sun. Moira Timms.
     www.atlantisrising.com/issue17/denderahserpentcrypts.html
Solar Discs. www.crystalinks.com/solardiscs.html
Zep Tepi, the Egyptian First Time. http://fusionanomaly.net/zeptepi.html

Ancient Egyptian Twin Soul Gods and Goddesses
http://www.vibrani.com/gods.htm
http://en.wikipedia.org/wiki/Ancient_Egyptian_religion

Apparitions of the Blessed Virgin Mary
Apparitions of the Virgin Mary and whether or not they are approved by the
     church. www.apparitions.org
Apparitions of the Virgin—links to many photographs and quotes.
     www.marylinks.org
Apparitions of the Virgin Mary with photographs. www.medjugorjeusa.org
Apparitions of the Virgin Mary and Jesus with links to web sites on specific
     visitations. www.apparitions.org
Apparitions of the Virgin as well as links to photos and illustrations.
     biblia.com/apparitions/mary.htm
Apparitions of the Virgin Mary with photographs.
     www.miraclehunter.com/marian_apparitions/visionaries/index.html
Apparitions of the Virgin.
     http://members.aol.com/UticaCW/Mar-vis.html
Apparitions of the Blessed Virgin. A list of many, many apparitions from 1061
     to 1996. www.catholic-forum.com/Saints/indexapp.htm
Apparitions of the Virgin Mary in the United States.
     www.mcn.org/1/Miracles/motherz.htm
Amsterdam, Holland. Our Lady of All Nations. Rue du Bac, Miraculous Medal.
     www.ladyofallnations.org/rudubac.htm
Bayside, Queens, New York City, USA.
     http://www.rosesfromheaven.com/
Betania, Venezuela. http://religion.info/english/articles/article_166.shtml
Cap-de-la-Madeleine, Quebec, Canada.
     http://www.michaeljournal.org/ndcape.htm
Cincinnati, Ohio, USA.
     http://www.spiritdaily.org/Our%20Lady%20Apparitions/Sr_Nuezil/fostoria.ht
     http://en.wikipedia.org/wiki/Paul_Francis_Leibold
Conyers, Georgia, USA.
     http://www.georgiaencyclopedia.org/nge/Article.jsp?id=h-750
Cuenca, Ecuador.
     www.dailycatholic.org/issue/99Mar/mar24dc1.htm

Fatima, the final secret.
www.vatican.va/roman_curia/congregations/cfaith/documents/rc_con_cfait
h_doc_20000626_message-fatima_en.html
Fatima, the passing of Sister Lucia, 97-year-old Fatima visionary.
http://news.bbc.co.uk/2/hi/europe/4267515.stm
Garabandal, Spain. www.garabandal.org
Guadalupe apparition of the Virgin painted on Juan Diego's tilma in 1531 in
Mexico—photograph. www.medjugorjeusa.org/guadalupe.htm
Guadalupe, the original written account, 1531.
www.ewtn.com/jp99/apparition.htm
Necedah, Wisconsin, USA.
http://www.pdtsigns.com/neuzil.html
Rue de Bac, Paris, France. Shows the Miraculous Medal and the gems from
which rays do not proceed. www.memorare.com/mary/app1830.html
San Damiano, Italy.
http://members.chello.nl/~l.de.bondt/SanDamianoEng.htm
St. James the Greater, martyrdom. www.newadvent.org/cathen/08279b.htm
Saragossa, Spain. At the Basilica-Cathedral of Our Lady of the Pillar.
http://en.wikipedia.org/wiki/Nuestra_Se%C3%B1ora_del_Pilar_Basilica
Zeitun, Egypt, actual photograph of Mary's appearance in 1968. This photo was
copied from a television broadcast, therefore, the photo comes from video
film rather than emulsion film.
http://members.aol.com/bjw1106/marian7.htm
Zeitun, more photographs of Mary's appearance.
www.apparitions.org/zeitun.html

Apparitions of the Blessed Virgin Mary in Asyut, 2000

Our Lady Appears in Asyut—Main web site with links to other web sites such
as the ten following. Plays music. Also has video clips of the flashes and
apparition including the sound of the crowd.
www.zeitun-eg.org/Asyut.htm
Asyut people opening their homes to pilgrims, especially the elderly and sick.
www.zeitun-eg.org/wa42-2028.htm
City of Asyut turned off the electricity in the vicinity of St. Mark's Cathedral
one night. www.zeitun-eg.org/Asyut_light.htm
Coptic priests in Asyut declare the apparition to be real.
www.zeitun-eg.org/declaration.htm
Eyewitness report with real photos of the Virgin's appearance in Asyut.
www.zeitun-eg.org/Asyut_witness.htm
Image of Virgin in Asyut gif file.
www.zeitun-eg.org/watani_international.htm

Luminous doves—article and photos—that flew over the apparition site in
    Asyut. www.zeitun-eg.org/wa43-2039.htm
Newspaper article on the Virgin in Asyut, includes two miraculous
    healings.www.zeitun-eg.org/watani_international2.htm
Photo of the apparition taken with an ordinary camera and no flash.
    Also reports of miraculous healings. www.zeitun-eg.org/wa42-2026.htm
"Pope H.H. Shenouda III approves the luminous apparitions that took place in
    Asyut at Saint Mark's Cathedral." Watani Report 10 December 2000.
    www.zeitun-eg.org/wa42-2033.htm
Population of Asyut. www.Asyut.gov.eg/EnglishSite/escanen.htm

Asyut, Egypt
Information about Asyut and Asyut University. www.aun.edu.eg/Asyut.htm
Tourist information on Asyut. www.touregypt.net/asyuttop.htm

Copts and the Copt Orthodox Church
The Copts in the United States. www.copts.com
The Copts and the Copt Orthodox Church.
    www.coptic.net/EncyclopediaCoptica/
The Copts, a description of.
    www.tiscali.co.uk/reference/encyclopaedia/hutchinson/m0005869.html

Djinn (Please see "Islam and the Djinn.")

Egypt
Statistics. www.cia.gov/cia/publications/factbook/geos/eg.html

Great Pyramids
Aerial view shows the relative sizes of the three Great Pyramids.
    www.greatbuildings.com/cgibin/gbg.cgi/Great_Pyramid.html/29.978041/31
    .132979/16/600/800
Great Pyramid. http://ce.eng.usf.edu/pharos/wonders/pyramid.html
Great Pyramid. The only pyramid with the burial chamber located above the
    entrance of the sarcophagus room. Also, that the weight on the roof of the
    King's Chamber is over 400 tons. www.ancientegyptonline.co.uk/kings-c-
    khufu.html
Great Pyramids and Great Sphinx Satellite Image.
    www.wikimapia.org/#lat=29.979286&lon=31.131048&z=15&l=0&mGreat
Pyramid. Queen's Chamber and Three Robots in Air Shafts.
    www.ancientegyptonline.co.uk/queens-c-khufu.html
Great Pyramid, Queen's Chamber. Gatenbrink's Robots
    www.cheops.org/

Great Pyramid. Controversies over the date of construction. Quotes archeologist
  Mark Lehner. www.cycle-of-time.net/constructiondateGP.htm
Great Pyramid Statistics. www.crystalinks.com/gpstats.html
Great Pyramid Measurements. www.earthmatrix.com/great/pyramid.htm
Great Pyramid. Interesting information and comparisons.
  http://ourworld.compuserve.com/homepages/DP5/pyramid.htm
Great Pyramid. Public Broadcasting System's NOVA on-line tour.
  www.pbs.org/wgbh/nova/pyramid/
Pyramid (Second) of Khafre or Chephren Height.
  http://en.wikipedia.org/wiki/Khafre's_Pyramid
Pyramid (Second) of Khafre or Chephren.
  www.crystalinks.com/pyrkhafre.html
Pyramid (Second) of Khafre or Chephren. Opened in July 2001 after extensive
  refurbishments.
  www.arabicnews.com/ansub/Daily/Day/010707/2001070721.html
Pyramid (Second) of Khafre or Chephren. Opened again in January 2005 after
  restoration work.
  www.arabicnews.com/ansub/Daily/Day/041231/2004123126.html
Pyramid (Third) of Menkaure. www.touregypt.net/featurestories/menkaurep.htm
Pyramid (Third) of Menkaure Height.
  http://en.wikipedia.org/wiki/Menkaure's_Pyramid

Great Sphinx
Great Sphinx. http://en.wikipedia.org/wiki/Great_Sphinx_of_Giza

Ixchel, Mayan Mother Goddess
http://en.wikipedia.org/wiki/Ix_Chel

Hookah Water Pipes
Hookah water pipes. http://hookahkings.com/hookah.htm
Hookah water pipes. http://en.wikipedia.org/wiki/Hookah

Immaculate Conceptions in Higher Vertebrates
http://news.nationalgeographic.com/news/2006/12/061220-virgin-dragons.html
http://news.nationalgeographic.com/news/2002/09/0925_020925_virginshark.html

Islam and the Djinn
Islam, chronological history of.
  www.usc.edu/dept/MSA/history/chronology/century7.html
Islam and Djinn. http://muttaqun.com/jinn.html
Islamic Mythology.
  www.absoluteastronomy.com/encyclopedia/i/is/islamic_mythology.htm

Pre-Islamic myth about the Djinn. http://en.wikipedia.org/wiki/Djinn

Jinn (Please see "Islam and the Djinn.")

Kitt Peak
Kitt Peak National Observatory on the Papago Indian Reservation in Arizona.
  Site includes the McMath Pierce Solar Telescope.
  www.mreclipse.com/Observatory/KPNO/KPNO2.html

Kwan Yin or Gwan Yin
http://en.wikipedia.org/wiki/Guan_Yin

Mary Crushes the Head of the Serpent
http://www.nd.edu/~wcawley/corson/serpent.htm

Maya Long Count Calendar, 2012, and the End of the World
http://planetpapp.com/br21december2012
http://www.usatoday.com/tech/science/2007-03-27-maya-2012_n.htm

Names and Their Meanings
http://www.babyzone.com

Robot in Great Pyramid Shaft
http://news.nationalgeographic.com/news/2002/09/0923_020923_egypt.html

Serpent Gods and Goddesses
http://www.reptilianagenda.com/research/r073101d.shtml
http://en.wikipedia.org/wiki/Serpent_(symbolism)
Australian Aboriginal Rainbow Serpent.
    http://en.wikipedia.org/wiki/Rainbow_Serpent
Seraphim Hebrew Serpent Gods.
    http://www.pantheon.org/articles/s/seraphim.html

Virgin Birth
http://en.wikipedia.org/wiki/Virgin_Birth
http://www.newadvent.org/cathen/15448a.htm

INDEX

AUTHOR BIOGRAPHY

 Carol Chapman is an internationally acclaimed author, lecturer, and media personality. A keynote speaker at weekend spiritual retreats, her seminars are not only informative and transformational but also fun and entertaining.

A frequent guest on talk radio shows, Chapman has been featured on CBS radio's Kimmie and Steve and The Maria Shaw Show as well as Coast-to-Coast AM hosted by George Noory and Art Bell.

She is the author of *When We Were Gods*, which is the revised, updated version of *The Golden Ones*.

As a freelance writer and photographer, her illustrated articles have been published in *Dream Network, Circle, Fate, Alternate Perceptions, Whole Life Times,* and *Venture Inward.*

She is also an award-winning photographer and the creator of the Edgar Cayce Calendar *Divine in Nature: With Inspirational Quotes from Edgar* Cayce. While a photojournalist under contract to NASA, her photographs appeared in publications throughout the world including *Air and Space Smithsonian, Koku-Fan* (Japan), *Aeronautique Astronautique* (France), *Aeronautica & Difesa* (Italy), *Details, Final Frontier,* and *Aerospace America.*

She studied photography and filmmaking at Ryerson University in Toronto, Canada, and has a bachelor's degree in journalism from Prescott College in Prescott, Arizona, United States.

Chapman and her husband love to travel. They live on a river in southeastern Virginia where they enjoy sailing.

Additional copies of

ARRIVAL OF THE GODS IN EGYPT
Hidden Mysteries of Soul and Myth Finally Revealed

can be purchased at

Amazon.com
BarnesandNoble.com
Your Local Bookseller

ISBN-10: 0-9754691-5-0
ISBN-13: 978-0-9754691-5-6

or by telephone from SunTopaz LLC at
(757)810-5347

For a Free Gift from the author, please visit her website at
www.CarolChapmanGifts.com

The author invites you to read her blog and make comments at
www.CarolChapmanLive.com

To contact Carol
please write to her at her blog email address
Carol@CarolChapmanLive.com

For media requests
please contact
Publicity@SunTopaz.com

Printed in the United States
128041LV00003B/4/P